MY LIFE IN WINTERS

The Extraordinary Tale of One Man's Journey
Through the Rise of the Ski Industry

Mike Ewing

7th Mind
Publishing

Copyright © 2022 by Mike Ewing and Britt Andreatta
All Rights Reserved.

No part of this publication may be reproduced, stored in a retrieval system, or transmitted, in any form or by any means, electronic, mechanical, photocopying, recording, or otherwise, without the written permission of the authors.

All maps of ski areas are publicly available on the web and are the copyright of that ski area.

7th Mind Publishing

Published July 2022.
7th Mind Publishing
Santa Barbara, California

For orders or bulk purchases of this book, please write Orders@7thMindPublishing.com.

ISBN: 978-1-7365898-7-8 (paper)
ISBN: 978-1-7365898-6-1 (ebook)

This book is printed on acid-free paper in the United States of America.

Special photos credits:
- Cover photo: Skiing at Big Sky Resort, Montana, in 2021 with Lone Peak in the background. Courtesy of Crystal Images at Big Sky Resort. Bigskyphotos.com
- Section photo: Skiing at Vail, Colorado, in opening year 1962-63. Courtesy of Fletcher Manley, Jr. Fletchermanley.com
- Photo of Mikaela Shiffrin racing at Lake Louise, Canada. Courtesy of Paul Bussi. Idealphotography.com

All reprinted with permission.
See page 183 for all photo credits.

This book is dedicated to the three women in my life.

Thelma June Tancik
June 6, 1913-January 12, 1980

Mom, thanks for encouraging me to try skiing. It changed my life. And thanks for saving everything written about me. It made writing this book easier than you could have imagined.

Barbara Ewing

My wife who made this life possible. Without you, I doubt that any of this would have happened to me. You have been my love and friend and companion through thick and thin. And your presence made me seem better than I really am. I could not have chosen any better and I am so glad you chose me.

Britt Andreatta

My daughter who convinced me that I had a story to tell. Without your help with editing and encouragement, I would never have recognized the value of this story. Thank you for making that phone call years ago that brought us together. Working on this book with you has been amazing.

CONTENTS

I. GENESIS
Introduction: 70 Years of Skiing..2
1. 1951-1952: Genesis..6
2. The 10th Mountain Division..11
3. 1953-1954: Monarch Mountain...15
4. 1955-1956: Eagle Scout..19
5. 1959-1960: National Ski Patrol...24

II. PATROLLING & TEACHING
6. 1961-1962: Arapahoe Basin..30
7. 1962-1963: Vail..34
8. 1964-1965: Mid-Vail..41
9. 1965-1966: National Ski Safety Research..45
10. 1966-1967: Crystal Mountain...51
11. Ski Racing Programs...58
12. 1968-1969: A&T Ski Company..64
13. 1969-1973: Lange Boot Company...71

III. THE SKI INDUSTRY
14. 1973-1974: K2 Ski Company..78
15. 1975-1976: The Cheeseburger Ski..83
16. Evolution of Ski Equipment...90
17. 1976-1977: MBA at U of VA...97
18. 1978-1979: Lake Placid...103
19. 1980: The XIII Olympic Games...109
20. Women in Skiing...116
21. The 1980's: Warren Miller Goes Big...124

IV. RETURN TO THE MOUNTAIN
22. The 1990's: Freestyle Goes to the Olympics.....................................130
23. The 2000's: Epic vs. Ikon..136
24. 2010-2011: Return to Teaching..142
25. Transformation of Ski Lifts..147
26. 2012-2015: Paying it Forward..152
27. History of the Professional Ski Instructors of America (PSIA)......158
28. 2015-2016: Tour of Montana Ski Areas..165
29. 2019-2021: The Pandemic...172
30. 2021-2022: Milestones and Medals..176

SKI AREAS & RESORTS

Loveland Ski Area, CO 5
Ski Cooper, CO 10
Mt. Rose Ski Tahoe, NV 14
Monarch Mountain, CO 18
Aspen Snowmass Ski Resort, CO 23
Hidden Valley Ski Area, CO 28
Arapahoe Basin Ski Area, CO 33
Vail/Beaver Creek Resorts, CO 40
Winter Park Resort, CO 44
Stratton Mountain Resort, VT 50
Crystal Mountain Ski Resort, WA 57
Squaw Valley/Palisades Tahoe, CA 63
Steamboat Resort, CO 70
Heli-skiing The Bugaboos, BC, Canada 76
Sun Valley Resort, ID 82
Heavenly Ski Resort, CA 89
Loon Mountain Resort, NH 96
Schweitzer Ski Resort, ID 102
Whiteface Mountain Ski Resort, NY 108
White Pass Ski Area, WA 115
Alpental Ski Resort (Summit at Snoqualmie), WA 123
Deer Valley Ski Resort, UT 128
Keystone Ski Resort, CO 135
Buck Hill Resort, MN 141
Big Sky Resort, MT 146
Jackson Hole Mountain Resort, WY 151
Bousquet Mountain Resort, NY 157
Red Lodge Mountain, MT 164
Lost Trail Ski Area, MT 171
Brighton Resort, UT 175
Cochran's Ski Area, VT 180

Acknowledgments 182
Photo Credits 183
References 184
Index 192
About the Author 203

I. GENESIS

"I think the most important thing in skiing is you have to be having fun. If you're having fun, then everything else will come easy to you."

Lindsey Vonn,
Olympic Gold Medalist

Introduction

70 Years of Skiing

This book began with a surprising phone call. At the beginning of Winter 2021-2022, I received a call from Herb Davis, the current President and CEO of the Northern Rocky Mountain Division of the Professional Ski Instructors of America (PSIA-NRM). He told me he'd received a message from the PSIA National Office that I had qualified for my 30-year pin. He asked when I was first certified, and I explained that I passed my associate exam in April of 1965 at Loveland Ski Area in Colorado. He asked if I had paperwork from that exam and, at the time, I told him that I didn't think so, but I still had my certification pin, which had my name and year of exam engraved on it. He asked me to take a photo and send it to him so he could have PSIA update their records.

Every winter, ski resorts around the U.S. hold pin ceremonies for their PSIA-certified instructors, presenting them with pins honoring their service to the sport. On December 28, 2021, PSIA-NRM held a pin ceremony at Big Sky Mountain Sports in Montana, where I currently teach. I was surprised when two of Big Sky's Board of Directors, Jim Mikulich and Ben Brosseau, presented me with my 30-year pin, and then followed that with my 40- and 50-year pins! My great friend and ski guru, Ursula Howland, put my new 50-year pin on my Big Sky instructor's uniform during the morning lineup, before we headed out with our students.

Ursula Howland pinning on the PSIA 50-year pin

It was quite the honor and also caused me to reflect on my lifetime of experiences with the sport and the industry. I have served in many roles, from ski instructor to ski patrolman, ski shop manager, racing coach, and salesperson for all of the biggest brands—I've even had a hand in designing skis and researching injury rates. Through all of it, I have had a front row seat to the rise of skiing in the United States, witnessing key moments that have made it what it is today. For example, I was working at Vail Resort during the first winter it opened and, on the day I'm typing this, I taught a lesson at Big Sky Resort on my 80th birthday. At the 1980 Olympics in Lake Placid, New York, our team handed Phil Mahre his K2 skis when he became the first Olympic ski racer to win a medal skiing on an American-made ski. I've worked for most of the major brands including K2 Skis, A&T Ski Company, and Lange Boots.

With urging from my daughter, Britt Andreatta, I decided to write this book about my personal journey, sharing key moments from my life and celebrating the 70th anniversary of my introduction to the great sport of skiing. In the research for this book, I actually found that PSIA exam paperwork in an album my mom had started during my high school years and continued until her death. It also had several other treasures that will show up in various chapters of this book.

As part of my 80th birthday celebration, my fellow instructor, Rich Noonan, and I decided to take off the last week in January to visit the two Colorado ski areas where I learned to ski—Ski Cooper and Monarch Mountain. They have both managed to stay as ski areas and not become resorts. There is no housing at the actual mountain, they have affordable rates for season passes and day tickets, and feature really nice day lodges serving good food at non-resort prices. Both have maintained their autonomy and are unabashedly proud of the fact that they are "family friendly" ski areas.

My college roommate and lifelong friend, Bob Shanks, and my godson, Tom Hove, met us and we had a fantastic week of skiing for fun. At both ski areas, we connected with mountain managers and key leaders. We were impressed at how welcoming they were and how they recognized what we were doing there. They all expressed appreciation for our comments about how much fun we were having. Both Ski Cooper and Monarch Mountain have really great terrain, rely on natural snow, and do not make snow or over groom their runs. It was truly a special trip down memory lane and reinforced the way I feel about why I love what I have done and what I still do.

This is how I got to where we are, and this book will cover my amazing series of happy accidents that allowed me to be totally immersed in the sport I dearly love. I've been able to craft a career that has every friend I know be amazed by the cool things that happened to me along the way. Being at the right place at the right time has become a mantra that keeps popping up for me. It is astonishing how many times I happened to benefit from serendipitous timing.

I hope you enjoy this book. Please forgive me if writing about things that happened over the past 70 years seems unbelievable. I have had a front row seat

Revisiting Ski Cooper in 2022 with Tom Hove, Bob Shanks, & Rich Noonan

to the birth and transformation of the ski industry, beginning as a quaint, small industry to billions of dollars now enjoyed by millions of people each year.

For example, in 2021, Vail Associates sold 2.1 million Epic Passes and were holding $1.4 billion in cash on hand. In Colorado alone, the skiing industry generates $5 billion per year in economic impact including 50,000 jobs or $2 billion in labor income not to mention the money spent on lodging, food, and equipment. Vail Associates recently purchased three resorts along the Atlantic coast to add to their collection of 35 ski areas around the world.

Globally, skiing is enjoyed in over 100 countries at 2,000 alpine skiing destinations. It is estimated that there are 135 million skiers in the world and there are 400 million annual skier days. History shows that humans have been skiing for the last eight millenia with archeological evidence of skiers in Russia, China, and Norway dating back 6,000 years. In the United States, the first resort was Colorado's Howelsen Hill Ski Area, founded in 1915, followed by Eaglebrook School in Massachusetts in 1922.

In this book, I'll share my experiences from the various roles I have held at ski areas and equipment companies in the United States. This book is organized around significant moments—specifically winters—that shaped the industry, my life, or both.

When I taught that lesson on my 80th birthday, I had the fortune to check off a long-awaited item on my bucket list. But I have more. I recently got in touch with the national office of PSIA and learned that they are soon going to grant a 60-year pin for the first time in their history. So, now I have a new item for my bucket list and I hope to receive mine during the Winter of 2024-2025.

Loveland Ski Area
Loveland Pass, Colorado

- Founded in 1936 by J.C. Blickensderfer, Loveland Ski Area currently boasts 94 runs over 1,800 skiable acres in the Arapaho National Forest.
- There are 11 lifts and a vertical drop of 2,210 feet. The average snowfall is 422 inches and they have the capability to make snow on 240 acres of terrain.
- Notably, Loveland was the first major ski area in Colorado to make snow. They leveraged the diesel compressors used to construct the Eisenhower Tunnel to create something that changed the sport forever.
- They just completed a massive expansion of the lodge at their beginner area, Loveland Valley.
- They offer private and group lessons for children and adults.
- Learn more at SkiLoveland.com.

Chapter 1

1951-1952: Genesis

Leadville, Colorado
39.2508° N, 106.2925° W
Base Elevation: 10,151 (3,094 M)

To understand how skiing became the core of my life and livelihood, we need to start at the beginning. I was born in Salida, Colorado in January of 1942, to Thelma and Levon Ewing. We lived in Salida because my mom's dad, my grandfather, was the blacksmith in the roundhouse located in Salida. As it happened, he was the last blacksmith employed by the D&RGW Railroad as they were going to convert to diesel engines in the mid-1950's.

My parents divorced when I was four years old and my father bailed on us. My mom was faced with the fact that he did not ever pay a penny of child support. I went to live with my grandparents and mom's younger brother, Uncle Bud. He was the youngest in the family and Mom was the oldest with a 22-year gap between them.

I have had people say to me that it must have been awful to leave my mother, but my view is that I had the perfect grandmother—she was a great cook, had a really good sense of humor, and was a perfect offset to my grandfather. He was the disciplinarian, in a good way, but never saw a shade of gray in his entire life.

In 1951, Mom remarried and we moved to Leadville, Colorado. Leadville was 57 miles west of Salida and was known as the two-mile-high city, meaning that it was 10,560 feet above sea level. My stepdad, Joe Tancik, was a shift supervisor for Utah Construction, which was trying to build a tunnel that would drain the water out of the many silver mines in the area. Joe's job was dangerous but he was really skilled at what he did and he made really good money. For the first time in six years, my mom felt financially secure.

Joe was a really great guy and he was totally invested in getting to know me and creating a family. He went to my grandfather and asked him how to get close to me. My grandfather told him to take me fly-fishing and hunting, which we did often together. He also came to all the school functions and he helped me with my Cub Scout and Boy Scout projects. All in all, he was my DAD and he became one of the nicest and most influential people in my life.

We lived in a place called The Pines, about 12 miles west of Leadville. I was enrolled in the 9th Street School, so every morning the school bus would arrive and pick us up to head off to school. Also living at The Pines were our neighbors, the Sakry family. They had five or six kids, including Cookie, who was in my grade and Paul who was two years ahead of Cookie and me.

One day in late October, it was snowing when the bus arrived, and we got on and headed to school. I noticed that there was a different vibe and level of excitement in the air. When we got on the bus to go home, the snow was about two feet deep. When we got home, the Sakry kids jumped off the bus and beelined it to the shed by their house. They opened the door and started bringing out skis, boots, and poles and putting on the gear.

In Salida, I had heard references to skiing, but save my buddy, Lance Stapleton, I had no idea what it was about. Salida rarely had snow on the ground, one of the blessings of the lower elevation. Lance had a pair of skis and we messed around with them a little bit, but not in the winter. We had skied off a dirt rock mound in the back of his grandmother's house, destroying the skis. I still remember how mad his dad was about that.

I stood there watching as they got their gear on and started sidestepping up the hill between the houses. They got to the top and skied down the hill. Mr. Sakry appeared and walked over to me and asked if I would like to try skiing. Without wasting a second I said, "YES! But I don't have equipment." He said, "We have extra and you can try some of it now if you like." I ran into our house and asked Mom if it was okay, and she said, "Yes, but put on your play clothes."

I raced back out and Mr. Sakry helped me get the boots on and showed me how to get into the bindings. He taught me how to herringbone (walk like a duck) up the driveway and then helped me get turned around and I slid down the hill. To this day, I can still remember that first slide and, I have to say, I was instantly hooked! Oprah Winfrey, who is an avid skier, said, "Skiing is the next best thing to having wings." And she is right.

About a half hour later, I was sidestepping up the hill and skiing down in straight runs. I heard my mom yell to come in and get ready for dinner. My dad was home and as we ate, I couldn't stop talking about how fun it was to ski. Until the day of his death, Dad couldn't believe that I would go out in the cold and spend hours skiing. He considered winter a big pain because it slowed down everything he did at work. But from that first day at The Pines, my life has always been calibrated by what happened in the winter. The Winter of 1951-1952 was the start of it all.

The Sakrys told me about Ski Cooper and how they went skiing every weekend and holiday. I wanted to go so I asked how much a ticket cost. They told me that if I went to the library, I could get a library card and a season pass to Cooper Hill. Do you know how much it cost in 1951? One dollar! I couldn't believe my luck.

It turned out that the U.S. Army had ceded Cooper Hill to Lake County when they closed Camp Hale after WWII. They stated in the document that

Cooper Hill was "to be used to benefit the youth of Lake County." And I can attest that they kept their promise.

Camp Hale was the training site for the 10th Mountain Division, America's response to the Axis countries of Germany, Italy, and Japan, all of which had Alpine Ski Troops as part of their armies. When they came home from the war, the members of the 10th were influential in creating the outdoor sports industry in the United States, which became a major driver in the post-war economy, especially in the late 50's and 60's. We'll explore the 10th Mountain Division in Chapter 2.

Cookie Sakry and Mike Ewing at The Pines

From that first skiing experience, all I wanted for Christmas was my own ski gear. Our family always opened gifts on Christmas Eve. So, when we got home from school, I went into the house and looked under the Christmas tree. I was really disappointed that there was not a package large enough to be skis or ski boots. We had Christmas Eve dinner and then we started to open presents— I remember that I got a new sweater, a pair of corduroy pants, and a new shirt for school.

Dad said he had forgotten something in the car for Mom and asked if I would go out with him to bring it into the house. He had a 1951 Buick and as they say today, it was the size of a Buick. He opened the trunk and there were skis, boots, poles, and three wrapped gifts, which we carried into the house. I don't think my feet touched the ground as we walked back in and saw the look on Mom's face. She was beaming and Dad couldn't stop laughing.

I opened the Garmisch ski boot box and, still today, the smell of leather boots is one of my favorite smells. Two of the packages were for me and they included a pair of black wool pants and a ski parka that was made of a lightweight canvas-like material. We soon learned that neither were waterproof and many a trip home from skiing were plagued by the smell of wet, steaming wool.

The skis were from a Seattle-based company, A&T Ski Company. They were the distributor for a lot of European brands and new companies trying to grow their distribution. They also had proprietary products, like Ome Daiber's SNO-SEAL, which is still used today to waterproof leather boots and gloves.

My first ski equipment was bought from Bill's Ski Shop in Leadville. Bill and Mary Jo Copper became fast friends that always took care of their customers. I am pleased to tell you that their shop is still in Leadville in 2022 and now owned by their son. Bill was a leader in the outdoor industry and started his long thriving business by buying army surplus that included 10th Mountain gear. One of my favorite pieces of equipment was a box of tanker goggles that had six different lenses and a frame that left a black mark under your eyes as the rubber deteriorated year after year. I used those goggles until I graduated from high school.

Paul Sakry and I skied together often during that winter. Once when I was skiing with Paul, we were messing around on the T-Bar and he lost his balance. He fell over backwards and, in the process, he managed to knock me over backwards too with my ski pinning his ski against the bar. One of the drawbacks of T-Bar lifts is that they are engineered to accommodate people between 5'6" and 6' tall. Neither of us fit that description. If your partner is taller than you, it becomes problematic to ride since one person has the bar at their knees or the other person has it in the middle of their back.

On that ride, we were essentially being picked up at every tower then slammed down as we cleared the tower's wheels. We were both laughing, but we could hear people yelling to get the lift operator's attention. We rode to at least 10 or 12 towers before he finally figured out why he was being yelled at and got us untangled.

After we got up, we realized that our parkas had been pulled up and our pants pulled down and both were loaded with snow. For anyone that has ever put on a wet swimsuit, you can imagine what it felt like. We skied to the bottom and went into the warming hut, formerly known as the Officer's Building. We grabbed hot chocolates and stood by the pot-bellied stove until we dried out a little. Fortunately, neither of our parents ever found out about that episode.

It's hard for me sitting here in 2022 to realize that it is almost exactly 70 years since that event, and I still vividly remember every second of that crazy T-Bar ride. It still amazes me that I was so lucky to find something that I loved and how it sent me on a lifetime of fun. With a lot of luck and serendipitous happenings, I have been able to ski and create a lot of lifelong friends because of that one day in October of 1951.

Ski Cooper
Leadville, Colorado

- Founded in 1942 by the men of the 10th Mountain Division, Cooper currently boasts 64 runs over 480 skiable acres in the White River National Forest.
- There are 5 lifts and a vertical drop of 1,200 feet. The average snowfall is 260 inches.
- Cooper offers snowcat skiing tours with 2,600 acres of open bowls and glades on Chicago Ridge.
- They offer private and group lessons for children and adults.
- Learn more at SkiCooper.com.

Chapter 2

The 10th Mountain Division

Camp Hale, Colorado
39.4351° N, 106.3255° W
Elevation: 9,200 Feet (2,800 M)

The soldiers who served in the U.S. Army's 10th Mountain Division started the outdoor sports industry in America. Those veterans and their children became the leaders in getting the baby boomers outdoors, with the need to recreate after a hard week at work. The weekends became "fun time" and an opportunity to have family time outdoors.

10th Mountain veterans founded iconic programs like Outward Bound and the National Outdoor Leadership School (both started by Paul Petzoldt), the Friends of the Earth and the Sierra Club (both David Brower). Bill Bowerman founded the Nike Corporation and another veteran established the High Alpine Avalanche Research Station.

But the place where they had the biggest impact, collectively, was the ski industry. The postwar economy of the 1950's was driven by infrastructure building for the outdoor sports industry. As a result, the federal government poured money into the Forest Service and Park Service, especially where recreational opportunities existed. Both the Forest Service and Park Service either built or leased land for ski areas. At one time, almost all ski areas in the United States were permitted by one or the other agency.

In the early days of skiing, almost every ski area was owned or managed by 10th veterans. In fact, they founded, managed or led the ski schools at 62 ski areas across the U.S. in New York (Whiteface), Vermont (Sugarbush), Nevada (Mount Rose), Washington (Crystal Mountain), Montana (Whitefish Mountain), and Colorado (Arapahoe Basin, Aspen Snowmass, Ski Cooper, Loveland, Vail, and Winter Park).

David Brower provided guidance on the environmental impact of ski areas. He was a staunch environmentalist and worked hard to prevent ski areas from destroying animal habitats. He advised resort leaders on best practices and also lobbied against those that would destroy key habitats or ecosystems.

One of the key ways the 10th veterans boosted the skiing industry was providing affordable equipment so cost was not a barrier. After the war, they put surplus military ski gear into the market, bringing prices down. This gave many families the start they needed to give this strange, new sport a try.

They also published ski magazines and started ski equipment brands. Many veterans participated in designing new equipment that was easier for the leisure skier to use. For example, Howard Head created the "Head Standard" ski in 1947 after seeking advice and input from many veterans.

Another critical role 10th veterans played was in ski instruction. They helped develop the early techniques and methods for teaching people the sport. Many veterans held leadership roles in the National Ski Association (NSA) and the Professional Ski Instructors of America (PSIA). Early ski schools were often led and staffed by 10th veterans as were the Ski Patrols. The National Ski Patrol (NSP) was founded in 1938 by 10th veteran Charles Minot "Minnie" Dole. Dole had actually been responsible for screening all soldiers who wanted to serve in the 10th, making sure they had the skills necessary to succeed.

In Colorado, many of the state's most iconic resorts were born from the efforts of 10th Mountain veterans. Arapahoe Basin was founded in 1946 by Lawrence Jump and assisted by Earl Clark, Wilfred Davis, and Merrill Hastings. That same year, Freidl Pfeifer, Percy Rideout, and John Litchfield opened Aspen Mountain. One of my favorite bosses, Pete Siebert, founded Vail in 1962. Fellow veterans Earl Eaton and Bob Parker helped to launch Vail, serving as Mountain Manager and head of Marketing respectively. I was lucky to have such great role models as I was beginning my own career in the ski industry.

One of Vail's runs, Riva Ridge, is named after a place where Pete was badly wounded in battle as a soldier in the 10th. Many 10th veterans that I knew shared stories about how everything they did was made more complicated because of the fog of war and bureaucratic mistakes that impacted their supply lines.

The most egregious mistake, in my opinion, came when they were assigned to the Po Valley Campaign and none of their climbing and ski equipment ever arrived. The days before the battle to take Mt. Belvedere, the 10th soldiers were going door to door in the Italian villages and borrowing mountain gear, most of which was antiquated. The Germans were so confident that the cliffs could not be scaled that they ignored one side of the mountain. To their surprise, they woke up to a full-on assault by the 10th.

Growing up near Camp Hale, I heard many interesting stories about the soldiers there. One of my favorites was the arrival at Camp Hale of a kid who weighed about 125 pounds and found himself going on a 10-mile ski with a backpack that weighed 90 pounds. That trip took place at 10,000 feet above sea level and capped out at 12,000 feet. He was from an east coast town at sea level. It is a miracle that he survived.

Almost all 10th troops volunteered for Camp Hale, but many a southern boy found himself assigned to a place he could only imagine because of Christmas tales and what they thought snow would look and feel like.

It was common that, after a snowstorm, the troops had to ski through new snow not in a line but spread out. This allowed them to make a wide packed swath for the muleskinners to bring the mules up with the artillery they were packing.

Camp Hale today, in the winter

One veteran, Fritz Benedict, created the 10th Mountain hut system because of his experience at Camp Hale. He said, "It's getting back to the way skiing started…it was simple and a lot of camaraderie…and to preserve that is so important." The hut system is a series of trails that connect Vail and Aspen with multiple huts along the way. It is still enjoyed by thousands annually. Benedict was helped by other veterans Carl Stingel, Pete Seibert, and Dick Wright.

The 10th was decommissioned right after WWII, but in the early 1960's they came back to Camp Hale for a short stint before those veterans went off to launch the ski industry as we know it. In the 1980's, the 10th Mountain Division was relaunched by the U.S. Army to help fight in areas that have mountainous terrain.

Today's 10th soldiers have fought in both the Afghanistan and Iraq wars since 2001. The 10th is now based at Fort Drum in New York, near Syracuse, an area known for its "lake effect" snowstorms that can drop four feet of snow in an hour.

In 2015, General Diana Holland became the first woman to serve in the 10th Mountain Division. She was also the first female commandant of West Point and went on to become a Brigadier General.

There are many books and movies about the 10th Mountain and below is a list of my favorites. I encourage you to read more about these amazing men and women.

Books
The Winter Army: The World War II Odyssey of the 10th Mountain Division, America's Elite Alpine Warriors by Maurice Isserman
World War II at Camp Hale: Blazing a New Trail in the Rockies by David Witte
Deep: The Story of Skiing and the Future of Snow by Porter Fox
It's Easy, Edna. It's Downhill All the Way by Edna Dercum

Movies
Climb to Glory by Warren Miller
Fire on the Mountain by Beth and George Gage
Mission Mt. Mangart, the Mighty Story of the 10th Mountain Division by Chris Anthony

Mt. Rose Ski Tahoe
Reno, Nevada

- Founded in 1939 by Wayne Poulsen, Mt. Rose currently boasts 60 runs over 1,200 skiable acres in the Humboldt-Toiyabe National Forest.
- There are 8 lifts and a vertical drop of 1,800 feet. The average snowfall is 350 inches and they have terrain parks for freestyle skiing.
- They offer private and group lessons for children and adults.
- Learn more at SkiRose.com.

Chapter 3

1953-1954: Monarch Mountain

Monarch Mountain, Colorado
38.5121° N, 106.3320° W
Base Elevation: 10,790 Feet (3,289 M)
Peak Elevation: 11,952 Feet (3,643 M)

At the end of the 1951-1952 winter, my parents decided to buy a house in Leadville because it would be at least another year before Dad's job was over. I don't exactly know the actual mechanics of how that came to be, but I think that my mom not driving was part of the reasoning. Dad had tried to teach her how to drive but she was never comfortable, so it was no fun for her to be stuck 12 miles from town. The house we bought was small with two bedrooms and a bath, and I think they bought it for $6,000. I did not realize that Dad had borrowed the money from his dad to purchase the house. I came to know this when my dad passed away in 1988 and his sister was the executor to his estate.

Shortly after we bought the house, the job in Leadville disappeared because the water inflow was thousands of gallons more than the tunnel had capacity to evacuate. Dad was offered another job with Utah Construction, but it involved us having to move to Australia where they had a huge contract to build a pipeline through the outback. It would have been a goldmine for us because we would be there for a minimum of five years, and housing and all expenses would be covered by the company.

But Mom said, "No way." She couldn't get over the fact that I would be out of the American school system. Because of Dad's skill set, he landed a pretty good job in a mine near Salida. So back to Salida we went. With the big job losses in Leadville, we rented out our house rather than sell it—we easily found another nice rental home near my old school and settled into our Salida life.

One day, one of the kids I walked to school with, Danny Espinosa, asked if I would accompany him to a Boy Scout meeting. Since I had been in Cub Scouts in Salida and Leadville, I said, "Yes." I met the Scoutmaster for Troop 65, Roman Fisher; he was about to play a big role in shaping my life. Early on, I found out that not only was he the Scoutmaster, he also was the General Manager at Monarch Mountain ski area, just 20 miles from Salida. He announced that all our scout winter outings would be at Monarch.

Once again, luck played a big role in my life. In the history of Salida, there had been only one Eagle Scout in Troop 65 and it was Roman's son. Another scout, Dewey Long, was well on his way to getting there, but he had at least one more year to go. It became a goal of mine to be the third Eagle Scout in Salida. I did not realize it was Mom's goal that I would also be the youngest. Everyone who knew my mom will attest to the fact that she was a powerhouse when she had a goal. We both got our wish.

I found that scouting was lots of fun and I soon realized that it was also a study in leadership and confidence building. Dewey and I really hit it off and he was helping me, and a lot of the younger scouts, get into the rhythm of acquiring the 21 merit badges required to become an Eagle Scout. Summer camps were held at a place called Indian Flats near Buena Vista, Colorado. Our project for the years I was in scouting was to dam the creek flowing through there and try to establish a fish friendly environment for that area. The last time I was there, I could still see remnants of our work from the 1950's.

Racing at Monarch Mountain wearing #117

The winters at Monarch were a kid's best dream. We got to ski every weekend and holiday, and although all we had was two rope tows and two ski runs, we made it all fun. Later in life, I came to know that Roman got the job as GM because he was in the Navy and knew how to splice ropes. This seemed to be an almost never-ending job. The Colorado Conservation Corps had built the area in the mid-1930's, one of the public works of the Roosevelt era. They used the logs from cutting the ski runs to build a really cool log cabin, named Inn Ferno.

It had concrete floors, log-based picnic tables, a kitchen, and a bathroom with running water. It was the property of Chaffee County and they leased it to someone who provided lunches and hot chocolate. All in all, it was a really homey place and, until 1958, it was quaint but not moving in an upward trajectory. So, the County put it up for sale. The Berry family bought it, very soon added a T-Bar, and it started to gain ground. The scouts were still a big part of it and we used to winter camp at Inn Ferno. We devised a way to night ski by using two-pound coffee cans packed with sawdust and soaked with kerosene, which we placed on the edges of one of the T-Bar runs. We'd light them and ski until midnight or later. It smudged the run a little bit, but it was well worth it.

One of the benefits of scouting for me was that Dad helped with the projects I had to do to acquire merit badges. He was a guy who could take your watch apart or fix a D8 Cat engine. When I was going for my skiing merit badge, one of the requirements was that you had to make a piece of equipment. We chose to make a pair of ski poles, so we went to Greenberg's Furniture Store and got two pieces of bamboo. In those days, every carpet came rolled up on a bamboo culm, so we had many to pick from. It took an hour per night for about two weeks before we finished them. One of my fondest memories is of my dad trying to figure out how to put metal on the tip of the poles. He took a can and one of his shears and started cutting and fitting the can metal so it abutted against itself and then he fastened it with copper brads.

After we were finished making them, one of the stores in Salida put them in their front window display for a week. I walked by every morning to make sure they were still there and I was so proud of what my dad and I had built. I skied with those poles until I graduated from high school.

During this time, I came up with a plan to make some easy money from my skiing friends. My grandmother did lots of food canning, so she had gobs of paraffin, which she would give me. I went to the secondhand store and bought three old ice cube trays. I would melt the paraffin and add food coloring to make red, blue, and purple bars of wax that I would sell to my friends for a quarter each. Of course, all the wax was the same, but they thought red was for warm conditions, blue was for cold, and purple was for the coldest. It was my first marketing project and a total scam, but not illegal because it was such a bargain compared to the commercial wax being sold at that time. Paraffin actually works really well on skis but does not last because it's soft and scrapes off easily. That's my story and I am sticking with it!

I first met Dan Cady when we were both in the fourth grade. At that time there were two grade schools in Salida—Dan attended Longfellow and I attended McCray. I met Dan on the first day of the ski season at Monarch Pass, probably Thanksgiving weekend. Dan was a really good skier and we hit it off.

I met Dan's parents, Jack and Jerry Cady, very early in the sixth grade. Dan's brother, Gary, did not like to ski, and Jack and Jerry couldn't keep up with Dan, so they asked me if I wanted to be Dan's ski buddy. I was really fortunate they chose me! My parents didn't ski and it was really neat for me to have somebody who went skiing in different ski areas; we had lots of adventures. Dan, his folks and I skied in different places like Arapahoe Basin and Aspen.

Dan and I became really close friends so, of course, I invited him to go fishing in the summer. It was one of the only times I found something Dan couldn't really do. I loved taking him fishing but he never caught any fish. Whenever we came home, we always had our limit, but it was because I caught everything.

I really cannot remember him actually catching a fish during all the summers we fished together.

One of my favorite stories of our childhood skiing days was the time he was skiing with a banana in his jacket so he would have a snack later in the day. We were probably in seventh grade and were the best skiers at Monarch. Hardly anyone could keep up with us and we were messing around jumping and Dan did what was called a Gelandesprung, a spread-eagled jump while in the air. The only problem was, if you didn't execute it correctly and your feet didn't get back together perfectly when you hit, your right ski went off to the right and your left ski to the left and you splattered right in the middle. That banana ended up all over his sweater in a patch about one foot in diameter. We laughed so hard we cried.

When Dan and I were in eighth grade, we were called into a meeting with the counselors to figure out what we should take in high school to get ready for college. They asked Dan what he wanted to do with the rest of his life and he said he wanted to be an airline pilot. They asked me and I said I wanted to be a ski instructor. Little did we know, we would both get our wish!

Monarch Mountain
Salida, Colorado

- Founded in 1939 and built by the Works Project Administration, Monarch Mountain currently boasts 67 runs over 800 skiable acres in the Pike San Isabel National Forest.
- There are 7 lifts and a vertical drop of 1,162 feet. The average snowfall is 350 inches and they also offer terrain parks, tubing, and cat skiing.
- They offer private and group lessons for children and adults.
- Learn more at SkiMonarch.com.

Chapter 4

1955-1956: Eagle Scout

Indian Flats, Colorado
38.4810° N, 106.1452° W
Base Elevation: 8,967 Feet (2,733 M)

By September of 1955, I had finished all of the requirements to attain my Eagle Scout status including my Eagle Project. I chose to do something to improve a stream up Ute Trail, north of Salida, which for years was flooding in the spring and eroding into the sand below the topsoil.

I approached the local Soil Conservation Office and submitted my plan to them. I asked them to give me 10,000 choke cherry saplings and I would organize our troop to plant them strategically along the riverbanks. With a little luck, they would take hold and stabilize the banks, especially in the turns. They said yes and my dad agreed to help me. We organized Troop 65 into teams of two, creating about 30 teams, including the other dads who volunteered to help. Each team had a 5-gallon bucket of water, the saplings, and a bar of steel to poke into the ground and pry open a 6-to-12-inch hole in the turf. A sapling would be placed into the hole, adding a splash of water to get it started, and then we'd close the hole by stepping on the turf. Our moms had packed lunches and it turned into a really fun outing. We had planned to do the project over three Saturdays but, with such a great crew, we finished in two.

For the effort, I received approval on my Eagle Project and a conservation award from the Soil Conservation Service. But the best reward came 45 years later, when I was home for my 50th Class Reunion and took a drive up there to see what it looked like. There now was a beautiful, giant meadow full of trees and beaver ponds. It turned out the Soil Conservation Service had relocated a beaver family there and they were thriving. The whole area was home to a myriad of birds and small and large animals.

I was awarded my Eagle Scout Badge on February 29, 1956. We decided to hold the Court of Honor on Mother's Day because my friend and fellow scout, Gerald Hagerman, was getting his Eagle Scout in March. It made for a great Mother's Day for both of our moms. I had achieved my goal of becoming the third and youngest Eagle Scout and Gerald was the fourth (Dewey had become the second the year prior). My parents were very proud!

The Eagle Scout is the highest honor that can be achieved through the Boy Scouts of America organization. Since 1911, only four percent of the scouts have achieved this level. It requires scouts to complete a substantial community service project—each year, Eagle Scout projects alone create three million hours of community service. Eagle Scouts must also complete 21 merit badges in the following areas: citizenship (community, nation, world), camping, communications, cooking, emergency preparedness, first aid, environmental science or sustainability, family life, fitness, personal management, and a sport like hiking, cycling, or skiing.

Eagle Scouts can qualify for a variety of scholarships ranging from $3,000 to $50,000. There are many notable Eagle Scout recipients including (but certainly not limited to):

- U.S. Presidents: Gerald Ford, John F. Kennedy, George W. Bush, Bill Clinton
- Nobel Laureates: Dudley R. Herschbach, Peter Agre, Robert Coleman Richardson, and Frederick Reines
- Astronauts (40): Neil Armstrong, Buzz Aldrin, and Guilon Bluford, the first African American to travel to space
- Civil Rights Leaders: Martin Luther King, Jr., Ernest Green
- Authors/Journalists: Walter Cronkite, Clive Cussler, Harrison Salisbury
- Sports All-Stars in the NFL, MLB, NBA and NASCAR
- Oscar Winners: John Wayne, Steven Spielberg, and Michael Moore
- Business Leaders: Bill Gates (Microsoft), Sam Walton (Walmart), Brad Tilden (Alaska Airlines), and Bill Marriott (Marriott Hotels)

During the school year, I had a job at the Salida Drugstore. I went in at 7:00 am and got the soda fountain ready for the day, going across the street to pick up baked goods for the mornings' coffee club, which consisted mostly of business owners in the downtown area. The owners, Riley and Hess Bartley, trusted me enough that I had a key to the back door so I could come and set up, and then go when I had to dash off to school. I made good money and I worked there all the way through high school. The Bartleys knew that, in the winter, I wouldn't be there on weekends and holidays because I would be skiing.

Once I had my Eagle Scout, I was going to quit the boy scouts, but Roman Fisher sat me down and explained that programs like scouting have to be paid forward. He told me he needed help with the younger scouts and I should help until I graduated from high school. I did the only thing I could, which was help with skiing. I started teaching the younger scouts and helping out when I wasn't working or playing football. I soon discovered that I really liked teaching, but I didn't realize I was gaining a skill that would lead me to a nice career.

Roman was a leader of men and I was really blessed having him in my life. He instilled in me the ethos of paying things forward and, to this day, I find myself trying to pass that on to young people I encounter in my skiing family.

At Monarch, the two original trails were Kanonen, which loosely translated to Gunbarrel, and the little hill named Snowflake. Gunbarrel was really steep, and it ran into a totally flat spot about 20 yards wide. It became a goal for us to go to the very top and straight-line schuss down, trying to make it across the flat and up to the top of Snowflake and Inn Ferno. The challenge was that the g-force, after hitting the flat area from the steep section, caused a compression that sat you back and you lost control of your tips, which would instantly either split or cross. Believe me when I say neither of those things at high speed ended without an extraction of pain. I can't tell you how many times I had the wind knocked out of me or the occasional bloody nose.

Gunbarrel in today's world would be at least a black diamond and, in some cases, a double black diamond. Dan Cady and I were the instigators of many a new guy at Monarch getting splattered from the compression of Kanonen.

One really big snow day came along. We had a group of scouts up at Monarch and it took about two hours to get Gunbarrel packed and ready to ski. Our packing crew consisted of 10 or 12 people, including Terry Campbell who was on snow shoes—he packed in an ever increasing circle while the rest of us sidestepped our way down the hill after a grueling ride up the rope tow. When we finally got it done, we went up to the top, skied down once, and then went back up.

Dan decided he was going to zoom across to Snowflake. I said, "You are going to eat it big time because the snow is really soft." Away he went and we all watched breathlessly as he approached the flat. To our great surprise, he made it all the way to Inn Ferno. Triumph!

In March of 1956, my buddy, Dan Cady, and I somehow convinced our parents that we should go to Aspen for spring break. I had saved enough money to pull it off and Dan's parents, Jack and Jerry, thought it would be a great idea, because they could drive us over to Aspen, ski for a day themselves, and then come back and ski another day when they picked us up. Both of us were 14 years old. Dan was a healthy 6'2" and I was a scrawny 5'6". Funny enough, he was eight months younger than me.

Unfortunately, Jerry Cady was hit by a skier in Spar Gulch (one of the fine runs on Ajax Mountain) breaking her leg. She had to have surgery that night in the Aspen hospital and they wanted to keep her for four or five days. Jack went home and Dan and I would visit her at the hospital, after skiing all day, before we went for dinner. Amazingly, she had a full recovery with a nice piece of titanium in her tibia. Jerry returned to skiing the very next year with no pain and no fear, and she skied well into her 60's.

Dan and I had the best time on that trip and we found a way to stretch our money for maximum fun. We found a hostel called Ed's Beds for $3.00 per night. It was a dorm with bunk beds and separate areas for men and women. It was also spring break for the University of Colorado and other colleges so we were there with lots of college students.

Dan and I had figured out the meals and, every other night after skiing, we'd go to the Jerome Hotel for the Skier's Special, which cost $5.00. We would order one and split it. Then the next night, we'd go to Pinocchio's Pizza and split a $3.00 pizza. On the mountain for lunch, we could get a burger and fries for $1.00 and it was really a big meal.

Dan had a quirk that was well known by all who knew him—he was a catsup addict. He would literally go through a whole bottle of catsup eating one burger with fries. I think his calorie count was probably in the high thousands. If it was today, where you get the little packets, he would have gone through the whole basket in one sitting. Being seventh graders, we were oblivious about tipping, so I think the waiters came to hate us.

We were the best skiers at Monarch and were really comfortable skiing anything, so by the end of the week we had skied every run on Ajax Mountain. On Thursday, they had a ski race that cost $1.00 to enter and it included a black and white photo that you picked up the next day. I am happy to say that I won that race and, more importantly, I beat Dan.

During that whole week, when we went into a lift line or ended up around the CU students, invariably a coed would approach Dan and say, "If you can ditch your little brother, I will meet you in the bar and we can dance." Remember, at 14 he was 6'2", blond and looked like a Greek God on the slopes. So, in the end, I really didn't win the race in Aspen.

Dan's dad came and picked us up on Sunday and we were back in school that Monday with our raccoon tans and memories that have lasted a lifetime. 1955-56 was a very good ski year for a lot of us, but it was an exceptional year for Dan and me!

This is my favorite photo of Dan. He was skiing at Vail in 1964, when we were both on the ski patrol. Dan skied off a cliff and this photo was used in a poster to promote skiing. It was hung in airports all around the U.S.

Dan Cady skiing at Vail in 1964

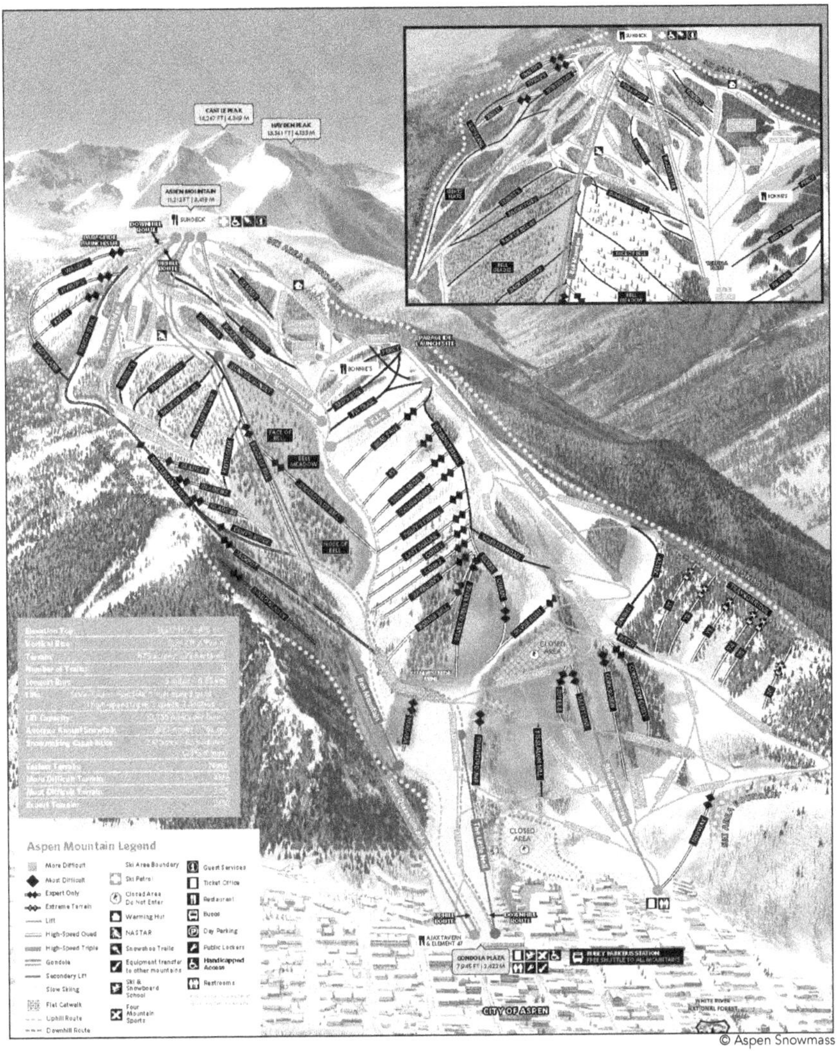

Aspen Snowmass Ski Resort
Aspen, Colorado

- The Aspen Ski Corporation was founded by Friedl Pfeifer, Johnny Litchfield, Percy Rideout, and Walter Paepcke. There are four mountains that now make up this resort located within the White River National Forest.
- Aspen Mountain (map pictured) currently boasts 76 runs over 675 skiable acres. There are 8 lifts, a vertical drop of 3,267 feet and an annual snowfall of 300 inches.
- Aspen Snowmass has hosted the X Games for over 20 years at Buttermilk.
- They offer private and group lessons for children and adults.
- Learn more at AspenSnowmass.com.

Chapter 5

1959-1960: National Ski Patrol

Estes Park, Colorado
40.3772° N, 105.5217° W
Base Elevation: 9,400 Feet (2,965 M)
Peak Elevation: 11,400 Feet (3,475 M)

In 1959, I had two goals. The first was to get my Senior Ski Patrolman test done so when I went to college, I could get on a volunteer Ski Patrol and ski for free. There are two types of ski patrol positions: professional, where you are a paid employee of that ski area, and volunteer, where you get a season pass in exchange for working your shifts. Dan Cady and I had been volunteer Junior Patrolmen at Monarch for two years and we were pretty sure we could pass, but we had to be tested.

My second goal was to graduate and get a good summer job so I would have enough spending money when I went to Colorado State University (CSU) that fall. Dan had applied to get into the University of Colorado and was accepted. We were heading in different directions, but fate would intervene, and our paths would merge in ways we didn't expect.

The National Ski Patrol (NSP) was founded by Charles Minot "Minnie" Dole in 1938. During WWII, Dole had established the 10th Mountain Division as the NSP screened all of the applicants. By the time of his retirement, Dole had expanded the NSP to 4,000 members working on 300 ski patrols. Today, there are over 31,000 members serving on 650 patrols throughout the U.S., Canada, Europe, Asia, and certain military areas.

The patrol test day rolled around, landing on my 18th birthday in January of 1960. The test was held at Monarch Mountain. In addition to Dan and me, there were six or seven other candidates along with three judges; one from Pueblo, Colorado and two from the Denver area. What I remember most about that test was the age of the other candidates and the judges. They all were in their 30's and 40's and most seemed to me to be okay skiers, but none stood out as being exceptional. In the skiing task, it was clear that Dan and I were above the bar that was expected in that exam.

Ski Patrol are responsible for safety on the mountain, dealing with emergencies, accidents, and injuries. We are the first ones on the mountain, making sure the terrain is safe, and the last ones off the mountain, ensuring no one is left on the mountain after dark. So, the test focuses on a variety of safety and terrain skills. This includes first aid, safely transporting injured people in toboggans, getting people off stopped ski lifts, and assessing for and resolving natural dangers like blizzards and avalanches.

Dan and I were test partners and we aced the task of getting the toboggan to the site of the staged accident and making the correct first aid decisions. When we had to ski the toboggan, loaded with the victim to the bottom of the steepest run, it was really easy because we had been practicing on that hill for at least three years. Some of the other candidates were struggling with the steepness and it was obvious that, wherever they skied, it did not have a run like the Gunbarrel at Monarch.

The last task was to find someone who was lost out of the boundary of the ski area. This entailed figuring out where they were most likely to be and then climb and get above that, so you could ski down to where they were and guide them back to the ski area.

Climbing through snow at 10,000 to 11,300 feet above sea level is no easy task, especially in ski boots and carrying gear. But Dan and I played on an intramural basketball team twice a week and we skied seven hours every weekend day. Plus this was familiar ground for us. We snuck out of bounds all the time to get to fresh powder, so we had a pretty good idea where someone would be. The task had a time frame of 90 minutes to be back at the base area. So, when the judges said "Go!" we took off like a shot and almost immediately found the tracks where they left the area. We charged up the hill to get above them and were back at the base in just over 40 minutes. The poor guys who worked at a desk all week and skied at areas of lesser altitude straggled in at the last moment. We got our badges and were set for the next year. I think only one other candidate passed the test that day.

My second goal was solved before the ski season was over because my grandfather's brother, Willis, was a superintendent at Climax Molybdenum Mine and he found me a job working in the miners' housing hotel. My job was to be a dishwasher five days a week and it was one of the dirtiest jobs I ever had. I was paid $3.00 an hour plus room and board from June 6th to August 30th.

The mine ran 24 hours per day, seven days a week. The first shift ate breakfast at 6:00 am and dinner at 6:00 pm, while the second shift had brunch at 12:00 pm and dinner at 12:00 am. The graveyard shift had breakfast at 9:00 pm and another breakfast at 9:00 am. Each shift had a wait staff of six to twelve people depending on how many diners were expected, and there were two or three of us dishwashers for each meal. My partner, Bob Foster, and I worked the day shift, so we started at 6:00 am and worked the 9:00 am, 12:00 pm, and 6:00 pm meals. If we had time from one crowd to the next, we would go to our rooms and nap or read or go outside and hike. It was a really good way to save money for college.

The workers in the mine all had a brass disk with their company number on it—when they entered the mine, they handed the disk to the shift supervisor who put it on a board. At the end of shift, it would be given back to the miner to ensure no one was missing. Those same disks were used when miners entered the dining hall so they would be charged for that meal.

One day we were working and, all of a sudden, we heard a lot of noise with chairs being knocked around and the wait staff came scurrying into our area. Apparently, someone flipped a serving spoon full of mashed potatoes on the guy across the table and a massive food fight broke out, turning into a riot almost immediately. Bob and I turned our sprayers on the highest heat and faced them toward the doorway so that anyone trying to get to us had to come through a wall of steam. Security showed up and herded the mob outside where everyone calmed down. We did not have to wash dishes that day because a professional cleanup crew handled all the food, broken dishes, and furniture. Every person who was in the dining room was charged for the damage done that day, which I suspect was thousands of dollars.

I was so happy after that summer ended and I went to Fort Collins to attend college. Part of our preparation included attending a special class on avalanche safety. The instructor had a slideshow of avalanche paths throughout Colorado. Imagine the looks on our faces when he showed a photo of an area that Dan and I had skied many times when we were in junior high and high school. We would sneak out of bounds and climb up to this great place with no trees and always good snow. He identified it as a very treacherous hazard. Dan and I looked at each other as we realized we could have been killed there many times.

At Christmas, I came home for the two-week break and went to Monarch to ski. As I was getting my ski boots on, the ski school director asked me if I wanted to teach skiing over the holidays. At first, I said I didn't know how to teach, but she cut me off and reminded me that I had taught her son when he was in the Boy Scouts. So I landed my first actual job as a professional ski instructor, getting paid to teach. Monarch was an easy place to reach from Kansas, Oklahoma, and Texas so we had a good crowd for those two weeks. I had an absolute blast teaching.

My first lesson was a 11-person group lesson and the students had never been on skis. They were all cadets from the U.S. Air Force Academy in Colorado Springs. Most were my age or slightly older, all were fit, and all were used to taking orders. I went through the entire teaching progression in four hours because they followed directions so well. I said, "This is a straight run," and then I demonstrated it. I'd stop and say, "Now you try it and come down to me." In unison, I heard 11 people say, "Yes, Sir!" and then they'd do it perfectly. Next was the snowplow—I'd explain it, demonstrate it, tell them to try it, and hear, "Yes, Sir!" We kept going and they were doing parallel turns by the end of the lesson four hours later.

I got paid $25 that day and at dinner my dad asked me if I liked teaching. I raved about how easy it was and how much I loved it. I still love it, but 62 years later, I have never had another lesson like that one. At the end of the 14 days, I went back to school with more money in my pocket than I made in 90 days of washing dishes.

Skiing powder in a favorite sweater that my mom knit

Back at CSU, I signed up for a skiing physical education class to further my career preparation. It was held at Hidden Valley in Rocky Mountain National Park—it closed in 1991 and is now known as one of the "lost resorts" (see sidebar). We took the bus every Wednesday and skied with an instructor. It was great fun, but the best part was that I met a guy, Bill Sears, who would become a lifelong friend, mentor, boss, employee, and confidant. As I was getting off the bus the second day, I had my Ski Patrol fanny pack on and, as I passed him, he grabbed it and said, "Where do you patrol?" I replied, "I am hoping to get on the patrol at Arapahoe Basin." He told me he was an A-Basin patrolman, and that he was going up that weekend and asked if I wanted to join him and a couple of friends. Of course, I jumped at the chance and met Bill and his girlfriend that weekend. Three years later, I was best man at their wedding!

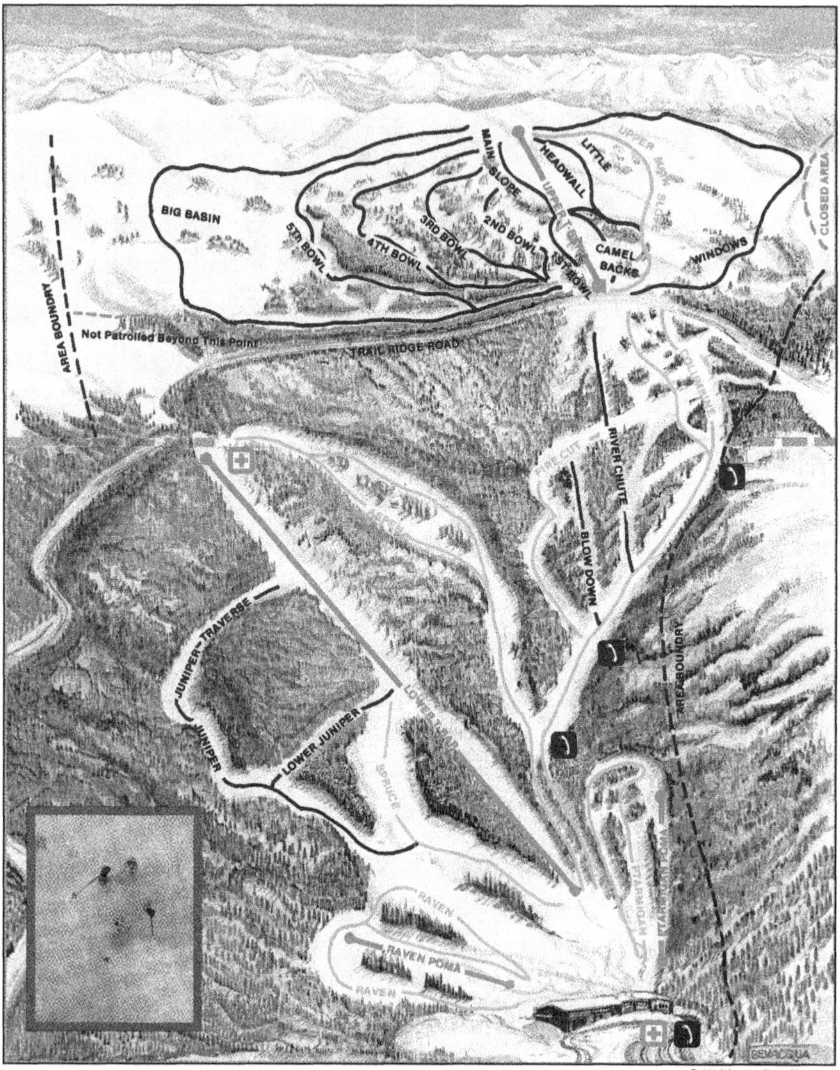

© Hidden Valley Ski Area

Hidden Valley Ski Area
Estes Park, Colorado

- Founded in 1955 and closed in 1991, Hidden Valley featured 27 runs over 800 skiable acres in the Rocky Mountain National Park.
- It is considered one of the "lost resorts"—one of 145 Colorado ski areas that are now dormant.
- There were 7 lifts (including two T-Bars and two Pomas) and a vertical drop of 2,000 feet. The average snowfall was 156 inches.
- Learn more at ColoradoSkiHistory.com/lost/skiestespark.html.

II. PATROLLING & TEACHING

"Powder snow skiing is not fun. It's life, fully lived, life lived in a blaze of reality."

Dolores LaChapelle,
skier, mountaineer, and pioneer
ecologist in the Rocky Mountains

Chapter 6

1961-1962: Arapahoe Basin

Dillon, Colorado
39.6425° N, 105.8719° W
Base Elevation: 10,520 Feet (3,206 M)
Peak Elevation: 13,050 Feet (3,978 M)

My time at Arapahoe Basin started with that fateful meeting with Bill Sears at Hidden Valley. I met him and his girlfriend that weekend and luck was in my favor because when we arrived, Dan Cady was there as it was his first day patrolling for A-Basin. The patrol director, Jerry Pasacani, approached us and said that there was some worry that since Dan and I were coming from Monarch, they needed to make sure we could ski well enough to join their patrol. He wanted to send us out with his assistant, Tom Anderson.

Bill jumped in and said, "This is ridiculous! They have already passed their patrol test." Dan and I both said we didn't mind and let's go. Tom took us to the Pallavicini run, which was covered with a foot of new snow. Tom said, "I will ski down and stop. When I wave, you guys ski down to me." Dan and I were busting a gut watching him bumble his way down. He waved and Dan peeled off and killed it. I jumped in and intentionally made figure eights over Dan's tracks. Tom didn't say much, but when we came in the door, Jerry asked Tom how we did. Tom replied, "FU Jerry! These guys are better skiers than anyone on this patrol."

Dan, Bill, and I had a good laugh about that. Thank God Tom didn't take us to moguls! Luckily, Dan and I were both assigned to the Ski Patrol at A-Basin, so we didn't have to part ways after all. And we had a great weekend skiing with Bill and Betty.

That was the winter that I quit being a forestry major at CSU and switched my major to skiing. I was taking a PE class that allowed me to earn credits for skiing on Wednesday and every weekend at Arapahoe Basin.

We had a friend from CSU who was ski patrolling and avalanche controlling at A-Basin, so we could bring our sleeping bags and couch surf at his house. Or we could sleep in the patrol room or on a cot in the bathrooms. When I got my grades at the end of spring term, it was obvious that I had checked out. But I didn't mind because I was living the dream and doing something I dearly loved.

When you love what you do, you care about the place and people in a deeper way. One day, I noticed that the patrol room door was in really bad shape. Which was no surprise, really, since it took quite a beating every day. When we brought a toboggan off the hill with an injured skier, we would detach the litter from the toboggan and pick up the litter to bring the injured skier inside. The front guy would kick the patrol room door open and, with help from the patrol room staff, we would unload the person and repack the toboggan to take it back up the hill. The patrol room door had seen many years of service and was badly in need of replacement.

Bill Sear's dad was owner of Sears Trostel Lumber Yard in Fort Collins, Colorado and Bill was (and still is) an innovative problem solver. His dad had just received a shipment of high quality doors and one was damaged in transit, so Bill talked his dad into giving it to the A-Basin Ski Patrol. Bill and I fixed the damaged part and put a stainless steel plate on the bottom panel of the door so that it would survive many more years of kicks. On a previous trip, Bill had measured the dimensions of the door so when we got there, we would be able to take the old door down and install the new door in a matter of minutes. There was only one problem left to solve...how do we get the door from Fort Collins to A-Basin? On a great weather day, it was at best a three-hour drive. We decided we would take it up the next Saturday and have it installed by 9:00 am.

At 5:00 am, Bill picked me up at my apartment and we headed out. Bill's car was a really cool, copper-colored, 1957 Chevy Bel Air Convertible with a ski rack on the trunk of the car. To fit the door, we had to put the convertible top down, place the door behind the front seats, and rope it to the ski rack. Needless to say, it was really cold; probably 30° Fahrenheit in Fort Collins and -20° at the top of Loveland Pass.

Being young and somewhat stupid, we really thought we had it all figured out. We had put on all the warm clothes we owned, including down sleeping bags wrapped around our bodies from our armpits down to our toes—except for Bill's right foot. Bill turned the heater on and the fan was blowing at the highest possible level.

Until the sun came up as we were driving through Georgetown, we were oblivious to other cars on the road. As daylight came, we started to get some really funny looks from cars passing us. We arrived at A-Basin a few minutes before 8:00 am and nearly frozen. But we still got that new door in place by 8:30 am. As I remember it, it took us a couple of hours to thaw out, but then we had a weekend of great skiing.

Another great memory of A-Basin was spring break in 1962 when we decided to ski 10 straight days. Bill and I, and another friend from CSU, Leo Eisel, put together a plan for how we could ski for 10 days on the cheap. We were three Eagle Scouts planning to "Be Prepared." We would split in thirds all the gas used. Bill made 90 sandwiches—one-third peanut butter and jelly, one-third baloney, and one-third ham. They were stowed in the trunk and, of course, frozen solid. We would grab one when we were hungry, put it inside our jacket, tucked under our armpit and, by the time we got to the patrol shack at the top, it was thawed enough to be edible.

Bill and I were patrolling so we each got a free pass for every day we worked. We gave one per day to Leo and we split the other passes among our friends who showed up to ski with us. Those two weeks were great fun.

A-Basin is one of the historic and iconic ski areas in the world. It was started by 10th Mountain veterans and former racers, Larry Jump and Sandy Schauffler. When they saw the range, they realized they could recreate the high, steep snowing they had enjoyed in the Alps.

A-Basin is Colorado's highest ski area in terms of elevation. As a result, it is usually the first area to open in Colorado and generally the last area to close. They have been open for skiing on numerous Fourth of July holiday weekends!

It was the first ski area to open in Colorado after World War II, started with all $25,000 of Larry's life savings. Max and Edna Dercum helped launch Arapahoe Basin. The couple had come to Colorado in 1942 as part of the second "gold rush" to launch new ski areas. They helped start both A-Basin and Keystone, along with Thor Groswold, who had a ski manufacturing business in Denver. His son, Jerry, would eventually become a long-time manager at Winter Park Resort.

A-Basin was the home for Willie Schaeffler, Head Coach of the University of Denver (DU) Ski Team, which won 13 of 18 NCAA skiing championships that they participated in during his career. Edna was also a competitor, competing in downhill racing and ski jumping events the first year she learned to ski. She wrote the book *It's Easy, Edna. It's Downhill All the Way*. Their son, Rolf Dercum, also skied at DU for Willie's team.

Another fine memory was one night we splurged and went to Max and Edna Dercum's Ski Tip Ranch for dinner. Afterwards, we schmoozed with their guests and listened to Max and a couple of people tell stories and sing for hours. The highlight of the night was watching Dale Gallagher climb up the fireplace and then traverse the high ceiling while Max belayed him. Everyone gasped and laughed. Like me, and most other male skiers I know, Edna was the reason Max succeeded and had such a blessed life.

Interestingly, both Max and Dale played major roles in the growth of the ski industry and the inception of the PSIA. Dale went on to be part of the Big 3 in avalanche prediction and control along with Monty Attwater and Ed LaChappele.

Most importantly to me, A-Basin was the place I learned from Max Dercum and his staff how to teach skiing as I prepared for my first PSIA exam in 1965. A-Basin is also where I proposed to my wife, whom I've been with for 55 years. Max and Edna were married 71 years and skied well into their late 80's—I hope to beat their records.

Arapahoe Basin Ski Area
Dillon, Colorado

- Founded in 1946 by two WWII veterans, Larry Jump and Sandy Schauffler. A-Basin currently boasts 145 runs over 1,428 skiable acres in the White River National Forest.
- There are 9 lifts and a vertical drop of 2,530 feet. The average snowfall is 350 inches and it was the first post-WWII ski area to open in Colorado.
- It is the third highest ski area peak elevation in North America.
- They offer group and private lessons for both children and adults.
- Learn more at ArapahoeBasin.com.

Chapter 7

1962-1963: Vail

Vail, Colorado
39.6433° N, 106.3781° W
Base Elevation: 8,120 Feet (2,476 M)
Peak Elevation: 11,570 Feet (3,527 M)

After two years of college, Dan Cady and I had been trying to figure out what we were going to do professionally…skiing won out. We heard about this new ski area, called Vail, that was looking for professional Ski Patrolmen. We applied for jobs and Dan got hired but I didn't, so I got a job at Breckenridge Ski Area instead.

Vail was founded by 10th Mountain Division veteran, Pete Siebert, who had worked at Loveland and Aspen ski areas before founding the mountain that he would develop into Colorado's largest resort. Investors included Jack Tweedy and Earl Eaton and early leadership included Morrie Shepard and Rod Slifer to run the ski school.

Vail opened on December 15, 1962 with two ski lifts and one gondola. Not even two weeks later, on the 27th, Dan called me and said they needed to hire two more patrolmen and that I should come for an interview. I did and got hired. I also recommended that they hire Jim Clarke, which they did.

Jim Clarke, or JC, and I first met in 1961 at A-Basin. He'd served in the U.S. Air Force in Europe and had returned to Colorado, working at night and skiing all day on the Ski Patrol. Jim and I had also been roommates. I was 20 years old and under the legal drinking age, but he served me a hot spiced wine with the comment, "If you're a ski patrolman, one of these won't do much damage."

Jim was an elegant skier who appeared in Head Ski advertisements and was one of the featured skiers in the Gerry Mountain Sports campaign for their down-filled ski parkas. Jim still lives in Vail and is on the Board of Directors of the Ski Museum there. Our friendship continues and I'll visit him for the 60th Anniversary of Vail in 2022.

But back to its start. Vail grew quickly. Within the first year, the village at the base of the mountain boasted a ski shop (run by Dick Hauserman and Joe Langmaid) and a ski boutique (run by Blanche Hauserman and Bunny Langmaid). Pepi Gramshammer opened a hotel and restaurant. But at first, we were all thinking that it wasn't going to take off! By the first week in January, the most lift tickets sold per day was seven. Total. In a panic, Bob Parker and Pete Seibert called all their friends in the press and ski industry, inviting them to come to Vail and ski.

Members of Vail's Ski Patrol: George Kelly, Joel Fritz, Carl Nelson, Mike Ewing

All the ski magazines and ski industry press showed up, but the main attraction was Warren Miller, who came to film Vail and the Back Bowls for one of his early movies. Warren asked for two good skiers—Pete was an obvious choice, being the founder. Bob suggested me, since Pete and I were about the same height and looked good together. Pete would wear his black parka and I would wear my red ski patrol parka.

We filmed on a bluebird day with new snow. We went to Milt's Face and Warren skied down to set up his camera. He waved and Pete and I took off and put on a show. About two-thirds of the way down, we got so close to each other that our boots actually touched and we both crashed. Warren was really nice and edited the crash out of the film.

On the lift out of Sunup Bowl, I rode up with Warren and he asked if anyone had jumped off the cliff underneath the chair from Mid-Vail to the Summit. I said, "I don't think so." He said, "Would you be willing?" Being 21 and bulletproof, I replied, "Of course!" He invited Pete to come with us but he declined. Warren set up his camera and I skied off that cliff and we headed back to the lodge. Warren left and business started picking up.

Imagine my surprise a couple years later when I went to a movie in Seattle. The previews ran, including a clip for the new Warren Miller movie coming out. There was a shot, in super slow motion, of a Vail Ski Patrolman skiing into view and then jumping off the cliff at Vail. The camera followed him until he landed

My Life in Winters   35

in four or five feet of powder. I realized it was me! When you skied with Warren for his films, he always gave a pin to the skiers. I still have mine. When Warren passed away, I wore that pin on my uniform in his memory.

Film shoot with Warren Miller at Vail

A few weeks later, midweek in late February, I was on Ski Patrol. We always counted on two or three National Ski Patrol volunteers to show up but none had on this day. At that time, Vail's patrol had 10 members and one was off so we had nine staff on the mountain. This was adequate on most weekdays because the volume was less than weekends when we had the volunteers. Vail was in its first year and had not yet been discovered by the masses.

At 1:15 pm, Patrol Headquarters (PHQ) was graced with the appearance of Don "Mother" Almond, the Ski Patrol Director. He was stopping by for a quick meeting with Milt "Uncle Milty" Wiley, the Assistant Patrol Director. In those days the Director spent most of his time coordinating with the other directors and managers while the Assistant Director ran the mountain part of the operation assigning openings, closings, and organizing the end-of-day sweep. Both Mother and Uncle Milty had come to Vail from Aspen along with the Ski School Director, Morrie Shepard.

In those days, Ajax Mountain at Aspen consisted of fall line trails connected by access road traverses. There was, at that time, virtually no glade or bowl skiing on Ajax and, as a result, the rescue toboggan was known as the "Aspen sled." It was designed to go down the fall line until you hit a road or reached the bottom of the mountain.

The Aspen sled was designed with handles set on a pivot that allowed the front patrolman to ski down the fall line and not get lifted off the ground by the toboggan as you went up one side of a mogul and down the other. The rear patrolman rode a platform made of steel that had brake teeth pointing down at an angle. There was a bar to hold onto with the off hand and a bar sticking up that you pulled back on to apply the brake. The upright bar had a rope attached to it that would apply pressure to the brake in case the back patrolman fell off. This had proven to work fairly well on many occasions and was, in fact, the perfect rescue toboggan for Aspen. For Vail, not so much.

Vail had been scheduled to open by Thanksgiving of 1962, but the weather had not cooperated and we finally got going on December 18th or 19th. By the end of Christmas week, it was obvious that the Aspen sled was virtually worthless in the back bowls and out on the Minturn Mile. Pete Seibert called his friend, Gordy Wren, the Loveland Pass Ski Area Manager, and purchased two Akia toboggans from him for the back side. The training on the Akias was done pretty hurriedly by some of us who had previous experience with these types of rescue sleds. The advantage of the Akia is that it can be skied in full traverse and turns can be made easily by a coordinated team.

However, Mother's and Uncle Milty's training consisted of them watching Dan Cady and I ski one down the Forever Trail in near perfect conditions. We were putting on a show. At that time, we asked them if they wanted to give it a try and they both said no. Uncle Milty probably added some jab like, "If you two yokels can do it, we can get monkeys to do it!"

So on that February day, we were short on patrolmen with two accidents on the front side. PHQ got a call of an injury on the nose of Milt's Face Trail. (Yes, resort founders get to name the trails.) Because we were understaffed, Mother and Uncle Milty were called into action! They grabbed an Akia and off they went. The snow conditions that day were pretty typical of the first years of Vail, loosely packed powder with some patches of wind crust interspersed. The ride to the accident was uneventful because it consisted of a short straight pitch to the injured victim. Upon arriving, they determined it was an injured knee and loaded up the victim, strapped him in, and started down the mountain.

Uncle Milty was on the front and Mother was on the back as they crested the flat to the steep pitch of Milt's Face. They immediately started to accelerate to Mach One speed. Whether or not they ever engaged the chain brake in the front of the Akia is up for discussion. In soft snow, it was virtually worthless as far as slowing down. These two Aspen boys did what they knew; they stayed in the fall line. It was getting scary because they knew if they reached the transition at the bottom, it was going to get ugly. So with Uncle Milty wondering why Mother was not applying the brake, and Mother hanging on for dear life, a high speed left turn was attempted and partially executed.

In those days there were several places on the back side of the mountain where there were snow holes created by the wind that were about 10 or 12 feet in diameter and as deep as five or six feet. It was great fun when we were skiing with some unsuspecting visiting patrolman to ski them into one of these. Joel Fritz, a patrolman from Winter Park, can attest to this because "I got him" the first time he skied Vail.

As luck would have it, Mother and Uncle Milty skied into one just after they started the turn. Mother must have thought that if he pushed down on the rear handles hard enough he could make it go slower. This is not the case, but it may have saved him from a serious injury. Uncle Milty must have seen the snow hole just before impact because he, too, pushed down on the handles just enough that he got his feet high enough to have the Akia pin him into the snow hole wall right at the back of his boots and not his legs. He described the crash as being "like a snowball thrown against a brick wall." Mother ended up running into Uncle Milty's back and knocking the wind out of both of them.

The victim in the sled, you ask? What happened to him? Mother said that he heard muffled cries that he couldn't understand and then realized he was hearing, "GET THE F&%# OFF ME!" Luckily, no one was seriously injured and Uncle Milty shared the story with me and a couple other patrolmen later. To my knowledge, neither Uncle Milty nor Mother ever touched another Akia toboggan again.

Dan and I had a great career at Vail. Several times, we were chosen to be part of press events and we'd later see our photos in ads for skiing in magazines and posters hanging in airports. We thought that was pretty cool! We loved skiing together, we loved working together, and we were a really good patrol team because we had been skiing together our entire lives.

Mike featured in an ad for skiing in Colorado

After the first year, when Vail closed for the summer, Dan, two other patrolmen, a nurse from Vail, and I went to Mazatlan, Mexico, where we lived on the beach for six weeks. This was before Mazatlan became the popular recreational area it is now. It was 1963 and there was hardly anything there—a little village and a great beach but very little tourism. We had a great time there. We spent very little money and had all kinds of fun.

Back in high school, I had taken Spanish for three years and was fairly fluent in the language, so I was doing most of the translating. Apparently, I was pretty cocky because Dan blew up at me about what a smart ass I was and told me in no uncertain terms that he did not need me to translate for him. The next night, we all got together for dinner and I sat there and let Dan order off the menu. I didn't correct him and, much to his chagrin, they delivered soup when he thought he had ordered something else. He slowly stirred the soup and you could see it had some kind of meat in it. Dan looked around and asked, "What is this?" and I said, "It's menudo....cow's stomach." I can still see the look on his face when he realized I knew all along what he was ordering. He turned beet red and the whole table was in convulsions. I thought he might kill me, but he eventually saw the humor and we all had a good laugh.

Later in his life, Dan earned his pilot's license and flew for the Air Force National Guard, teaching others how to fly. He flew for Aspen Airways, Frontier Airlines, and US Airways. In the meantime, I had gotten my certification to be a ski instructor, managed a ski shop, and ended up working in the ski business.

When I was working for K2 Skis, I was flying to Aspen when the pilot came on the loudspeaker and made the typical speech just after we were in the air. I asked the flight attendant if that was Dan Cady—it was and he invited me to come sit in the cockpit. As we flew into Aspen, I was hanging on for dear life as he laughed—flying was so normal for him and so scary for me.

The last time I saw Dan was at the Patrol Party at Vail's 50th Anniversary celebration. He acted just like he always did when we were together—having a great time with lots of smiles and laughter. I thought it was the best moment because Dan and I knew how much we meant to each other and were not afraid to express it. Unfortunately, Dan passed away on October 26, 2014, but I will never forget my dear friend and all that we shared.

Vail & Beaver Creek Resorts
Vail, Colorado

- Founded in 1962 by Pete Siebert, Earl Eaton, Harley Higbie, Bill Brown, Bob Parker, and others. With 5,317 skiable acres, it is the fourth largest skiable terrain in North America and is located in the White River National Forest.
- There are 31 lifts, a vertical rise of 3,450 feet, and an average snowfall of 354 inches.
- Vail (map pictured) has 3 sections: Front-Side, Blue Sky Basin, and the Back Bowls. It also includes several terrain parks for freestyle enthusiasts.
- Beaver Creek is a sister resort located 13 miles away. It has 24 lifts, 167 trails over 2,082 skiable acres, and a vertical rise of 3,340 feet. It gets an average snowfall of 325 inches and has a tubing park.
- Both resorts offer private and group lessons for children and adults.
- Learn more at Vail.com.

Chapter 8

1964-1965: Mid-Vail, Colorado

Mid-Vail, Colorado
39.6433° N, 106.3781° W
Elevation: 10,250 Feet (3,125 M)

Two more incidents happened at Vail Resort that changed my life forever. The first was that Vail paid for Jim Clarke and me to attend the U.S. Forest Service's Avalanche School. I came away from it with a great deal of knowledge and, on more than one occasion, it has saved my life and the lives of others.

The second happened after Christmas. I was in the Ski Patrol Headquarters at the top of Vail, when a call came in from a phone on Riva Ridge from an instructor with 10 kids stuck on Tourist Trap, a run that has a steep pitch. She was stressed because it was especially cold and she couldn't get them moving. I decided to take the challenge, so I grabbed some extra goggles, hats, and gloves and skied down to find her.

Sure enough, there she was and it was a mess—the kids were missing equipment and many of them were cold and crying. I took care of getting the equipment on the kids and we got them moving with her leading and me bringing up the rear. We finally got them off the steep pitch and everyone calmed down, so we played a game of leapfrog the rest of the way down to the meeting place for the parents to pick up the kids.

As I was leaving to go to the patrol room, the instructor called out and invited me to meet her after work at the Copper Bar so she could buy me a beer. The first rule of being a ski patrolman is "never pass up a free beer," so we went and got a beer or three. I am always curious about people, so I started asking questions about her skiing and how she came to be teaching kids at Vail.

Well, it turned out that Georgene Dunn was a Winter Park Eskimo and had been a gifted racer, winning the 1952 U.S. Junior National Ski Championship, the same year that Buddy Werner won. He was 17 and Georgene was 16. Buddy went to the 1956 Olympics, but Georgene couldn't go because you had to be 18 by the time the Games began. Right after the Olympics, Georgene had a chance to race against the Olympic champion and she beat her by six whole seconds. There is no doubt in my mind that she would have won Olympic Gold if she'd been allowed to compete.

Sadly, Georgene became a victim to the dangers of crashing on the flats. At Winter Park she broke her leg in 14 places with a spiral fracture down her tibia and fibula, a common injury at that time due the stiffening of the ski boot. She had surgery and her bone was repaired with metal bands, but she could not heal well enough to get back to racing. Instead, she became an instructor and actually started the children's ski school at Vail.

What was amazing about Georgene's skill was that she only skied on the weekends at Winter Park; whereas her peers skied every day on more advanced slopes. Around Colorado it was a known fact that watching the ski train arrive for skiing at Winter Park on a weekend was an event to behold. For a few minutes the train seemed to be trembling, then the doors would open, and the area would fill up with colorful, hyper-excited kids from Denver. Heaven forbid if you were caught in a lift line when they arrived.

Georgene's success in racing led Steve Bradley, the General Manager of Winter Park, to leverage her accomplishment to get investments for expanding the ski area. It is the exceptional resort that it is today because of her talent.

We finished up our beers—she was a little older than me and was wearing a wedding ring, so we went our separate ways. A few days later, I bumped into her on Bridge Street on my way to a party and she asked if she could come with me. Honestly, I was trying to hook up with a new nurse in the clinic, but I didn't see any harm in letting her come along so I said yes.

We enjoyed the party that evening. At some point, Georgene came over and said, "I'm ready to leave and since you brought me, you should leave with me." We headed back to my apartment and talked. It was then that she disclosed that her husband, Pete, was a U.S. Air Force pilot stationed in Canada. She said he was having an affair with a nurse and she was trying to make sense of what was going to happen when he came home on furlough in mid-March.

I told her that I was not too interested in being part of that scene. She put her coat on, I walked her to the door, and she turned and embraced me. Then she kissed me and said, "Thanks for understanding," which was crazy because by then I was totally confused about what I was feeling. As expected, we started seeing each other and started seriously dating, spending nights together at my apartment or hers.

On January 10, 1965, Glen Yarborough held an evening concert at Mid-Vail to raise funds for a school. Mid-Vail is a large restaurant built halfway up the mountain at the top of Gondola #1. I volunteered to be the patrolman on site in case first aid was needed. Georgene and several other instructors volunteered to work the event as well. After the concert, we helped get the attendees loaded on the gondola and Georgene and I were there until the last gondola reached the bottom of the hill. We had brought our skis and head lamps, so we called the lift operator at the bottom and told him that we were going to ski down. But we stayed a bit longer and made love on that moonlit night.

The last week in February, I was at Arapahoe Basin ski area training for the PSIA exam. I was in the lift line and looked up and saw Georgene's car pull into the parking lot. I skied over and she got out of the car and walked over to me and said, "I have either good news or bad news; I can't figure out which. I am pregnant." All I said was, "How can that be bad news? I will head home and we can figure out what we are going to do."

We spent a couple of days talking it over and I said, "Let's get married and make a life at Vail." Her response was, "Yes, but it will be complicated until I see Pete in March." To my surprise, he did not try to kill me when he arrived in Vail and learned about us and the baby. Also, to my surprise, he told Georgene he wanted to stay married, which set up the two worst months of my life.

I was torn with the fact that I really wasn't ready to settle down and I didn't think marrying a woman nine years my senior was a great decision, but I was also in love with Georgene and excited to be a father. Pete and Georgene decided to work with a marriage counselor in Denver to try to fix their marriage.

In the meantime, I took my PSIA test in April at Loveland Ski Area and passed. Loveland first opened in 1936 by J.C. Blickensderfer. In 1955, Pete Siebert was hired as General Manager before he went on to found Vail. Loveland is near the Eisenhower Tunnel, which opened in the 1970's and crosses the Continental Divide. Otto Werlin was inspired by the pumps and compressors used to dig the tunnel and innovated their use for making snow, an invention now used at ski areas around the world. With the increasing threat of global warming, this might just be the thing that saves the ski industry. More on that later.

In the meantime, Georgene and Pete kept popping up to Vail, which put me in some awkward situations. On one of their visits, they said that their marriage counselor would like me to come in and have a talk with him. I was not comfortable with the idea, but I agreed to go to their counselor.

It was one of the most interesting hours of my life. The counselor asked about my life, how I saw myself, and all kinds of questions that seemed like he was trying to lead me to walk away. But we ran out of time and he asked if I could come back for another session. I agreed, but I came to the next session with questions of my own. He did not take kindly to being challenged. He ended the session by telling me that all my life I had the opinion that I was a good guy. But he saw no possible way I could come out of this without being the villain.

I told Georgene that I was not going to any more sessions. I asked that she make her decision and let me know as soon as possible. Unfortunately, fate played a pivotal role in the final decision. Two days later, her car was rear ended by a dump truck filled with sand at a stoplight in Denver. She was injured quite seriously and doctors told her it was going to be a long-term recovery. She was forced to choose between a life with me, a ski bum, or an officer in the U.S. Air Force who could get her the best medical care available.

Three weeks later, she and I met at her family's cabin on Red Feather Lakes to say goodbye. We agreed that our child would be told the truth about being born from love and that she had a birth father. There was no phone at the cabin and that afternoon her mother unexpectedly showed up to inform me that my grandfather had just passed away and I needed to get home.

Six months later, Georgene called to tell me that our daughter, Britt, had been born at the USAF base hospital in Canada. I had no communication with Georgene until six years later when we met in a chance situation at the ski show in Denver. We talked and I got an update on my daughter. After that, we did not communicate until 1978 when we bumped into each other at Vail while I was working for the K2 Ski Company.

I did not meet my daughter until 30 years later when Britt contacted me. We both had been waiting for the other person to reach out. I'm pleased to say that we started our relationship in 1998 and have been in each other's lives ever since. In fact, she's the one who encouraged me to write this book.

Winter Park Resort
Winter Park, Colorado

- Originally founded in 1932 as Hideaway Park by Linus Oliver "Doc" Graves and his wife, Helen, it was incorporated in 1978 and renamed Winter Park. It currently boasts 167 runs over 3,081 skiable acres in the Arapaho and Roosevelt National Forests.
- There are 23 lifts and a vertical drop of 3,060 feet. The average snowfall is 327 inches and it is the closest resort to Denver.
- They offer lessons for adults and children as well as tubing, snow biking, and snowcat tours.
- Learn more at WinterParkResort.com.

Chapter 9

1965-1966: National Ski Safety Research

46.9282° N, 121.5045° W
Base Elevation: 4,400 Feet (1,341 M)
Peak Elevation: 6,872 Feet (2,094 M)

In the Winter of 1965-66, I decided to leave Vail and work for the Ski Safety Research Project. My friend, Dr. Jim Garrick, and his colleague, Bill Sears, had received a research grant from the federal government to ascertain the economic impact of injuries suffered while skiing. Jim was a Mayo Clinic Fellow in Orthopedic Surgery and Bill was a doctoral student at Colorado State University.

At this time, almost every ski area in the United States operated under a lease agreement with the U.S. Forest Service or other similar agencies managing public lands. The injury rate as far as anyone knew was anywhere from five percent to as high as 12 percent, but there was really no data to support these numbers. Garrick's proposal was to staff a group of knowledgeable skiers, mostly Ski Patrolmen, and gather data at twelve ski areas in the United States including Vail in Colorado, Stratton in Vermont, Crystal Mountain in Washington, and Buck Hill in Minnesota.

The goal was to gather accurate information about the frequency and severity of injuries and, ultimately, to make skiing a safer sport. The timing of this research coincided with the push to create recreational opportunities for the growing families in the baby boomer surge. The government had just finished a program called Operation 66, which doubled the camping and picnicking areas managed by the federal agencies. By making skiing safer, more people would likely join in winter recreation, and specifically skiing, throughout the public lands managed by the federal government.

I was lucky and told that I'd get my first choice of ski area to which I'd be assigned. I knew it was going to be a western state, but I was not sure which one I should ask for, so I called my friend Billy Marolt. Without a second of hesitation, he told me to go to Crystal Mountain near Mt. Rainier National Park. It turned out to be one of the luckiest decisions I ever made.

I showed up at Crystal right after New Years 1966, on a clear day with 20+ inches of new snow. I went into the office to see Huck Paulson, the General

Manager, who had no idea what I was talking about. It turned out that the Chief Financial Officer had approved the deal without notifying his team.

I had met Huck before when he attended an event I had chaired at Vail for the National Ski Patrol. We had invited ski industry people to come to Vail to look at newly developed rescue equipment to make evacuation of injured skiers safer and faster.

Huck grasped what had happened and said, "Grab your gear and go to the patrol room. Go ski with some of our patrolmen and when you get back I will have this resolved." I went over and introduced myself and the Pro Patrolman on duty said he would show me around the mountain. Boy, was I in for a surprise! Of course, he took me to the toughest trail on the mountain for my introduction to northwest powder. The name of the trail is... wait for it... Exterminator! It has the steepest terrain on Crystal Mountain and is an active avalanche path. Near the bottom, they had built a mound about 25 feet high to deflect avalanches away from the base lodge, which had a moat about 20 feet deep between the mound and the building.

We skied to the top of the run and I noticed two more patrolmen had joined us. Of course they wanted me to go first, so I did. On my first turn, I fell over backwards from the snow resistance on my skis. Remember, I was from Colorado and used to dry snow. They all broke up laughing at me. They said it was pretty funny to watch people try their first run on what they called "Cascade Cement."

At that time, I was skiing what was then called Alta turns, which today are called compression turns. During that era, most skiers were going into turns in deep knee bends and rose up to initiate the turn. But the guys from Alta, Utah, where the powder snow was often chest deep, learned another way. They would keep their upper body stable and lift their knees to initiate the turn. None of the Crystal guys had ever seen that technique before. When we got to the bottom, we went back up and out to more terrain. By the end of the day, I had not only figured out the snow, but I had also created a couple of new Alta turners.

When I went to the office, Huck said, "I got it fixed and your housing is going to be at Green Water," which was a cabin camp about eight miles from the ski area. I also was supposed to have an office, so he took me to a desk and said, "You can work from here." I set up my desk, moved a few things around, and settled in. Boy was I surprised the next Saturday when I came in to find all my stuff neatly stacked on the floor and Grace Devin sitting at my desk.

It turned out that Crystal Mountain had about 300 to 500 skiers a day during the week and 6,000 on the weekends and holidays. Grace was the manager of one of the most profitable parts of the ski school and Huck had given me her desk without telling her. This turned out to be the second most important thing that happened to me at Crystal Mountain. Grace and I became lifelong friends and her family got me into lucky positions that helped me have a great career.

To this day, Grace and her family are some of my most cherished friends. The desk thing worked out perfectly because on weekends I was super busy interviewing every injured skier that went through the ski patrol room, along with other healthy skiers who were randomly selected.

Very quickly, the data was busting some long-held myths. The first myth was that the last run of the day is the most dangerous. Of course, if you started skiing at 9:00 am and broke your leg at 10:00 am, that was your last run of the day! What we did find was that, if you were the weakest skier in your group, you were likely to get exhausted. While the group will wait for their weaker partner to catch up, they often take off again, never allowing the person who needs it most to get a rest.

The second myth was that people were more likely to get hurt on the steep slopes. But, in fact, we were finding that the better skiers were actually getting injured on flatter terrain. Because they were going faster, they would get injured falling as their momentum caused more blunt force trauma. This was true for Georgene, my daughter's mother. She was a talented ski racer but broke her leg in 14 places with a crash on the flats.

One weekend when it wasn't too busy, I happened into the office and Grace was putting her ski boots on and I asked, "Are going out to ski?" She said yes and then asked me, "Do you actually ski?" I jokingly said, "Yes, a little. I'll go get my gear and we can go together." We went out on the hill and rode the lift up and skied down the run and then went up to a run called Green Valley, which was a little steeper and had great snow. Grace told me to lead so I took off and skied down about 25 turns and then watched her ski down to me. When she got there we both said, almost in unison, "Hey, you really can ski!" Grace said, "I can't wait to tell Doug (her husband). He should have you coach in his Mighty Mites program." He was the supervisor of the Mighty Mites program, a Jack Nagel racing program. I'll tell you more about that in Chapter 11.

Skiing epic powder in the Rocky Mountains

My association with Doug and Grace opened a lot of doors for me in the ski community in the Pacific Northwest. Doug Devin worked for a large check printing business but, as a sideline, he imported Haderer Ski Boots from Kitzbuhel, Austria. He also was a rep for A&T Ski Company and Scott Ski Poles.

The Ski Safety Research Project was set to continue for two years and I intended to return after the summer. As the season was winding down, I was packing up all the study results when Huck stopped by my desk with Mel Borgerson, Chairman of the Board of Directors for Crystal Mountain. They invited me to go to lunch with them and we walked over to the Alpine House to eat.

Huck said, "We want to talk to you about a job with Crystal Mountain for next year. We just found out that the Ski Patrol Director has accepted a job with another ski area and we would like you to take over the patrol." I was flabbergasted and honored, but I needed time to think about what it would mean for my career and the study. So I said, "Thank you. I would like to set up a separate meeting where we can discuss the job, what it pays, and your expectations." They agreed and we set up a meeting for the following week.

I immediately called Bill Sears, my supervisor for the research project, to discuss the best outcomes, both for the study and my career. Bill and I had become friends at Colorado State University and he was a trusted voice when I needed help making decisions. We discussed the job description, pay, relocation and a myriad of "what ifs?" We agreed that I could supervise a replacement researcher and do my job as Ski Patrol Director.

I went to the meeting with Huck and Mel and was surprised to hear their comments because I did not remember either of them paying much attention to what I was doing over the winter. They said that I was very respected by both the professional and volunteer ski patrolmen as well as the leadeship of the National Ski Patrol (NSP). They also said the word was out that Jack Nagel, the Ski School Director, had his eyes on me because the Devins thought I would make a good Mighty Mite coach.

I went into that meeting with a salary number in mind as well as ideas for how the conditions in the patrol should work. One of the sticking points for me was how their avalanche control was set up. They had a world famous mountain climber from Austria, Leo Scheiblener, in charge of that program. I had come to know him and was highly impressed with his knowledge and work ethic, but their group was autonomous from the patrol and he brought in Austrian climbers and mountain guides to work for him.

This presented two problems for me. One was the fact that they were paid more than the American Patrolmen and, more importantly, they refused to let the other patrol go with them when they were making their morning rounds. Blasting and skiing for avalanche control is hazardous, but it also creates opportunities for some fun skiing, which my future team was currently being denied.

Mel and Huck arranged for Leo and me to meet. He agreed to enforce an expectation that his team collaborate with the patrolmen. By the time we opened, all was fine and we became good friends and trusted colleagues.

I accepted the job and left for the summer with a plan where I could see a successful career in the ski business. I was 23 years old, the Ski Patrol Director of a significant new ski resort, and a clear path to becoming the mountain manager or, possibly, a general manager in the future.

In addition, it was obvious to me that our data gathering for the National Ski Safety Research study was going to make a real difference in the sport. Once we concluded the study, it was published in a variety of places. One was a chapter in the winter sports section of a book titled *Sports Safety, Accident Prevention, and Injury Control* by Charles Yost. In it, Dr. Garrick and Bill detailed our main findings. These included:

- Skiing had a much lower injury rate than anticipated. The data showed the injury rate was half of one percent (.05%), far lower than the 20 to 30 percent in high school and college contact sports.
- While rates were low, the sources were many and included injuries while in the act of skiing (falling, colliding with another skier, hitting obstacles like trees, and avalanches) as well as passive injuries that occur while getting to and from the trail (ski lifts, car accidents).
- Because skiing occurs in cold weather, injuries tend to create less pain and swelling than similar injuries in warmer climates.
- Injuries were most correlated with three factors: age (most in 19-22 age group), ability (injuries decrease as you get better), and gender (with women experiencing a marked increase at puberty). This was a puzzle at the time, but research has shown similar patterns in many sports. As females go through puberty and their hips widen, the angle to the knee changes, making knee injuries more common than in males.
- Improvements in equipment can reduce injuries and its particularly important that ski bindings be appropriately calibrated for the skier's weight and ability. This is still true today. Always have your bindings checked and tested by professionals before you ski.

Considering that skiers have a lot of leeway to move around a mountain and end up in circumstances beyond their abilities, Dr. Garrick stated, "As skiing is one of the most vigorous athletic activities and is practiced mainly by non-athletes, its safety record is admirable."

It was an honor to work on this project and get to know Dr. Garrick. He went to medical school on a Navy ROTC scholarship and served two tours in a Navy MASH hospital in Vietnam. He was there for the Tet Offensive where he was in surgery for 96 straight hours. He said he did more operations in those four years than he did the rest of his life.

He published many articles on athletic injuries in all types of sports. Many PAC12 team doctors owe him for his injury healing protocols for athletes. He established a Sports Medicine Department in San Francisco, where he culminated his career as Chief of Staff. He was also the world authority on ballet injuries and ballerinas from around the world came for his treatment, rehabbing injuries that, before his research, would have been career ending.

Bill Sears finished his Ph.D. and taught at CSU for several years and also served as a consultant to many businesses. In 2019, we attended Arapahoe Basin's reunion event for ski patrollers and were pleasantly surprised to see old friends and talk over the fun times we had there. Bill, Jim, and I keep in touch a couple times every month. I am the only one still skiing.

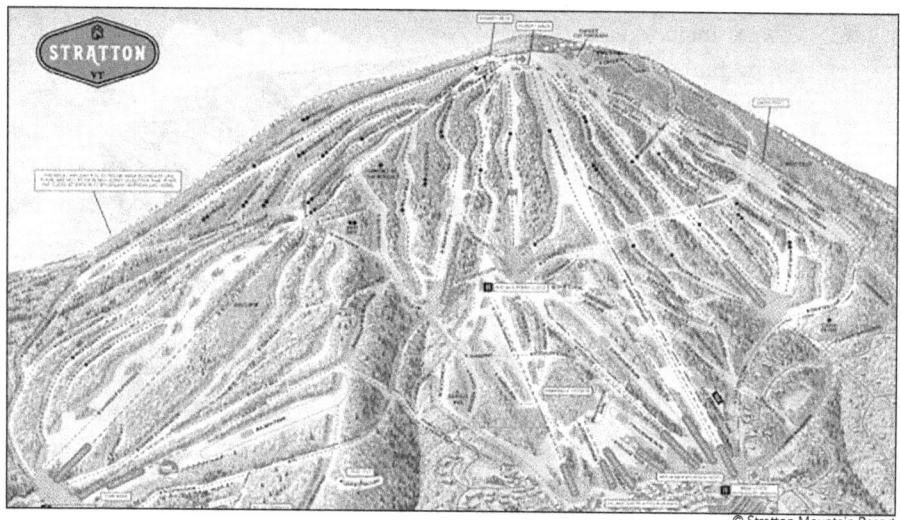

Stratton Mountain Resort
Stratton, Vermont

- Founded in 1960 by 10th Mountain veterans Robert Wright and Frank Snyder, Stratton Mountain currently boasts 99 runs over 670 skiable acres in the Green Mountain National Forest.
- There are 11 lifts and a vertical drop of 2,003 feet. The average snowfall is 180 inches and they also have terrain parks and tubing.
- They offer private and group lessons for children and adults.
- Learn more at Stratton.com.

Chapter 10

1966-1967: Crystal Mountain, Washington

46.9282° N, 121.5045° W
Base Elevation: 4,400 Feet (1,341 M)
Peak Elevation: 6,872 Feet (2,094 M)

After the eventful 1965-66 ski season, I headed back to Colorado and skied Vail and Monarch. I also secured a job lifeguarding at the Boulder Reservoir. It was the perfect summer job for a ski bum and I was secure that I had a job for the coming winter.

The summer went by very quickly and I had to return to Crystal Mountain so I could start putting things in order as the new Ski Patrol Director. So, the second week in September, I returned to the Pacific Northwest for the next big surprises in my life.

I arrived in Seattle and stayed overnight with the Devin family before heading up to Crystal Mountain. The next day, I went to work on the mountain and was on the same crew as Leo Scheibleiner. It gave both of us a lot of time to get to know each other and get comfortable with the collaboration between the Ski Patrol and the Avalanche Control Team. To this day, I think it was a great idea, especially given the size and scope of the physical mountain and the habit of Pacific Northwest storms to dump large amounts of high-water content snow.

In the second week of October, we got a pretty good snowstorm, which drove us off the high mountain down to the lower area, where we decided to burn brush piles from new trails that had been cut over the summer. One day just before lunch, Ross Gregg, one of my patrolmen came trudging up the hill and said to me, "You have got to go to the office and get a look at Huck's new secretary." Huck was the General Manager at Crystal Mountain and our boss.

My curiosity peaked, I headed down to see the new person in the office. I walked in and spotted her sitting at her desk. At the time, I was covered in soot and soaked with fuel oil from the brush pile burning. She looked at me and took out a cigarette. I rushed over, took out my Bic lighter, and lit her cigarette, risking spontaneous combustion while thinking I was being so smooth.

Huck introduced us and that was the first time I met Barbara Wilson. I was standing there thinking about my next great move when I noticed that the newest edition of the *USSA Ski* magazine of the month was sitting in stacks on the table. I was the cover photo skier and blurted out, "Hey, that's me!" She didn't say anything but I could tell she was not convinced. I flipped the page and sure enough it was there in print: Skier Mike Ewing at Vail, photograph by Fletcher Manley, Jr. At last, some street cred!

Mike on the cover of Ski News magazine from November, 1966

Barbara was commuting from Seattle and staying with a friend who had a cabin at Silver Springs. I had a date with a woman who was attending the University of Washington so we both left for the day. On the way down the mountain, I kept coming back to the attraction I felt at first sight of Barbara—it was like there was something special there instantly.

It turned out that I was not the only guy who thought she was good looking. At Crystal Mountain there was a ratio of Neanderthal males to cute girls of about twenty to one. I instantly figured out that if I was going to have a chance, I better have a plan in place pretty damn quick. My plan started with the fact I had a secret weapon in the form of Grace and Doug Devin, who held apres ski gatherings at their condo. It turned out that Barb's friend, Marlys, was dating Len Gerber, nephew to Sid Gerber who owned A&T Ski Company and a friend of the Devins. I asked Grace to invite Len and his date to their party. We all had a lot of fun and it was easy to see that the ski crowd at Crystal was accepting me as one of their own.

I still had to overcome a hoard of guys asking Barbara out on dates. I knew that Barbara liked movies, so for our first big date I asked her to a movie in Auburn, Washington, which was the nearest town with a good selection of theaters. We had a nice dinner and, while I don't remember the movie, I clearly remember that driving back, Barb was really animated, and we laughed a lot as we discussed the film. I was over the moon. She was everything I wanted.

Over the following weeks, I started falling in love with Barb. She had a great personality and could socialize with anyone. She was very smart and had a witty sense of humor that kept me on my toes. Most importantly, she was not easily impressed by me and kept my ego in check. Somewhere in here, I had decided that she was "the one." However, she had not gotten to the same notion about me...yet.

Barb had grown up in Seattle with her lifelong and best friend, Marilyn. Her Seattle roots meant she grew up with the Nordstroms, Gordon Bowker (founder of Starbucks), and the creators of pickleball—Joel Pritchard, Barney McCallum, and Bill Bell. She was athletic and enjoyed the outdoors and sports as much as I did. All my friends and colleagues liked her, she was really good looking, warm and funny, and exactly the right size that was easy to hug and kiss. I certainly didn't have a checklist, but if I had, she ticked everything that would have been on it.

We continued juggling our work and our budding relationship. Because I had committed to Doug and Grace Devin to coach Mighty Mite skiers on my days off, I had to go to the November hiring event at Rainy Pass and compete for a job in the Jack Nagel Ski School and CMAC race team. Jack and his staff of supervisors were there to judge the applicants and come up with the top 16—10 or 12 would be full-time ski instructors and a maximum of six would be hired as coaches. To this day, I am proud to say I tied for number one with a guy my age out of Seattle, Roger Ryanen. Since my commitment was to the Mighty Mites, I chose the coach position.

About five days later, we had a big dump of snow and the season began in earnest. The second weekend we woke up to a foggy morning and decided to open the lower lifts, while Leo, Bill Savery (Volunteer Ski Patrol Leader) and I went up to see what it was like on top. When we got up there, it was worse than expected. We decided to ski down Green Valley, which looked like a giant bottle of milk, to decide whether to open it or not. We got lost and almost skied off a cliff before we got oriented. Needless to say, our decision was to keep the top closed until the fog lifted or we closed for the day.

I was in the Ski Patrol room when I got a call from Huck to come to his office. He told me to open the top and I asked why he wanted to go against our judgment. He informed me that a board member had called Mel Borgerson, the Board Chair, and Mel gave the order to open the upper mountain. I quit on the spot. Thankfully, no one suffered an injury in the fog that day.

I trudged over to the Ski School and told Jack Nagel what happened. I asked if I could teach to finish out the season. He said, "Of course, but I have another idea so let's talk tomorrow." The next day, Jack and I met and he told me that he would like me to come work full-time for him and his wife, Donna. He wanted someone to be the hard goods manager of his recently expanded ski shop at Crystal Mountain. He said I would still be coaching Mighty Mites on the weekends and, if the shop was not busy, I could also teach and pad my income.

Another great memory from Crystal Mountain was when Doug Devin asked me to ski for him so he could photograph a powder day. We went to Snorting Elk Bowl and I jumped off the cornice. Doug went below me and photographed me as I skied a 25+ turn sequence down a track-free snowfield. These photos show a great morning run and one of my favorite core memories!

Skiing Snortng Elk Bowl on a poweder day at Crystal Mountain

By now it was pretty much established that Barbara and I were a couple, and we were set for the winter. I was still welcomed in the office as Huck had explained that he thought I had made the right decision and it was a mistake to overturn the decision made by the experts on the mountain.

In my role managing the ski shop, I reached out to Lange Ski Boot Company. While I was at Vail, I had the good fortune to be a boot tester for Lange ski boots when Bob Lange was starting his company. I had been a friend of Morrie Sheppard, the ski school director and, in turn, Bob was one of his former clients. We did not know it then, but it had been obvious that the plastic ski boot was going to revolutionize the sport of skiing. I called Bob and became the on-mountain tech guy for Lange.

Lange sent Jimmy Simonson to Crystal Mountain to show me how to fit plastic boots. He was surprised that I'd figured out a way to bend the plastic boots by heating our boot tools in hot water, thus saving the plastic shell from being melted in the process. We became great friends and, until his premature death from a brain tumor, we were colleagues and ski buddies for over 20 years.

While Barb was clearly the main reason this was the most epic winter of my life, the second was my Mighty Mite group for that year. They were all nine- and ten-year olds that I would have the privilege of skiing with for the next four years. This amazing racing program deserves its own chapter so read more about it in Chapter 10.

This was the beginning of my career changing from a full-time instructor/coach to a person interested in the growth and opportunities of the ski industry. I am so thankful that I had both Doug and Grace Devin, as well as Donna and Jack Nagel, to help me through the decisions I made at that time.

As the season was coming to an end, I talked Barbara into coming home to Salida to meet my parents and do some spring skiing. We met some friends in Fort Collins, then went home to Salida and met my parents. Bill and Betty Sears were gracious hosts and they were impressed that Barb fit into the conversations and activities we did while visiting them. Betty and Barb went into town to shop and Bill and I had a long conversation about my future and how Barb fit in the formula. He asked if I was serious about her and I told him I was planning on marrying her if she would have me. He agreed that this was a great decision.

Barb and I hung around Salida and decided to ski Arapahoe Basin on May 8th. It was a bluebird day and there was about 10 inches of new snow. We went up the two lifts and skied down Lennaway Meadows. By the time we went up the lift again, the wind had erased our previous tracks. Hardly anyone was there and it was like having our own private ski area. We skied our legs off and then enjoyed a burger and a beer at the Ratskeller .

Barb said she had the best day ever and couldn't believe how light the powder was at 11,000+ feet. I told her I wanted to ski the Pallavicini Trail and then we could head out after that. As I entered the roll-over into the Pali, I saw two skiers at the bottom of the run in A-Basin instructor uniforms. The powder was perfect and I skied nonstop to them.

As I approached, I realized it was Max and Rolf Dercum, both legends in Colorado skiing. Max turned to Rolf and said, "I told you he was a former A-Basin instructor!" I said hello and Max introduced me to Rolf who was racing for Denver University under their coach, Willie Schaeffler. Willie and Bob Beattie were locked in a rivalry for the best ski team in the NCAA. In my opinion, Bob Beattie won because he was a better recruiter.

I met up with Barb at the base and we headed to the parking lot. Barb was flying home to Seattle the next day so we were going back to have dinner with my parents. Barb was going home to find a summer job and I was returning to my lifeguard job.

At the airport, as we said our goodbyes, I said, "I will see you next fall" and Barb replied, "Maybe." I asked what that meant, and she said, "I am not going to just hang around and wait for you to show up." I said, "Why don't we get married and both go to Boulder?" I thought I was being cool, but I have since realized that I hold the record for lamest proposal ever. Luckily, she said yes!

Her flight was boarding and she had to go. Her flight was three hours and my trip back home was two and a half hours. I was waiting when she called and we talked through the details. I had to be in Boulder by Memorial Day so we only had a short timeframe to work with. We decided I would fly to Seattle on the 17th and we would get married on the 20th.

My Mom and Dad overheard the conversation and, when I hung up, my dad said to Mom, "I told you so!" I asked what he meant, and he said, "You are different with Barb than any of your previous girlfriends." He was correct.

Barb had 10 days to pull together a wedding. Grace Devin's son, Steve, was my best man and Barb's best friend, Marilyn, served as her maid of honor. In what I have since come to learn as her typical Barb fashion, she organized an amazing wedding, complete with minister, venue, dress, and guest list. It was the first of many times that Barb would take a crisis created by me and turn it into something wonderful. It was a beautiful day.

Barb (right) on our wedding day with her best friend, Marilyn Hove

There is no possible way I could have the life I do if Barb was not my wife. I'm grateful for her willingness to move to support my career. Until we moved to Bozeman, Montana in 1987, I think we lived in 25 different houses and she sometimes had to leave great jobs so that I could go do mine.

Some of our friends thought we had married too quickly and, therefore, wouldn't last. In 2022, we celebrated our 55th Anniversary. I consider marrying Barb to be the absolute best decision of my life and that's why 1966-67 is my all time favorite winter of all.

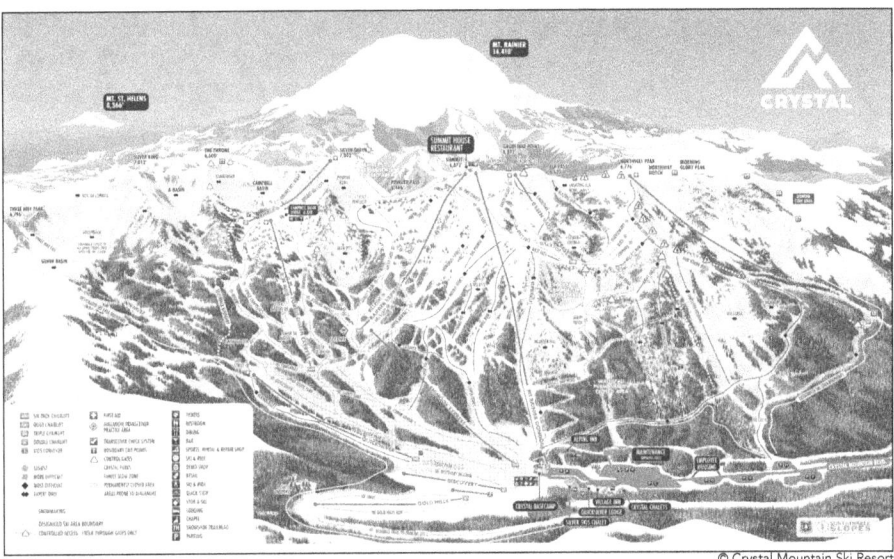

© Crystal Mountain Ski Resort

Crystal Mountain Ski Resort
Crystal Mountain, Washington

- Founded in 1955 by a group of investors, Crystal Mountain currently boasts 85 runs over 2,600 skiable acres in the Baker-Snoqualmie National Forest.
- There are 11 lifts and a vertical drop of 3,100 feet. The average snowfall is 486 inches. Also, it is only two hours from Seattle in the heart of the Cascade Mountains.
- They offer private and group lessons for children and adults.
- Learn more at CrystalMountainResort.com.

Chapter 11

Ski Racing Programs

Squaw Valley/Palisades Tahoe, CA
39.1976° N, 120.2354° W
Base Elevation: 6,200 Feet (1,890 M)
Peak Elevation: 9,050 Feet (2,758 M)

Crystal Mountain Athletic Club (CMAC) was the ski team that Jack Nagel put together to try and make the Pacific Northwest more present in the ski racing world. Jack had been on the 1952 U.S. Ski Team representing the United States at the Olympic Games in Oslo, Norway. The U.S. Ski Team had hired Émile Allais to be the head coach of the team and he chose Squaw Valley, California for the training site.

The team showed up right after Christmas and started training. The first 10 days were spent skating on their alpine skis on the cross-country course in the meadow at Squaw Valley. This not only strengthened their legs, it was also Émile's method for teaching skiers how to gain speed. It made such an impression on Jack that, for the rest of his life, he skated between every turn gaining speed on each skate. At the end of the Olympics, Jack took his experience and began a career producing world class racers for at least two decades.

Émile Allais was later hired by the French Ski Team and put his method of how to ski fast into a program that brought the French to a pinnacle at the 1968 Olympic Games in Grenoble, France. They were the dominant team and captured all three gold medals in Men's Alpine—Downhill, Slalom, and Giant Slalom—and they put two athletes on the podium in all three ski events.

Émile's theory was if you put a large number of good athletes together in a team setting and give them four to six years to train and race, you would end up with a great team of about 12 to 15 elite skiers. He wanted to increase France's chance of dominating at the Olympics and the FIS World Cup events. Jean Claude Killy proved his theory in spades—he became a triple Olympic champion and won the World Cup titles in 1967 and 1968.

Jack brought the same techniques to create the CMAC ski program, putting six athletes on the U.S. Ski Team in a period of five years: Cathy Nagel, Judy Nagel, Steve Devin, Betsy Devin, Alan Lauba, and Carole Miller. Since then, many more have come out of the Pacific Northwest to race and medal in sub-

sequent Olympics. It was one of my best experiences to be chosen to coach in Jack's CMAC program and team system. Jack created three levels based on age groupings:
- Papa Bob's Bunnies for 5 to 8-year-old kids
- Mighty Mites for 9 to 14-year-old kids
- CMAC Racers for 14 to 18-year-old kids

At every level, coaches had goals that their assigned group should reach every year. Technically, each group had to focus on specific skills that would lead to their ultimate success.

I coached the Mighty Mite level and was tasked to have all the kids skiing with their hands in the perfect position for slalom and giant slalom. If you watch the Olympics or FIS World Cup races, you will notice that all advanced ski racers keep their hands in a forward position, almost like holding a steering wheel, which allows them to move gates or recover from mistakes. I also had to get them comfortable with tucking in the perfect egg position.

Tactically, one of the really fun things for the coaches and young racers was teaching them to embrace speed in that egg position. We used the Jump Hill at Crystal Mountain where we had dug a trench for the coaches to stand in. We'd start with the six-year-olds and get them pointed down the hill in that tuck position. We would do a countdown and release them—they'd go flying down the landing hill into the flat and across to the uphill stop.

The idea was to get them used to speed—each group had an age terminal velocity, which was about 20 miles per hour for the six-year-olds, but it was as fast as they could go. When they got to be 17 and weighed 160 pounds, they would go 60 miles per hour, also as fast as they could go. I often laugh about how many parents came to us to ask how they could be skiing with their little racer one weekend and unable to keep up with them the next.

I was assigned to the Mighty Mites level and coached a group of 10-year-olds that was half girls and half boys. Each coach had to come up with a group name. After the first day of skiing with my kids, I decided to call them the "Charm School Dropouts" or CSD's.

I had the great fortune to ski with this group for four winters and, to this day, I have never been more challenged or had more fun than those days with them. We free skied, we raced, winning many and losing some, but we always had fun. Fifty years later and I still hear from some of them. This group had many great skiers but I want to highlight a few that you might recognize.

Steve Devin—made the 1973-1974 U.S. Ski Team. He skied for my friend, Billy Marolt, when he was coach at the University of Colorado. (I had a hand in getting Steve a scholarship there.) Steve went on to coach the University of Utah women's team to a national championship. Steve continues to manage the myriad of family-owned businesses.

Betsy Devin—was a member of U.S. Ski Team in 1976-1977 and was a four-time All-American skier at the University of Wyoming. She went to veterinary school at Washington State University. She is a U.S. Ski Team coach in biathlon and para-cross country skiing and had one athlete who competed in the 2022 Paralympics in Beijing, China. She now goes by Betsy Devin Smith and her son manages the family business.

Betsy Devin Smith and Mike before her athlete competed in the Beijing Paralympics

Bill "Tres" Gates—yes, the same Bill Gates who co-founded Microsoft. He went by Tres because he's actually Bill Gates, III. He was a good skier, a great person, funny, and smart! When he was nine, I took the group to ski some powder and he asked me, "Why do you sink lower than we do?" I replied with a simple explanation, "Well, I weigh more." Without missing a beat, he said, "But your skis are longer, which would offset that." The other kids could barely keep their mittens on and he was already analyzing the engineering of it all. His mother, Mary, was one of the parents who showed up for every race, volunteering as a gatekeeper, timer, or whatever needed to be done.

Paige Paulson—the daughter of Beege and Huck, Crystal Mountain's GM. Paige was a great skier and part of a trio who were always plotting to get me to fall or run into tree limbs. I have to admit that they were really good at getting it done! The last I heard, she was an executive with IBM and highly successful.

Kristy Peterson—also part of the trio and now lives in Sun Valley, Idaho. Her dad was a manufacturer's representative in the ski and outdoors business and became a great friend when I finally got into the selling side of the business. I ran into Kristy skiing at Sun Valley and told her I was very impressed with her skiing. She told me, "I learned from the best!" That really made my day.

Carol and Carl Prothman—twins and their parents, Gregg and Marge, worked for the Nagels, running the ski school. The twins were good skiers, but a bit disorganized, often showing up without gloves or goggles. The twins were always game for whatever we were doing. Their mother was an Olympian for the Canadian Ski Team and a revered ski racer.

Alan Lauba—a great skier with high energy and focus. He made the 1977-1978 U.S. Ski Team. He is now the CEO of the Crystal Mountain Athletic Club. I saw him in 2021 and he told me that I was his parents' favorite coach. I asked him why, and he said, "Because you made me do things I didn't want to do." We had a great laugh at that!

Mike Ewing and Alan Lauba at a Big Sky ski race

Like Crystal Mountain, nearly every ski area or resort had a children's ski school and a racing program. My own daughter learned to race in Aspen's program, taking after her mom. But then she tried an ice skating lesson and found her passion, eventually winning medals and doing triple jumps.

Every international skier you see at the Olympics or the World Cup got their start in a youth racing program somewhere. Here is a list of U.S. Olympic alpine medalists from the past few years and where they started:
- Julia Mancuso— Medalist at the 2006, 2010, and 2014 Games. Learned to ski at Squaw Valley Ski Area in California. She currently has the most Olympic medals (4) of any female American skier.
- Bode Miller—Medalist at the 2002, 2010, and 2014 Games. Started skiing at the Cannon Mountain Ski Area in New Hampshire and a ski racing academy in Maine.
- Ted Ligety—Medalist at the 2006 and 2014 Games. Began skiing at the Park City Ski Area in Utah. He is a five-time World Cup champion.
- Lindsey Vonn—Medalist at the 2010 and 2018 Games. She was on skis at the age of two and began racing at Buck Hill Ski Area in Minnesota.
- Andrew Weibrecht—Medalist at the 2010 and 2014 Games. Born in Lake Placid, New York, he learned to ski at nearby Whiteface Mountain, home to the 1932 and 1980 Winter Olympics.

- Mikaela Shiffrin—Medalist at the 2018 Games. Born in Vail, Colorado, Shiffrin learned to ski there and also attended the Burke Mountain Ski Academy in Vermont. She is the youngest slalom Olympic champion in history.

In recent years, sports at the Winter Olympic Games have expanded to include additional skiing and snowboarding events, featuring men's, women's, and team competitions. The six current International Ski Federation (FIS) disciplines are:

- Alpine skiing, which includes downhill, super-G (or super giant slalom), slalom, and alpine combined
- Cross-country skiing, which includes various distances, sprints, and relays
- Ski jumping, which includes two sizes of hills
- Nordic combined, which as the name implies, is a combination of ski jumping and cross-country skiing
- Freestyle skiing, which includes aerials, moguls, halfpipe, slopestyle, big air, and ski cross
- Snowboarding, which includes halfpipe, parallel giant slalom, snowboard cross, slopestyle, and big air
- The Paralympics hosts modified versions of alpine skiing, cross-country skiing, and snowboarding

Ski areas and resorts have expanded to include facilities and teaching programs for all of these options, giving families a plethora of programs from which to choose.

At Big Sky, Montana, where I currently teach, we have a very vigorous and well-supported program for the youth. We have wonderful terrain parks that are maintained and frequently used by the local programs. PSIA has created a certification for freestyle and we are very fortunate to have one of the Demo Team members, Matt Larson, on our staff. Our race team is very active and Big Sky hosts many ski racing and skiing events throughout the year. This includes local and regional events where really accomplished racers and competitors from out-of-state come and train or race for a week at a time.

In 2022, Big Sky hosted an event for 14- to 18-year-old ski racers from Montana, Idaho, Washington, Oregon, and California. I went to the race course and bumped into Alan Lauba from the Crystal Mountain Athletic Club (CMAC). After we had a photo taken together, he introduced me to all the coaches and told them that I had taught him how to tuck and jump when he was eight years old.

I asked him what the current cost is for being in a program like CMAC. He said, "Over a six-year racing career, the families probably spend about $400,000 if they don't have sponsors." He added that coaches for the NCAA ski teams were scouting here and his program has had good results in getting scholarships for some of his kids. For most families, the low return on investment makes it prohibitive, especially for those that are middle- or low-income. We both lamented how hard it is for U.S. skiers to compete against the European athletes who are sponsored by their governments.

With that said, there are still many affordable options to learn the joy of skiing and the thrill of racing. Near Big Sky is a non-profit local ski area called Bridger Bowl. The whole community supports this program and they have successes at all levels from Mighty Mites all the way to college bound skiers. Over the years, it has produced many collegiate racers. Montana State University is 17 miles away in Bozeman and their ski team is a powerhouse in NCAA ski racing.

But the goal is not always to become a racer. My own life and career is proof that a love of skiing can take you far. I've been successful in various roles, on and off the mountain, including the ski equipment part of the industry. I've traveled around the world and witnessed some of skiing's greatest moments.

© Squaw Valley/Palisades Tahoe

Squaw Valley/Palisades Tahoe
Olympic Valley, CA

- Founded between 1943-1949 by Wayne Poulsen and Alexander Cushing, Squaw Valley is now known as two resorts—Palisades Tahoe and Palisades Alpine Meadows.
- Tahoe currently boasts 170 runs over 3,600 skiable acres in the Tahoe National Forest. There are 29 lifts and a vertical drop of 2,850 feet. The average snowfall is 400 inches.
- Alpine Meadows was established in 1961 and currently features 100 runs over 2,400 skiable acres. There are 13 lifts and a vertical drop of 1,802 feet. This resort is the smaller, sister resort to Palisades Tahoe.
- They offer private and group lessons for children and adults.
- Learn more at PalisadesTahoe.com.

Chapter 12

1968-1969: A&T Ski Company

Seattle, Washington
47.6062° N, 122.3321° W
Elevation: 174 Feet (53 M)

In the Winter of 1968-1969, Barb and I were both working for Jack and Donna Nagel; Barb in the ski school and me in the ski shop along with coaching the Mighty Mites. I also was available to teach lessons if needed. I got lots of private lessons on rainy weekdays because the other instructors didn't like teaching in the rain. Barb would call the ski shop and, if I wasn't busy, she would tell me to come take out a person waiting for a lesson.

As newlyweds, we were a tad money hungry. The extra money from the lesson and maybe a tip usually was enough that we could afford to go to Ivar's Acres of Clams restaurant on the waterfront where I would have steamed clams and Barb would have the crab-stuffed halibut.

Barb's mother, Elinor, had been living alone since 1967 when Barb's dad, Cecil, was killed in a freak accident at work. Because of that, Elinor was receiving compensation from the State of Washington along with a life insurance policy. She had some insurance as well. While Elinor was financially secure, she had suffered from agoraphobia her adult life. We went into town every Wednesday and shopped for her and brought her dinner. All the neighbors checked in with her and, if she needed anything, they would take care of her or call us with a heads up.

Back at Crystal Mountain, we were having a great time being part of a small community and living in a winter wonderland. We had snow by Thanksgiving and the shop and ski school were busy—it looked to be an epic winter.

Unfortunately, a few days before Christmas, we had the Chinook of all Chinooks. The temperature rose to 50° Fahrenheit and it rained cats, dogs, and elephants for four consecutive days. Every river in Washington and Oregon flooded and the ski areas all shut down. Needless to say, we went into a state of depression that was harder on me than Barb, because I had never seen anything like that.

Around the 28th, it turned cold and snowed enough that the ski areas opened up and the winter normalized. But I was spooked by Washington's weather and contacted Vail—I learned they would welcome me back if I wanted to go. I was relieved and somehow the word got out that we were contemplating that move. I don't know who let them know, but Bill Kirschner and Russ Butterfield came to Crystal and took us out to dinner. They told us that K2 skis were going to be distributed by A&T Ski Company and they were sure that I would be hired by A&T as a salesperson if we could hold out until October.

As I am sitting here typing this, I just realized that the Devins and the Nagels had probably championed us to Bill and Russ. I had been testing K2 skis for them and, in fact, had talked them into making a kid's racing ski that they let me name. That ski became a big seller for them and I am proud of the fact that the XR-10 was successful. I named it after my expert 10-year-old Mighty Mite racers!

I contacted the local Forest Service office and the District Ranger, Dalton Dulac, gave me a summer job working out of the Green Water Station. Barb got a job cleaning hotel rooms for the summer at Crystal. One of the funny benefits of that summer was we didn't have to buy a single bottle of beer, wine, or liquor because she got to keep whatever was left in the rooms. It was astounding how much alcohol people left in their rooms.

I spent the summer driving to campgrounds and making sure the occupants were putting their $3.00 fee in the containers at the entrance of each campground. I also interacted with campers and answered a lot of funny questions. One of my favorites was when I visited a campsite that had giant old growth Engelmann Spruce trees and was asked if they were above timberline yet. In fairness to them, they were from Nebraska on their way to Mt. Rainier National Park. By noon the next day, they were most definitely above timberline.

In mid-September, we planned to move to Seattle and rent a place to start our business life. We got a call from the Devins saying one of their neighbors was going to Europe and needed house sitters. So we got free rent and lived in Laurelhurst, one of the best neighborhoods in Seattle. We were close to Barb's mom and it gave us time to look for a rental without feeling stressed.

Barb applied for a job at the Battelle Research Facility in Seattle and became the administrative assistant to the operations manager. Battelle hosted Nobel Laureates and operated as a Think Tank. She loved working there—it was a great working environment.

October 1st came and I started work as a sales representative for A&T Ski Company, located near downtown on the western side of Lake Union. I was the new guy for two days and then they hired Knut Martinsen. We were both enrolled in the Western Winter Sports Representative Association. I was Member #414 and Knut was #415, a fact that we laughed about the rest of our careers. The owners of A&T were Henry (Hank) Simonson and John Woodward; they were the nicest people anyone could work for.

John was a 10th Mountain veteran who had led ski instruction for the troops and became a Bird Colonel by the end of the war. Hank was the Chairman of the Board of Directors of the Seattle Ports Authority as well as the

Consul of Norway and Sweden for Seattle. Both were highly respected in the ski industry and many successful ski reps had gotten their start working for A&T.

John managed most of the sales functions and Hank managed the import accounts with Salomon Ski Bindings, La Trappeur Ski Boots, and the new K2 Ski Company. The catalog was 25+ pages with everything from shoelaces to ski wax and ski poles to ski racks. Literally, every ski shop had to buy something from A&T, so it was the perfect place to learn the ski business.

A&T had all their reps live in Seattle and each was assigned a territory plus one or two of the local ski shops. I had everything east of I-5 for Washington, Oregon, and all of Northern California. My Seattle account was OU Sports who operated four shops in Seattle and one in Portland. The main store was at the corner of 2nd Avenue and Seneca and the big boss there was Yoshitada "Yosh" Nakagawa.

Yosh was a force to be reckoned with in the industry. The first call I made to Yosh, I went in with sweating palms. I introduced myself and Yosh invited me into his office. I was about to meet the smartest and most complex person in my entire life. He started the conversation by asking me about my time at Crystal Mountain and said he had heard about me being a good ski boot fitter. I was flabbergasted that he knew so much about me. We discussed his relationship with A&T and he said he really respected Hank and John. At the end of the meeting, he told me that, in the future, I should schedule meetings with him so we could go to lunch next door at his favorite Chinese restaurant, which I agreed to do.

John and Hank had some interesting ways to incentivize us as a group. First, they did not pay on commissions—they gave us a fixed salary and then paid year-end bonuses. They also provided a company car and credit card and allowed us to charge gas for personal trips. The cherry on top was a perk that every winter we could take a week-long vacation at any ski area of our choice and they would pick up the tab. Barb and I made the most of that perk. One time, we went to Colorado and borrowed Bob Shanks' car for our ski adventure. Barb's lifelong friend, Marilyn Hove, and her husband, Ralph, joined us for a week of skiing—two days each at Vail, Winter Park, and Steamboat Springs.

Unfortunately, our time at Vail was plagued by temperatures of -15°, so we drank lots of hot chocolate in between runs. We skied about three total hours each day. Luckily, when we got to Winter Park, it had warmed up so we had two great days of skiing at the iconic ski area that was part of the park system for Denver, Colorado.

We then went to Steamboat Springs to ski the champagne powder that Billy Kidd was promoting. Billy was the first American man (along with Jimmie Heuga) to win Olympic medals in skiing. In the 1964 Games in Innsbruck, Austria, Billy won silver and Jimmie Heuga won bronze in the slalom.

In the early days, Steamboat was known for its jumping hill—Howelsen Ski Hill was internationally known and is the oldest operating ski area in North

America, founded in 1915. Steamboat Springs was where the Werner skiing family called home. From the name of the mountain to the trails and glades, the Werners influenced every facet of this great resort.

Gladys "Skeeter" Werner played a vital role in the birth of Steamboat, working in several different capacities. She was an Olympian and married Doak Walker, a Heisman Trophy winner. Along with her younger brother, Loris "Bugs" Werner, they developed a very successful ski school.

In 1964, Bugs won the coveted Ski Meister Award from the NCAA National Championship—it goes to the skier scoring the most points in all five disciplines: slalom, giant slalom, downhill, jumping, and cross-country or Nordic skiing. He participated in the 1964 Olympics and 1968 Olympics.

Wallace "Buddy" Werner was an American Olympian, NCAA Champion, and the original ski hero of my generation. He was the first American to win the Hahnenkamm Ski Race in Kitzbühel, Austria. He was injured just weeks before the 1956 Olympics and again before the 1960 Olympics. Tragically, Buddy was killed in an avalanche in Switzerland in 1964.

After Buddy died, a group started a new ski resort in a place known locally as Storm Mountain. They got the Forest Service to change the mountain's name to Mount Werner.

When we were at Steamboat, we had fantastic skiing and perfect weather. Today, Steamboat is a great area with lots of loyal fans who won't ski anywhere else. It's also part of the Ikon Pass, but more on that in Chapter 23.

Barb skiing through powder at Steamboat Springs

I really loved my job and was learning a lot about dealing with the various personalities in the ski industry. I was soon the number one salesman in production at A&T, but it wasn't a fair fight because I had OU Sports and Yosh as part of my territory. I have a plethora of Yosh stories, but I suggest you Google his name and be sure to have tissues close at hand.

When he was a child, his family was imprisoned at the Minidoka Internment Camp in Hunt, Idaho. He has been a leader in the ski industry and other outdoor sports, the Vice President of American Baptist Churches, and a tireless advocate for diversity and equality. In 2011, he worked with the U.S. National Park Service to build the Minidoka Internment National Monument, which remembers the internment of Japanese Americans during World War II. I am lucky that he became a lifelong friend and mentor.

One of the cool things that happened in my time at A&T was the ski rack business. Every year, we had to get the specs on every new car released by Detroit and figure out how to attach our racks to the top of each car. One salesman, Dick Savage, was charged with that task and he was really good at what he did. We actually had these racks made in our facility and it meant we always had inventory on hand. Our main competitor was Barrecrafter, headquartered in New England, and they supplied OU Sports with their racks.

For some reason unknown to me, Barrecrafter had not made a rack that would fit a new Chevrolet model, but we had, so I saw an opportunity. I put together a sales pitch to make to Yosh so I could get a foot into the door for A&T ski racks. I called Yosh and arranged our typical call, lunch first and then business in his office. I made my pitch and, after some negotiating, Yosh said he'd take 50 and see how they did, but he'd only pay for them after they sold.

I went back to John, who resisted at first because he saw it as a consignment and not a sale. But I reminded him that he had told me that my job was to get the order. He finally agreed and I loaded 50 racks into my wagon and delivered them to Yosh's warehouse. Interestingly enough, when I left A&T to work for Lange Ski Boots, the rep who replaced me inherited a ski rack business which had grown to be 40-50% of A&T's business.

As Knut and I thrived on the salesforce, we started looking toward the future. Because A&T distributed K2 skis, we thought we could eventually move to that division, probably sometime in the mid-1970's. But K2 hired Chuck Ferries and Chuck immediately hired Dick Zue from Head Skis who was their hotshot sales manager. I don't remember how I found out, but K2 had negotiated an early release from the distribution agreement for a promise not to hire any of the A&T reps for a two-year period. Knut and I were really disappointed. In the meantime, I had been offered a job with Lange Boots to run their repair and warranty department. It was intriguing, but I had figured out that in a growing industry, the money was made by the salesforce and shareholders.

Coincidentally, John and Hank figured out that I was restless and made me an offer to go to Denver and run one of their warehouses that involved a distribution deal with Dynastar Skis from France. Barb and I discussed this, but fate intervened one evening when I got a call from Yosh. He said, "Lange has decided to replace their rep who was living in Sun Valley. They are going to hire someone from the Seattle area and I think you should interview for that job." I agreed and about 30 minutes later he called back and said he had set it up.

The interview was on a Tuesday and I went to the meeting to meet with Bob Collins, the Sales Manager. Bob had owned or managed a ski shop in Fort Collins when I was at CSU, so the meeting was comfortable at first, but took a turn when he started to tell me how easy the job would be. I had been in the field for more than two years and had listened to dealer after dealer discuss how difficult it was dealing with the arrogant Lange salesforce and management.

In my usual, straightforward style, I said, "No, this is not an easy job. I'm actually okay where I am." Bob asked me what it would take to get me to leave so I threw out a figure and conditions that were absurd and we shook hands. When I got home, Barb asked how it went, and I said, "I blew it and won't be hearing from Bob again."

The next day, a couple of us from A&T went skiing at Crystal Mountain and we bumped into John Peterson, the Gerry Mountain Sports rep for the Northwest. He said, "Hey Mike! Congratulations!" I asked him what for, and he replied, "I heard you got the Lange job." I laughed and said there was no way that was going to happen.

We finished skiing and I came home. Right after dinner, the phone rang and it was Bob Collins saying, "Welcome to the Lange Gang!" He told me that he had made some calls and Lange was actually hiring me for more money than I had asked for. I said, "Give me a day to talk this over and I will let you know tomorrow." Barb and I sat there and talked about what an opportunity this was and how we should give A&T a chance to match.

The next day, I went straight to the office and met with John and Hank. I told them exactly what I had been offered and they both said that there was no way they could match it because of the margins they worked on as distributors. I felt awful because they were such great guys. We worked out the details of my departure and they were very generous. They said I could keep the car for three months and they would pay me a pro forma bonus on the profit at the end of the year. By the time we were done talking, I was in tears. From that day, every time I bumped into them skiing or at trade shows, they always went out of their way to praise me about how my career was going. I've always been grateful for their support and guidance.

Because I had some free time before my first sales meeting at Lange, I decided to make a run down Interstate 5 and call on my new-to-me Lange accounts. This included South Washington and North Oregon to Eugene, Oregon. Because this was my first Lange trip, I was wearing my copper colored corduroy jacket with a green tie and my new 1970's bell bottoms pants. I thought I looked really professional.

Along Interstate 5 my first stop was at a shop in Longview, Washington. As I was leaving there, I realized I would be in Portland at lunch time so I stopped at McDonald's and had a quarter pounder with cheese meal. I then visited my five Portland accounts plus another in Vancouver, Washington.

When I got to my motel for the night, I took off my coat and started to undo my tie. As I was looking in the mirror I was shocked to find a nickle-sized pickle welded to my new tie with a mixture of ketchup and mustard! To this day, I cannot believe one of the guys I called on didn't point out my pickel tie tack! But of course, after that, every time I saw or heard from those guys, they loved to make me cringe about the pickle incident!

Those last weeks zoomed by, then I headed off to my first Lange sales meeting. Let me tell you, it was an eye-opener. The cultures of these two companies could not have been any farther apart than day and night. But more on that in the next chapter.

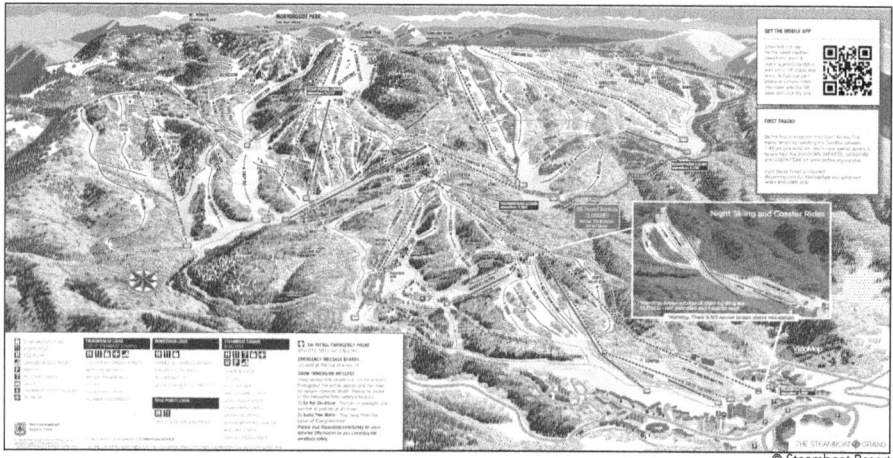

© Steamboat Resort

Steamboat Resort
Steamboat Springs, Colorado

- Founded in 1915 by Carl Howelson and expanded in 1958 by James Temple, Steamboat currently boasts 170 runs over 2,965 skiable acres in the Medicine Bow-Routt National Forest.
- There are 17 lifts and a vertical drop of 3,668 feet. The average snowfall is 314 inches and they also have three terrain parks.
- They offer private and group lessons for children and adults.
- Learn more at Steamboat.com.

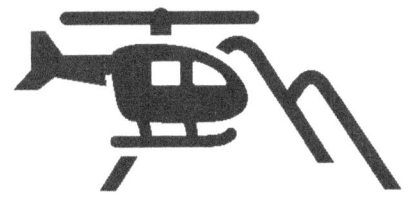

Chapter 13

1969-1973: Lange Boot Company

Bugaboos, British Columbia, Canada
50.7535° N, 116.7057° W
Base Elevation: 4,888 Feet (1,490 M)
Peak Elevation: 10,007 Feet (3,050 M)

I went to Denver a couple of days early so I could meet with Lange Boots Management and, most importantly, the sales and marketing department staff. I was curious about how they structured the support staff for the sales reps. I already knew Bob Collins and I also met with Morrie Shepard.

Morrie had been fired by the new ownership at Vail. In a move to glamorize the ski school, they had replaced him with Roger Staub, an Olympic gold medalist from Switzerland. This was a big mistake because they didn't realize how much respect nearly every person at Vail felt for Morrie. The ski patrol hated it, the current teaching staff hated it, and the ski press hated it. I felt sorry for Roger because he was innocent in that fiasco. Roger was a great racer but had no business experience and very little knowledge about how to run a ski school. Tragically, Roger was killed a year later during a hang glider accident in Switzerland.

During that first day at Lange, Bob told me that Yosh had called him and strongly suggested they should hire me as the new Lange rep. Morrie said, "Since OU Sports is the largest Lange dealer in America, we thought we should probably listen."

I was introduced to the other players in the company and discovered that most were either Bob's relatives or racers from the Canadian National Ski Team coaching staff. Everyone made me feel right at home. The other reps arrived and we went to dinner at a great restaurant in Denver. Lange had recently moved from Dubuque, Iowa to Broomfield, Colorado so everyone was enjoying seeing the new set up. The atmosphere was collegial and I was introduced to the salespeople I didn't already know, some of whom became friends for life. But after dinner, I got a hint that all was not well in Lange Land.

The next morning, we went to the conference room and the meeting started with Bob making a speech about how the new factory coming online would make the salesforce rich. The next to speak was Dave Jacobs, a Vice President.

One of the east coast reps stood up, interrupting Dave, and said, "I think you guys need to know that we are unhappy about being lied to and you need to explain why you have chosen to try to gloss over what you have just done to us." Dave told him to sit down, but the rep charged the podium. Luckily, he was intercepted and stopped. Bob Lange took charge and the meeting was adjourned.

We all went out to the lobby where I grabbed Dick Swan, who I knew from Northern California, and asked what was going on. He grabbed one of the east coast reps, Terry Fletcher, and we went to a quiet place. They explained that Lange had promised them that as the business grew, they would not lower the reps' commissions. It turned out that not only had they lowered the commission rate, they also hired new reps and reduced the territories in size, further cutting into their compensation. This explained why Jack Gray had quit and Lange had hired me and Bruce Morse. My Lange territory was Washington, Oregon, Alaska, and Montana. Bruce had Idaho, Eastern Oregon, and Utah, which had been taken from Tim Carter. Apparently, the same thing happened on the east coast where Terry Fletcher and Gub Langdon had lost territory. Things were now starting to make sense to me.

The meeting resumed and Bob and Morrie promised to hear grievances in person that evening. The rest of the meeting went smoothly and I learned a couple lessons that would help me later in my career. The first was that any change in compensation must be done in a private session and justified. Second, all things negative should be resolved in private and, if you have to clean up a mess, keep it as simple as possible.

Toward the end of the meeting, the year's results were shared—because a performance goal had been reached, the salesforce would be going to the Bugaboos in British Columbia for a week of helicopter skiing (aka heli-skiing) with Canadian Mountain Holidays (CMH), a ski business started by Hans Gmoser. He was widely known as the founder of modern mountaineering in Canada. Just like in the U.S., Canada was aggressively developing their outdoor sports industry, including skiing.

I assumed that I would not be included in this amazing reward because I was just joining the staff. After the meeting, Bob and Morrie approached Bruce Morse and me and told us that they were giving us their trips because they were taking their families to Hawaii instead. We were both over the moon!

The first week in April, we all flew into Vancouver, B.C. and were accompanied by the Henderson brothers who were fresh off the Canadian Ski Team and starting their post-racing careers. From there, we caught the next plane to Calgary and then took a bus to the CMH Bugaboo Lodge.

The ski magazines had known about our trip and two professional photographers accompanied us to shoot photos for Lange and the magazines. Norm Clasen and Fred Lindholm had about a thousand rolls of film and were planning to capture every moment on film. I had heard of them before, but Tim Carter, the Colorado rep for Lange, knew them both really well.

On Wednesday, we awoke to a great treat because it had snowed about 10 to 12 inches and there wasn't a cloud in the sky. We were skiing in two groups that day and Hans Gmoser accompanied our group. We went to the top of the main mountain and skied a relatively short run and then headed to the top of a run named Widgeon. When we landed, Hans said, "If we ski this trail all at once we will get one run, but if we ski figure eights, we can get two or maybe three runs." Needless to say, we all agreed to do figure eights. To my surprise, Hans pointed to me and said, "You in the yellow suit, you are my partner." My friend, Dick Swan, was in our group and he got a great shot of me leading the legendary Hans Gmoser down Widgeon.

Mike Ewing leading Hans Gmoser down Widgeon in the Bugaboos

"A person should have wings to carry them where their dreams go, but sometimes a pair of skis makes a good substitute."

Johann Wolfgang "Hans" Gmoser,
Founder of modern mountaineering in Canada

When we first arrived and started skiing, Tim and I partnered up. We knew that Lange had paid for 80,000 vertical feet, but anything over that, we had to pay the difference. It became obvious that the guides were paid bonuses for extra vertical feet. It also became obvious that some of the reps from the Midwest and Eastern territories were struggling to keep up with the guide's pace. Tim and I agreed we needed to slow down or someone was going to get hurt. One of the Midwest reps had paid for his girlfriend to come with him and it created two problems for us. The first was that he was married to one of Lange's customer service reps and we all knew her and couldn't believe he had done this. Jimmy Simonson made it his mission to harass that rep any time he could. On two separate occasions after skiing, when Jimmy saw them canoodling on the sun deck, he filled up a waste basket with water and doused them from the second floor of the lodge.

The second problem was that she was not a good enough skier to handle the terrain we were skiing. We had an event when one of the Huey choppers broke down at the bottom of the mountain and we had to use a two-passenger helicopter to get 16 people to the top to ski back to the lodge. Dick and I rode up together and realized we were running out of daylight. As soon as the sun set, it was going to be really sketchy skiing on the track to the lodge.

When the last group came up, they all started down. Tim and I intentionally brought up the rear, since we were the strongest skiers. As we were descending, we saw them all gathered in a big group. When we reached them, we saw that she was injured. Our guide had a packable Akia that he quickly assembled while the other guide was splinting her leg. Since I was familiar with running an Akia, I took the back position and the guide took the front. The other guide had taken all but six of us and headed back down to the lodge so they wouldn't have to ski out in the dark.

We finally got to a place where the smaller chopper could pick her up. It hovered just off the snow and four of us loaded her into the chopper and laid down in the snow while the pilot backed away from the mountain so he could turn and head for the lodge. The two guys who were above us watched this move and later told Tim and me that it looked like we were going to be hit by the rotors as it backed away. Lying on the ground, it felt like the blades were clearing us by mere inches. They bussed her and her boyfriend out the next morning. She made a full recovery but the other reps never really forgave him for his poor choices.

When I started at Lange, my territory was in 10th place out of 11. But 18 months later, my territory was first and Gub Langdon's was second. While I was successful at Lange, the company was struggling. Due to a great snafu by the Lange fitting system, called Lange Flow, Lange was soon in financial trouble to a point they couldn't defend their patents when Nordica Boots infringed and actually started taking market share away. Besides the fact that I had OU Sports and really loyal accounts, it felt like we were going to go out of business.

Lange fired Dick Swan and split his territory between Jimmy Simonson and me. Luckily, Dick was immediately hired by Rossignol Skis and didn't miss a beat in doing well there.

After Labor Day of 1973, I decided to make a pass through my territory and set up training clinics for my dealers. The first call I made was to Anderson's Sporting Goods in Salem, Oregon run by Harvey Fox who was a great friend and one of the most ethical dealers in the business. I walked into the store and told him I was setting up training clinics. He shook his head and said, "Let's go get a cup of coffee." He told me he just got off the phone and was told that Abu Garcia Company was buying Lange and their sales rep would be taking over my territory. I couldn't believe it and drove home to call Morrie.

He was apologetic and said that because of our contracts, Gub and I were going to be fired while the rest of the salesforce would be retained. I immediately called Gub; he had received the news the same way I had. He was retaining an attorney and suggested I should, too. Apparently, Jack Beattie (VP of Sales at Abu Garcia, and brother to Bob Beattie, U.S. Ski Team coach) was telling everyone that by firing us, his reps would collect our commissions. I called a business attorney and he laughed when I told him that. He said Colorado had a state law that any company not paying commission could be sued and, if you won, you got triple damages plus attorney fees. I called Gub and he had the same information, so we agreed to meet in Denver the next Monday and go to Lange.

When we got to Bob's office, Morrie was there as was Jack. He was looking a little peaked; apparently his attorney had read the contracts and knew the Colorado commission law. Morrie and Bob looked embarrassed. Jack attempted to shake our hands but we just stared at him. We reviewed our sales data and travel expenses and came to a deal that we felt good about. We would be paid for what we had sold and could take the leftover equipment samples we had on hand and do what we wanted with them. We stood up, shook Bob's and Morrie's hands, nodded at Jack and left.

We had to contain ourselves in the parking lot because we didn't want them to see how happy we were. We felt like we had just gotten off a sinking ship! Gub went back to New York and accepted a job with Beconta, the distributor of Nordica Ski Boots, Volkl Skis, and Look Ski Bindings. Two weeks later, I was hired by Dick Zue to be the K2 rep for Northern California and Northern Nevada.

But that didn't happen by chance. Because Harvey Fox had tipped me off, I had a friend create a card announcing that I was leaving Lange because of the Lange Garcia marriage. Dick Zue had been looking for an excuse to fire his Northern California rep because dealers were complaining about lack of service. He received the card I sent him and called me that afternoon. My contract with K2 was really great and it showed the difference between companies that respect their salesforce and those that don't.

In Seattle, there was a great used equipment store called the Ski Rack. It was owned by friends of ours, so we had an outlet to get rid of the sample equipment. All of it sold and, by the end of October, we got a big check and the people who bought it got some really good gear for bargain prices. Big wins for all concerned.

© Danny Stoffel

Heli-skiing the Bugaboos
Canadian Rockies, British Columbia

- Started by Hans Gmoser in 1965, heli-skiing the Canadian Rockies is an epic adventure.
- Photo by Danny Stoffel and courtesy of CMH Heli-Skiing & Summer Adventures.
- Helicopters deliver you to various locations on the range, providing 251,000 acres of skiing terrain.
- Locations include: Bugaboos, Cariboos, Adamants, Gothics, Kootenay, Purcell, Revelstoke, Bobbie Burns, Galena, Monashees, Nomads, and Valemount.
- Located in the Purcells Mountain Range 208 miles (335 km) east of Calgary, the five-star Bugaboos Lodge offers incredible views and amenities.
- Learn more at CMHHeli.com.

III. THE SKI INDUSTRY

"A pair of skis are the ultimate transportation to freedom...The best place in the world to ski is the place you are skiing today."

Warren Miller,
Ski filmmaker and friend

Chapter 14

1973-1974: K2 Ski Company

Sacramento, California
38.5816° N, 121.4944° W
Elevation: 30 Feet (3 M)

When Dick Zue and I met to finalize my K2 sales rep contract, he offered a nice package. They put me on salary until the sales cycle was over and then I'd switch to commissions. They set me up with a new car and paid our moving expenses to Northern California. He also told me he'd pay a $50 bonus every time I called on an account. I agreed because I knew that most of the dealers had not been given a clinic on K2 skis for at least a year. I bought a 1973 Chevy Blazer because it would allow me to remove the rear seat to stow demo skis and gear and travel around the territory in sunshine, rain, or snow.

When my car was delivered, it didn't have air conditioning, which was problematic since it got to 110° Fahrenheit in the Sacramento Valley. K2 had just been sold to Cummins Diesel, whose president loved skiing and was in an acquisition mode. He'd acquired Jani King, maker of aftermarket air conditioners. I met with one of their dealers, got a great price on it, and had it installed. I sent the receipt to Dick and I was shocked when he refused to reimburse me.

Dick Zue was married to the sister of my good friend, Dick Swan. When Rossignol Ski Company hired him, they gave him the same territory that I had with K2. Dick told me to call him when I made my first trip into San Francisco and he would take me around and introduce me to the dealers I didn't know. I called him and we agreed to meet at Sam's Grill in downtown S.F. Dick was friends with the owner, Frank Seput, so when we went in for lunch, we got a table instantly. Frank let me know that he was a big fan of U.S. Ski Team member Spider Sabich, a California native, who also raced on K2 skis. Frank and I became great friends; I actually took Spider and his girlfriend, Claudine Longet, to his restaurant for lunch about three weeks before she shot and killed Spider in Aspen.

Dick took me around and I was really surprised at how complex the layout of San Francisco was. I would have wasted hours trying to find some of the smaller dealers within the city. Most of the dealers were amazed that the Rossignol rep was helping the K2 rep learn the territory. Dick and I are still great friends and we have spent many a day pursuing our passion for fly-fishing.

I set up clinics and worked very hard to gain the trust of the K2 dealers in my territory. I was doing four or five dealer calls in a day and collecting $50 on each call. One of the dealers that I called on just before Christmas grabbed me and said, "Let me take YOU to lunch today." So we went to Sam's where he asked me, "I have carried K2 for three years now and I was lucky to see my rep in my store once a year. You've been here for three months and you have called on me five or six times." I said, "Today is seven." I never told him about my bonus, but when I got his pre-season order, it was double the previous year's. Dick and I both knew that relationships matter–I would have made those visits even without the bonus. I'm glad Dick recognized that time spent with dealers had direct value to him, too.

That spring, right after the ski shows and getting preseason orders, I got a call from Dick Zue. He asked if I would meet him at the San Francisco Airport, take him to a meeting with a dealer, and then take him to Reno to see his brother-in-law. I said, "Sure!" and we went to lunch and then drove to Stan's for Sports in Santa Rosa and met with their GM. Dick told him that K2 had made a mistake on the top skins of a special entry-level ski and needed to dump 400 pairs of skis. They normally sold for $72 wholesale and $125 retail. Stan jumped in and said he would buy them all for $40 each.

I got to watch Dick at his finest. He asked, "Why $40?" and Stan said, "That fits a price point I don't have a good ski in right now." Dick started talking about the other price points, what each K2 ski priced at, and which other brands occupied that price point. We did not drink alcohol at that lunch, but I could see that the Stan's guys were getting confused the more that Dick talked about pricing. About an hour later, we had an order for those skis at $57 a pair.

As we left the Bay area and started toward Sacramento, it went from a pleasant temperature to a warm day and by the time we hit Vacaville, Dick was sweating. He reached over and turned the AC on. I reached up and turned it off. Ten miles later he turned it back on and I turned it off again. He asked what I was doing, and I told him. "Since you wouldn't pay for the AC, you're not allowed to use it." He glared at me and then laughed. He reached up, turned it on, and said, "Fine. Send me the bill."

K2 was really cooking in the market and had built a brand-new factory to increase production, so we became a consistent supplier. The factory was on Vashon Island in Puget Sound and accessed by ferry boat. It was a 30-minute ferry ride to the island and then a 15-minute drive from the dock to the building.

The reason Bill Kirschner started K2 was that he was too cheap to pay $125 for a pair of Head skis. He and his brother had a company named Kirschner Scientific and their big product was fiberglass animal cages for veterinarians and research labs. Bill was running K2 and his brother was managing Kirschner Scientific. A lot of skiers think that K2 was named after the Himalayan Mountain range peak by that name. It was actually named after the Kirschner brothers, two of them, hence K2.

They chose to sell Kirschner Scientific to an investor group that was acquiring assets in that field—they merged it into one of their businesses called Hazleton Laboratories, located in the Washington, D.C. area. It later became famous for having an outbreak of Ebola virus within a few miles of the White House. This story eventually became the best-selling book *The Hot Zone*, which later was made into a movie and TV series.

About that time, Bill Kirschner and Chuck Ferries (President of K2 and former Olympic skier) met with Terry Heckler and Gordon Bowker from Heckler Bowker Advertising Agency. At the first meeting, Terry sat there doodling to a point that Bill was becoming annoyed. When the food arrived at the table, Terry handed Bill a napkin with the red, white and blue K2 logo still used today. Bill and Chuck both were taken aback by how that logo gave the brand such a made-in-America presence. Terry and Gordon were hired on the spot. Terry told them, "The logo is free, but we will be charging from here on out."

Heckler Bowker was one of the best things to happen to K2. They not only remade the brand with that new logo, they also called for a new look in the K2 lineup. The era of Holiday, Elite, and XR10 ski lines was about to be over as we got more production capabilities. All the reps came to Seattle for a sales meeting set up to introduce the new skis for next season's delivery. The meeting was run by Terry and Gordon with Chuck, Bill, and Dick sitting in front and looking like the cats who just ate the canaries.

The room was set up like a lecture hall with the stage full of displays all covered in black curtains. Terry said that they were unveiling the first of many changes going forward that they hoped would establish K2 as a worldwide player in the sport of skiing. Gordon pulled the curtain off the first display and revealed the red, white and blue skis with a spotlight coming on and dazzling the salesforce. Chuck took over the microphone and explained that K2 would be selling four skis next year. Ski #1 would be the entry level ski and would replace the Holiday. Ski #2 would replace the Elite. Ski #3 was a new ski designed to compete with the Head 360 ski and would appeal to the all-around ski market. Ski #4 would be a full-blown competition ski to compete with the Rossignol Strato, which at that time was their top selling ski.

The room was charged with electricity and Chuck turned the microphone back to Terry who said, "Now we will reveal the advertising campaign to support this new step." Gordon pulled the curtain off the easel and the room went absolutely silent. He had revealed the now iconic barn with a daisy in the foreground and a big K2 logo painted on the barn—the text read "Chew K2." He stepped to the microphone and said, "We have a slideshow to explain our thoughts about this." He turned it on and went through editions of both *Ski* and *Ski Magazine*, showing every ad from the previous year. They all looked the same, either a racer skiing or someone skiing powder snow or jumping off of something. He explained that with all sameness, ads disappeared, but the Chew K2 ad would be read because of its uniqueness. To this day, that imagery is still used with K2's booths at ski shows.

The Chew K2 ad and trade show booth design

It was the beginning of a business relationship that would benefit K2 and Heckler Bowker for many years to come. Dick Zue took the microphone and announced that we would be having our winter sales meeting at Sun Valley, Idaho, where we would have the opportunity to ski on all the new models before the selling season and the annual ski show at Las Vegas. There was some doubt about the ads, but Gordon turned out to be right and we heard lots of good things from our dealers telling us the marketplace was responding to the idea of an American company making quality skis for all levels of skiers.

In my territory, between Rossignol and K2, we were pushing some of the European brands out of the first-tier shops. They were stocking more of the best-selling skis and eliminating the ones that were hard to sell. It took me a little time, but I figured out that these weaker, European brands were not going to go away because they were being subsidized by their governments, which resulted in a lot of inventory being dumped into the U.S. market. This was disconcerting because many of the dealers we had taken care of were now suddenly having sales on skis that were competing with our entry level skis.

I started to think about how we could solve this problem. Having worked in the Crystal Mountain ski shop for the Nagel's, I started thinking about what would discourage a dealer from purchasing dumped ski brands. I had an idea and presented it to Dick Zue. I suggested that we get ahead of these guys by offering an entry level ski from K2 that we would only sell to dealers willing to buy 300+ pairs and we would let them design their own graphics. We'd offer these deals at the ski shows and ship the skis so they would be in stock for the Labor Day sales. The invoices would come due on December 1st, guaranteeing them income at the launch of the ski season.

Dick liked this and further fleshed out the details. It would be a short selling season with an absolute deadline on the placing of orders and would allow K2 to build the ski blanks early. The dealer could name the ski and select the color of the graphics, which would come from K2's art department. They could price it where they felt it would sell quickly but, in the event that it did not, it would be easy to dump before Thanksgiving. The program was named SMU for Special Make Ups. It accomplished what we wanted and, to this day, K2 still has that program. It also changed how dealers defined the term "Hot Ski." Prior to this program, it used to describe a fast model that was fun to ski on. But now "Hot Ski" means a model that the dealers buy, make a great profit on, and sell out by Labor Day weekend.

© Sun Valley Resort

Sun Valley Resort
Sun Valley, Idaho

- Founded in 1935 by Count Felix Schaffgotsch of Austria, Sun Valley was built by the Union Pacific Railroad. The area consists of Bald Mountain and Dollar Mountain. Together, they offer 121 runs over 2,054 skiable acres in the Sawtooth National Forest.
- There are 18 lifts and a vertical drop of 3,400 feet (Bald) and 628 feet (Dollar). The average snowfall is 102 inches.
- They offer private and group lessons for children and adults.
- Learn more at SunValley.com.

Chapter 15

1975-1976: The Cheeseburger Ski

Vashon Island, Washington
47.4473° N, 122.4599° W
Elevation: 381 Feet (116 M)

During the next selling cycle, Dick came to San Francisco to help out at the Nor Cal Ski Show. We had a spectacular show and Dick had brought his tennis gear, so we played a couple of sets every morning before breakfast. On the day after the show, we played a three-set match and Dick was as animated as I had ever seen him—he looked great and was in fine form. This was on a Thursday. On Sunday, I got a call from Jackie Van Guilder, the customer service guru and department head at K2. She told me that Dick had a pancreatitis attack and was in the hospital, not expected to live through the night. We all got a call the next day and were told the service would be on Wednesday on Vashon Island. Every one of the sales reps came; it was probably the largest funeral ever on Vashon.

The entire company was in shock and it started a chain of events that changed my life forever. Barry Gordinier was named as Dick's replacement and, in less than three months, Dick "Mac" McNamara was named Eastern Sales Manager and I was named Western Sales Manager—our territories defined by the Mississippi River. I had to fill my own position and hired Brian Snelson, one of our tech reps. He became a superstar salesperson, staying with K2 for 25+ years as part of his spectacular career.

To replace the So Cal rep, I went to one of our biggest accounts in Los Angeles, Pats for Sports. I sat down with Pat, explained my plan to hire someone with retail experience, and asked if he had any recommendations. He sent me to Paul Ingle, whom I interviewed and hired. Interestingly, Mac hired the Rossignol rep from his territory, which showed our different sales philosophies. His guy became #1 sales rep in the East and Paul became #1 in the West, proving that there is more than one way to peel an apple.

Everything was looking great for K2. We had started taking market share from Head and Rossignol and the dealers were making K2s their second or third choice of skis to stock.

Our plan was working except we rapidly got ahead with sales, but manufacturing couldn't keep up. We had three consecutive years where we missed

My Life in Winters 83

delivery deadlines on our three top selling skis. The salesforce didn't like it, the retailers didn't like it, and the CFO really didn't like it. K2 moved the factory to three shifts a day and seven days per week to try to catch up. The factory was running so hard that the walls felt like they would come apart.

The only good news was that the market was still growing and there was a new segment emerging in the ski industry. "Hot Dog" or freestyle skiing started to take off. As a sales manager, I was watching a big-time shift from racing being the king to, all of a sudden, hot dogging taking off in America. K2 was fortunate that we had hired Wayne Wong, a Canadian skier, in 1972. He was a great freestyle skier and had a super charismatic personality, so he got lots of media coverage. I can remember being in the room when we learned that the Wayne Wong ski had outsold the Spider Sabich ski.

While we should have been celebrating, it was a somber occasion for most of the management who had all been racers. I also remember a Hot Dog contest at the Heavenly Valley Ski Area at Lake Tahoe, California where Bill Kirschner, Chuck Ferries, and Gordy Eaton (a former U.S. Ski Team member) were standing at the bottom of the mogul hill. A freestyle skier really laid down a great run and all the competitors were clapping by clicking their poles together and Gordy leaned in and said, "I think I am going to puke!"

It was a harbinger for what was about to happen that almost put K2 out of business. We went to a sales meeting at Sun Valley and again Heckler Bowker staged an unveiling of the next year's product line. This time, we had already skied on the new products for two days and we were blown away at how good the short skis were performing. So, at the unveiling, we knew we were going to have two separate lines. The first was the standard line with our competition skis plus a new model to round out that line. The graphics had changed a little, but they were very sellable.

We took a bathroom break and, when we came back in, the new short skis were there wrapped in aluminum foil and had restaurant-style heat lights pointed at them. Gordon started at the bottom of the line with the "Shorts," which was a standard K2 looking ski in red, white, and blue. He unveiled the next ski, named "Briefs" and it was lime green and orange. I remember thinking, "Huh. Interesting choice."

The next ski was called the "Cheeseburger" and was orange on lighter orange, followed by the "Cheeseburger Deluxe" with orange on yellow. Then Gordon unveiled the new ski poles and announced that they were called... wait for it... "Fries." I thought, "Uh oh."

The room was deadly quiet and then it exploded as the salesforce realized that this was the racer mentality disrespecting a large segment of their ski market. Bill and Chuck calmed everybody down and said that it would all work out. The sales reps would not relent because we knew that our dealers would not buy those skis. It was suggested that new graphics be put on hold. That was when the news got worse—they were already in production and had produced fairly big quantities.

Things happened just as we expected—the K2 dealers supported us very cautiously with that part of the line, but sales were minimal because of the graphics, which was really sad because those were really great skis. I skied most of that winter on Cheeseburger Deluxe and they were great in the powder and at high speed they were amazingly stable. They were forerunners to today's skis minus the under foot component.

The greatest damage of that event actually was the loss of trust by the shop employees of our dealers. One indicator of a product's success is how many retailer employees buy it, given all their choices. I doubt that we sold more than 10% of the shop employees' skis that year.

I later asked Gordon how that fiasco had happened and he told me that he and Terry thought they were poking fun, in a good natured way, at what was seen as the "fun" segment of the ski population. But I think that what really happened is that the racer side of the sport put pressure on them and it backfired.

Once it was clear that we had lost the faith of our dealers' employees, I was tasked with coming up with a plan to win them back as quickly as possible. I decided to go all in and met with Fred James, our advertising manager. When she answered her phone, people would hear her voice and assume she was Fred's secretary. They'd say, "Please connect me with Fred James in Advertising." And she'd reply, "You are talking to her."

I explained that I needed some of her budget to woo the shop employees back to K2; I was going to put a program together to blow up Rossignol's, Head's and Kneissl's shop employees' programs. Here is what I planned to do. I would not publish our program until I knew what those three companies were offering and then I would fix our prices to match theirs, but we would include a free binding of their choice at no extra cost. At that time Marker, Look, and Salomon controlled about 85% of the binding market. She agreed and we put that plan in play. We were so successful that we surpassed the sales from the pre-Cheeseburger year by more than 20%!

At the next Las Vegas ski show, I bumped into Henry Patty, the Head of Rossignol U.S.A. He walked up to me, shook my hand, and said, "You are a very clever person." I knew instantly that we had gotten one over on our competitors. A big part of our recovery took place when we held an event at Heavenly Valley Ski Area and brought in key dealers from all over the country. At the opening meeting and dinner, Bill Kirschner took the stage and apologized to the dealers and thanked them for continuing to support K2. He was sure that the new lineup would bring the K2 buyer back into their stores.

Having been with Lange during the Lange Flow fiasco and seeing how dealers and the consumers reacted to Lange versus what we were seeing at K2, it dawned on me that the humility that Bill conveyed compared to the arrogance of Lange's management was the difference between the market wanting you to survive (in K2's case) and everybody wanting to kick you when you were down, which Lange experienced.

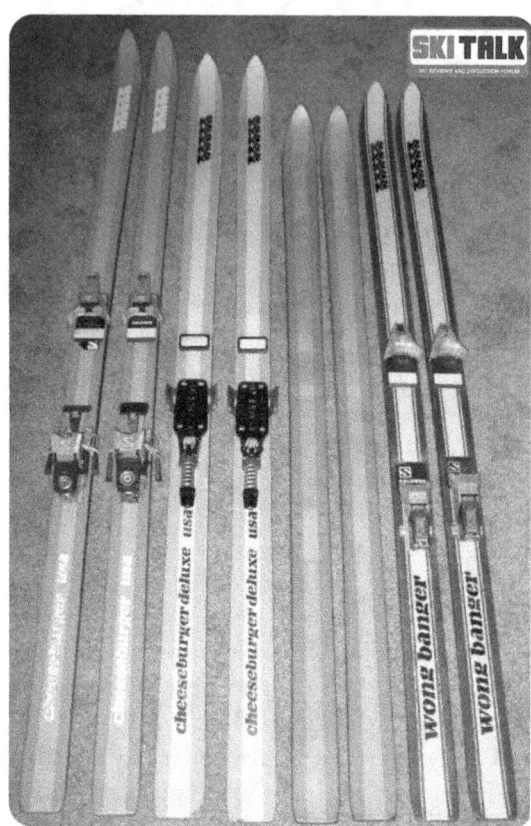

K2 Cheeseburger ski lineup—photo courtesy of SkiTalk.com

Things seemed to be going better at K2, but we were blindsided by a Cummins Board of Directors meeting. They decided to divest themselves of all the companies they had acquired that were unrelated to the primary business in the automobile and truck industries.

Bill and Chuck told them that if they sold K2 to anyone but the companies they approved, they would leave. In fact, the entire management team was prepared to leave if they didn't have the final say in the transaction. The Cummins BOD agreed to let them find the right home.

Bill and Chuck called the investor group who had bought Kirschner Scientific and asked if they wanted to buy K2. They came to look at what was for sale and couldn't believe the leverage they had just with the location of the manufacturing and office facility. They purchased K2 and we became part of GGCON, which is the initials of the last names of the five investors:
- Steve Garvey, an attorney in Seattle
- Jim Garrison, PhD, from Harvard University in Business
- Kirby Cramer, CEO at Hazelton Laboratories
- Wally Opdyke, CEO at St. Michelle Winery
- Leslie Nielson, CEO at U.S. Tobacco

Jim Garrison, the only investor not managing a business, became CEO at K2. I was very interested in the changes, so I got a copy of Garrison's doctoral thesis. It was all about team building, so he seemed like a safe bet to lead K2.

When Jim Garrison came to K2, the Board did several really smart things. The first was to appoint Bill Kirschner as Chairman of the Board and give Jim the title of President and CEO. Chuck Ferries was made Executive Vice President.

Next, they empowered Jim to launch a detailed evaluation of the business and create a plan for rapid growth, so we could take advantage of the heating up of the American ski industry in general.

The marketing team was in place with the addition of Ned Post, a Harvard MBA with experience from the wine industry and a stint at Procter and Gamble. Before his arrival, we were shooting from the hip most of the time and the marketing and sales department was calling all the shots. Ned teamed up with Heckler Bowker and created a really good image of what an American-made ski company should look like.

After Jim finished the business evaluation, he brought us together and informed us that the theoretical factory capacity was 300,000 pairs of skis per year. We were currently selling and manufacturing about 225,000 pairs. We were told to reach at least 75% of capacity as quickly as possible.

After that meeting, Jim came to Barry, Mac, and me and said the BOD had approved a one-week all expenses paid trip to Maui, Hawaii for the three of us and our wives to brainstorm how to get to that number. That was another great BOD move because we had a ball in Hawaii and came back with three goals and a plan.

First, we needed to expand our dealer base without disrupting our current dealers. If we did it right, we could set a way to grow in the overall ski industry, which would benefit K2 and all our dealers. We decided to do this by creating two new brands; these would each create the additional pair numbers to get to the 275,000-300,000 range needed to make the factory efficient.

Second, we needed to explore the technology we were using to make skis and see if we could translate that into a new line of products that would serve another marketplace or industry.

We then launched a plan to accomplish our goals. To start, we singled out our best and biggest dealers and hosted them on a trip to Las Vegas. We wanted their input on the current industry climate and their thoughts about where we could grow. We were amazed at the response. I remember hanging out in the swimming pool at the Sands Hotel on the Strip and realizing we were surrounded by 60% of U.S. ski retailers.

We asked them to identify the market segments that constituted a large percentage of their total business. And then tell us what we could provide them that would consolidate those vendors into a cooperative partner. The exchange of ideas was impressive and, while we didn't get any firm commitments, we accomplished our goal of starting the conversation.

We were not surprised when Jerry Gart of Gart Brothers in Denver, Colorado called us and offered to host another meeting in Denver if we would listen to his thoughts. We quickly agreed and were eager to see what they had in mind.

In the meantime, we promoted the plan to create three new brand names to sell to different markets. One was a brand we called Pre. It would be sold to non-K2 dealers and a few carefully selected K2 dealers. Here is an example of what we did in Idaho. We had five really good dealers in Boise and we had carefully sold to three of them, which helped them stay profitable and promote the fact they were an authorized K2 dealer. The new plan was to sell a line of four or five skis to our number one dealer in volume and then also the two dealers who were not currently selling our products.

It became obvious that this would only work if Pre looked like an independent entity and were trying to figure out how to pull this off. We were surprised when Chuck Ferries said he would resign from K2 and become the Pre CEO. It turned out that he wanted his own business and parlayed Pre into a solid company. Eventually, he also ended up owning the Schwinn bicycle brand. He retired and his son and son-in-law are currently running that thriving business from Sun Valley, Idaho.

The second brand we launched was Killy, named after the French racer, Jean Claude Killy, who won all three alpine events in the 1968 Olympics in Grenoble, France. He was now a member of the K2 Pro Race Team and had a contract with us and General Motors for the use of his name in North America. The third brand was Dynaglass, which was the defunct company that Bill Kirschner originally bought to make prototypes in the early days of K2.

In the meantime, Jerry Gart organized his meeting in Denver. Barry, Mac, and I attended and, honestly, that meeting bordered on the bizarre. Jerry had brought in 12 dealers with whom he had cooperative agreements. This included Morrie Mages, whom we had never sold to because of his creative business practices. Also at the meeting was Nate Gart, Jerry's father, who provided some comic relief. Their proposal was they would take on the Killy and Dynaglass brands, if we could offer them exclusivity and not sell those brands to any of their competitors. This was what we had always planned so we signed that deal.

In the meantime, we had great success with our third goal of leveraging our technology to expand into other markets. K2 started manufacturing cross-country skis and water skis. K2 also acquired JanSport, a backpack and climbing company based in Snohomish, Washington. This led Lou Whitaker to launch an expedition to Mount Everest, where he hoped to join his brother, Jim, as a summiter of the world's highest mountain. While bad weather prevented his summit, JanSport packs and tents were on the Everest attempt and the press coverage made it a valid mountaineering brand.

As an active white water kayaker, I tried to get K2 into the kayak paddle business because it was growing in popularity, but no one else saw the same thing. Today, 18.1 million participate in kayaking in the U.S. alone. As the saying goes, you win some and you lose some. Hard to know who lost in this case.

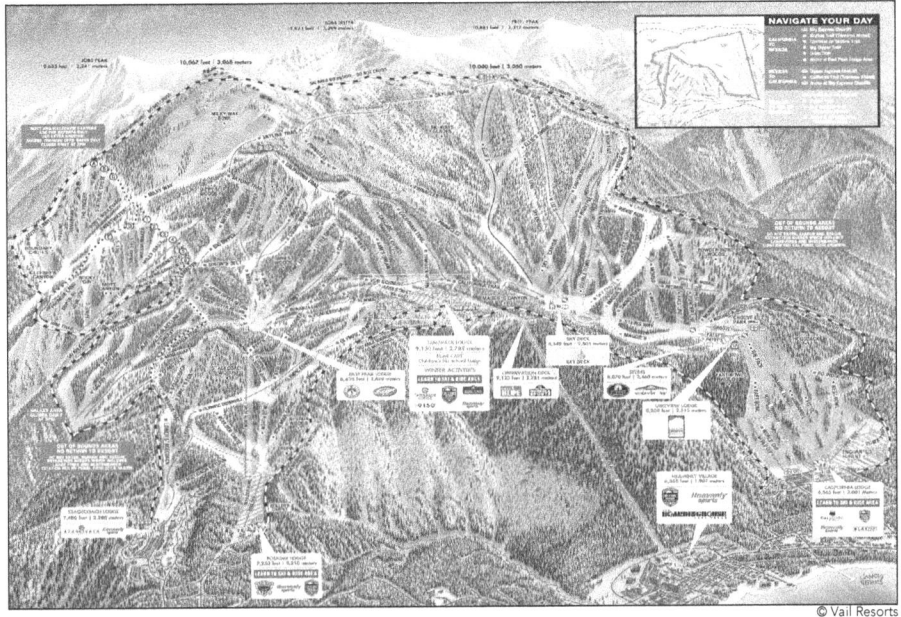

© Vail Resorts

Heavenly Ski Resort
Lake Tahoe, California

- Founded in 1947 by Lee and Daisy Miller, Heavenly Valley currently boasts 97 runs over 4,800 skiable acres in the El Dorado-Toiyabe National Forest.
- There are 28 lifts and a vertical drop of 3,500 feet. The average snowfall is 360 inches and they also have terrain parks.
- They offer group and private lessons for both children and adults.
- Learn more at SkiHeavenly.com.

Chapter 16

Evolution of Ski Equipment

Loon Mountain Resort, New Hampshire
44.0563° N, 71.6336° W
Base Elevation: 950 Feet (290 M)
Peak Elevation: 3,050 Feet (930 M)

Since I started skiing in 1951, the mountains have not changed nor has the human body, but ski equipment has evolved exponentially! Ski equipment falls into five main categories—skis, poles, boots, bindings, and helmets. The latter was added once skis evolved enough to generate great speeds.

While skiing is depicted on cave drawings as far back as 5,000 years ago, the modern era of skiing began in the 1800's. We can think of today's equipment as evolving through four main eras. I'm going to give you the highlights here but, if you want a detailed analysis, read the posts by Seth Masia on the SkiingHistory.org website.

Pre-Depression Skiing (1850-1920)

The skis in this era tended to be really long, made of wood, and the bindings were leather straps that held your boots to the ski. The wooden skis were difficult to turn because the wood provided nothing to grip if the snow was not soft. So skis were mainly used as a form of transportation across snow in the winter. Gentle hills could be managed but skiing down steep inclines for sport was not a thing yet. In 1868, the telemark ski was invented by Sondre Norheim, which coupled with a stiffer binding, gave people the first real ability to control a ski by turning.

Throughout the late 1800's, various Scandinavian inventors developed new types of telemark skis using different kinds of wood and laminating different woods together. But waterproof glues were not yet invented so the skis would come apart after a few uses. The size and shape of skis did not change much—they were long and straight.

Throughout this time, ski boots were really just leather boots generously slathered in animal fat to create waterproofing. Boots were held on by leather straps and people moved much in the style of today's cross-country skiing, with their heels coming up as they strode across the flats. One invention of the time was to add a curled tip to the front of the boot (think elf shoes), which kept the boot from sliding out of the binding strap. In 1888, Fridtjof Nansen added a buckle loop to keep the heel strap in place.

Poles were also made of wood and leather with their overall shape being similar to today. However, most skiers skied with one long pole that was used to help turn the ski. It also served as the brake—skiers would put it between their legs and sit on it, thereby digging it into the snow, which slowed or stopped their forward momentum.

Depression-Era Skiing (1920-1945)

In 1926, Austria's Rudolph Lettner invented the steel edge, which radically changed skiing. Skis could now grip to harder snow and steeper hills. In 1928, Switzerland's Guido Reuge invented the Kandahar binding that holds the heel down. These two nearly simultaneous inventions opened the door for alpine skiing because it gave skiers the ability to navigate hills and ski down them for fun or sport. Also during this time, aluminum skis and poles went into production in France. Similar advances were being made in glues, lamination techniques, and wax.

Skis became shorter and the Dover Toe-Iron was invented, which gave skiers a bit more control. This showed itself in the Hannes Schneider Arlberg technique where the skier sunk down and then rose up to take the weight off the skis and the skier rotated his upper body to affect a turn.

This technique came to the U.S.A. in the 1930's as the European ski countries started emulating the success of the golf pros from Scotland and Ireland. Many had come to the U.S. and made a living teaching golf and designing courses in the late 1800's. Many alpine skiers saw a similar path that could help them escape the depression economy and the oncoming wars.

The great advances for the ski industry in the U.S. came as a result of the New Deal that created agencies to provide government-backed projects. These projects drove short-term economic recovery and created infrastructure that benefitted the public for years and decades to come. The Citizens Conservation Corps and the Works Progress Administration ran from 1933 to 1942.

During this period, hundreds of new ski areas were built on federal lands and thousands of people were put to work. When the project was finished, it generally became property of the county that it was built in. Almost every town in snow country had a town hill and it was very economical to access these areas. In my hometown of Salida, we had Monarch Pass which was 17 miles from downtown. Pre-WWII, tickets to ski were $.25; by the time I was skiing there in 1954, it had gone up to $1.00.

During World War II, 1939 to 1945, ski equipment was focused on military uses and navigating European mountains during battle. See Chapter 2 for more information on the 10th Mountain Division.

Post War Era (1945-1960)

This is the era that saw the birth and early rise of the outdoor industry in the United States. The Greatest Generation came home and started building what would become the ski industry as well as the camping and mountaineering industry. This era really kickstarted innovation in equipment and federal expansion of recreational opportunities as the middle class expanded and became more mobile.

During this time, several inventions had an epic impact on how we ski today. First, Georges Salomon invented an interlocking steel edge that could easily be installed on army surplus skis, which were plentiful and, therefore, inexpensive. My friend, Kenny Smith, and I installed the Salomon edges on A&T surplus skis that we bought for $20.00 a pair. We bought the edges along with an A&T base finish that was blue and dried to a hard plastic-like material when painted on the ski. These edges really changed the way people skied, making possible carved turns on hard packed snow. It was not too long after that ski manufacturers started installing steel edges in the production process.

Second, the 1950's brought about the invention of plastic skis reinforced by fiberglass. These skis were coated in polyethylene, eliminating the need for wax and making it easy to repair minor dings by simply applying more polyethylene. Howard Head used this approach and released the Head Standard ski. By 1960, plastic fiberglass skis essentially replaced wood and aluminum skis, both for racing and recreational use. However, aluminum/fiberglass skis remained popular for recreational use, especially in deep powder.

Third, Hannes Marker invented a ski binding that released when too much tork was applied to the ski. Before releasable bindings, fear of injury was a roadblock for some people to take up the sport. Marker Bindings created a reliable system for the boot and ski to work as a team, giving people a sense of increased safety.

Fourth, Bob Lange invented the plastic ski boot. Before Lange, all boots were made out of leather and very labor intensive to manufacture. For the average skier, a pair of leather boots would last four or five years. For the average ski patrolman or instructor, they would be lucky to last an entire season. The culprit was water—melting snow and sweat would soften the leather and the boots would break down, losing the stiffness that allows the skier to control the ski.

Skiers would try a range of things to get more time out of their leather boots. I remember heating shoe polish and painting it on my boots just to bring back some stiffness and add temporary waterproofing. What a mess it was!

I was working at Vail with Morrie Sheppard, the Ski School Director, when his friend, Bob Lange, walked into our office and showed us his prototype plastic boot. He asked Morrie to test it for a week. Luckily for me, I am not bashful so I asked if I could test it too. He said, "Yes. I'll meet you at Morrie's house tonight to fit the boots."

Fitting consisted of heating the boots to 200° in the oven, then putting them on, lacing them up, and running outside to cool them off to harden them.

Morrie and I could not believe how great they skied. After three days, I changed back to my leather Molitor boots and could not believe how much trouble I had turning. Bob gave us those boots and I skied on them the rest of the year and then some.

Lange's plastic boot had the most impact on ski racing. They gave racers the ability to lean much harder on their edges, especially on hard or icy hills. It only took a few seasons before all the winning racers were in plastic boots, either Lange or Nordica, or some other manufacturers who quickly followed suit.

Fifth, chemists working for the U.S. Army invented nylon and other synthetic fabrics and insulations that completely changed outdoor clothing. Before this revolution, skiers wore wool, canvas, and sometimes down, none of which were waterproof. My ski clothing today weighs approximately one-third of what I wore skiing when I started in 1951. Again, I can't help but think that this whole industry exists because of the 10th Mountain Division.

Finally, this is the era when safety helmets entered the sport. Mainly because the advancements in skis, bindings, and boots allowed people to ski much faster, thus leading to an increase in impact injuries. In 1955, Winter Park became the first ski area to outfit its crew with helmets when Steve Bradley provided Bell Toptex helmets to their groomers. Very soon after, the U.S. Ski Team outfitted their skiers with the same helmets. There were no standards so many teams still wore leather helmets but that all changed in 1959 when John Semmelink, a Canadian skier, died after hitting his head on a rock while wearing his team-issued leather helmet. The 1960 Winter Olympic Games in Squaw Valley mandated that all downhill racers wear the hard-shell helmets.

Modern Era (1960-Today)

While all of the previous inventions made recreational skiing possible, and intensified the competitiveness of racing, recent developments have made skiing much more enjoyable and safe.

Today, we have a system called DIN, which is an acronym for the German Institute of Standards. It creates a system to ensure that all types of boots fit all bindings exactly the same. This standardization allowed consumers to pick and choose their favorite brands, knowing they would all work together. In addition, the DIN system combines weight, age, skiing ability, and standardization of materials to ensure that the safety settings are perfect for each individual. For those of you who walk around in your boots on concrete or dirt, you are compromising your DIN settings.

All skiers should remember to have their DIN settings checked annually. This is why renting your ski equipment can be a good deal. You not only get customized fitting (they check your DIN settings there in the store), you also get to ski on the latest and greatest developments the ski and boot manufacturers have to offer.

Speaking of ski boots, innovations here have been more focused on comfort. Boots now have comfortable inner linings made of memory foam; some even include battery-charged heating elements to keep your feet warm. Some brands have played with a walking boot that fits inside the outer shell, making it easy to transition around the ski area. I'm sure this was inspired by snowboarders who seem to be the most comfortable on the mountain with their walking boots and roomy clothes.

The evolution of the modern ski is the combination of the petrol chemical advances coupled with the downturn in the aerospace industry that took place in the late 1970's and again in the mid-1980's. A lot of carbon fiber experts suddenly became available to the ski industry and their experience in high tech design led to a lot of great skis and snowboards. They were able to combine kevlar, carbon fiber, glass supplants, ceramic fiber, and other strong materials into new combinations that improved speed, flexibility, and torsion.

I was at K2 when Boeing lost a government contract and we were able to hire two people from Boeing's helicopter division, specifically the rotary carbon fiber blades division. It didn't hurt that both engineers were really great skiers and had thought about how to create more efficient and predictable skis. Jim Vandergriff and Al Davingon, along with Bucky Kashiwa, revolutionized how K2 skis are built.

Several advances also came from other serendipitous events. In the 1960's, Émile Allais came up with a formula for making skis. He decided to design a slalom ski, a giant slalom ski, and a downhill ski. His thinking was that this would cover all skiers, including the elite racers. The first company to adopt this method was Dynastar, followed by Dynamic and then Rossignol. Whether it was fate or luck, the 1968 Olympics was dominated by the French team who had two athletes on all three events podiums.

In the 1970's, new shaped skis hit the market. Ski designers at Elan Ski and K2 Ski incorporated a radical side cut to mimic the excellent carving that snowboards produce. Bode Miller won several races skiing on K2 skis with that design inclusion. Elan gained a really strong following because their skis were the easiest skis to turn and carve with, until other companies mimicked their designs.

Another crazy innovation happened when Seth Morrison, a K2 big mountain skier, bent one of his skis during a fall while filming backcountry skiing. He noticed that the bent ski was easier to turn, so he bent the other ski to match, and the term "early rise" crept into ski design conversations and was adapted by most manufacturers.

Racing skis continued to develop, becoming faster and capable of handling steeper and harder terrain. In 1990, K2's Walter Knott created the aluminum GS race ski that had a 10mm sidecut. The Velocity, the version for recreational skiers, made high-speed skiing on groomed snow a real joy. Volant shortly came out with a 12mm sidecut and, in 1991, Elan's Jurij Franko and Pavel Skofic created a super fast GS ski, the SCX. It had a 22mm sidecut, more than three times what other racing skis had. Soon after, skiers on the SCX ski held eight of the top 10 places and other companies quickly followed suit.

For recreational skiers, the "Albert" ski, considered the first modern shaped ski, was created by Frank Meatto, an engineer at Olin Ski Company. One of their executives was having a hard time learning how to ski and asked Frank to make a foolproof beginner's ski. The fat tip and deep sidecut make turning a breeze and this shape has continued to be adapted by most brands.

Today's "powder fats" are another innovation to serve the recreational skier. Designed by Atomic's Rupert Huber, who repurposed one of the snowboards they were building into the first Atomic Powder Plus. Right now, all the boutique brands are leading the charge with more and more radical designs to make powder skiing easier, such as 100+ millimeters underfoot.

With the current growth in the ski industry, powder skiing is fast becoming a rare thing except for backcountry skiers and wealthy skiers who can afford to heli-ski or cat-ski (where you ride the snowcat grooming truck) at remote locations. In today's world, if you have the money, you need at least four pairs of skis to cover the different snow conditions you can encounter in a week of skiing. These are:

- All-mountain skis for most conditions
- 100+ MM underfoot for powder
- 80- MM underfoot for hardpack or ice
- 88 MM under foot for high-speed cruising (the length needs to be more than your height)

My guess is that innovation will continue, more people will become better skiers, resorts will be more and more expensive, and you will need to be willing to travel for your season pass to pay off financially.

Skiing was, and will continue to be, the most family friendly sport you can participate in. It is the only sport I know that is fun at all levels, so it's something the whole family can enjoy. As people improve in their skills, along with boosts from advances in equipment design, it only gets easier and more fun.

If you are not having fun while skiing, I am certain you are using the wrong equipment. Get support from a professional ski rental shop, ideally at the base of the mountain you are skiing. This allows you to try things and get immediate help until you find the perfect match, something you can't do if you rented from a place that is now miles away.

Also, spend the time and money on a lesson with a PSIA-certified instructor. Even one lesson can catapult you forward, boosting your confidence and enjoyment by leaps and bounds. If you don't have that experience with an instructor, get a new instructor!

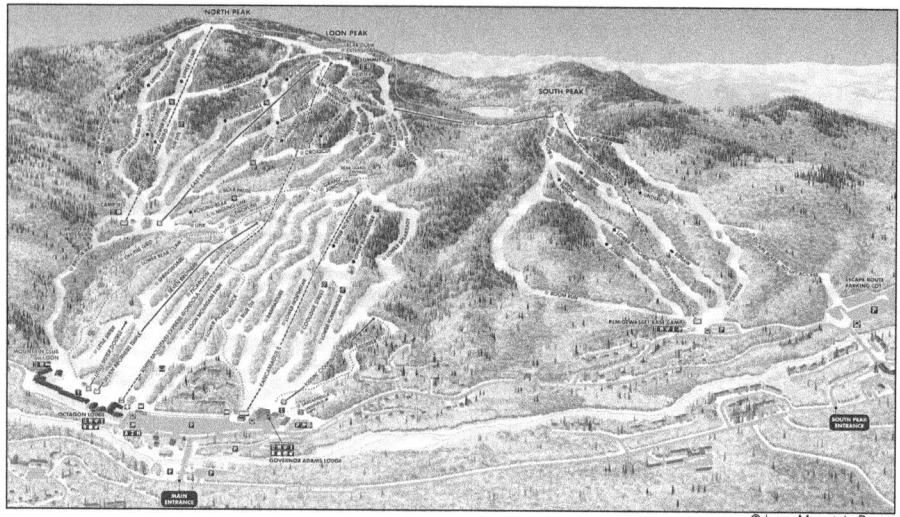

© Loon Mountain Resort

Loon Mountain Resort
Lincoln, New Hampshire

- Founded in 1966 by Sherman Adams, Loon Mountain Resort currently boasts 61 runs over 370 skiable acres in the White Mountain National Forest.
- There are 11 lifts and a vertical drop of 2,100 feet. The average snowfall is 172 inches and they also have six terrain parks, a 425-foot superpipe, and snow tubing that's open during the day and night.
- They offer private and group lessons for children and adults.
- Learn more at LoonMtn.com.

Chapter 17

1976-1977: MBA at U of VA

Charlottesville, Virginia
38.0293° N, 78.4767° W
Elevation: 594 Feet (181 M)

Jim Garrison proved to be a great leader for K2. One of the things I really appreciated was that he invested in his team. Because of his Harvard degree in business, he was familiar with a program at the Colgate Darden School of Business at the University of Virginia. They offered a seven-day intensive training program and he sent Mac and me to it. It was a non-degree granting MBA program, where the regular faculty gave the participants different case studies each day.

The best part was that it was a residential cohort model, so we got to network with other professionals as well as our faculty. Each person there was a leader in their company or industry and we learned as much from each other as the faculty. Our class had several people from the pharmaceutical industry as well as federal government departments. Of course, when they found out Mac and I were from a ski company, everyone who skied wanted to talk to us about the sport. Mac also had a fun sense of humor and could do about sixty different voices as he told jokes, so we spent a lot of time entertaining the group.

The whole experience was really eye-opening for me. Each day featured five case studies of real companies and the problems they needed to solve. We would read the assigned case study and then meet the professor in a lecture hall on campus. The professor would review the information, summarized on a giant whiteboard, and we would all start proposing changes or solutions to turn the company around. At the end of the day, they would reveal what the company actually did and how it impacted them, for better or worse. It was a great way to learn different strategies and also calibrate your instincts.

Many of the case studies involved problems with sales and it was interesting to see how the various leaders addressed that. The pharma guys would not tolerate any hint of a salesperson not performing, so their first move would be to fire them. On the other hand, the government agency folks knew that they were bound by policies that made it difficult to fire people, so they would focus on transferring the problem out of their department. And no surprise, Mac and

I would suggest helping the salesperson improve through more training and mentoring them through various situations.

This pattern played out for a couple of days until one day, the professor challenged Mac and insisted the salesperson should be fired. They got into an argument that turned into a shouting match that ended with Mac saying the salesperson should be saved and the sales manager should be fired. The room suddenly became very quiet. The professor revealed the real case study and it turned out that Mac had nailed it. The sales manager had been fired and the "problem" salesperson was promoted to sales manager. This person had made many critical changes and the company was still in business and thriving. And guess what? They had instituted new training and mentoring programs for the salesforce, which had made all the difference. Needless to say, Mac and I felt pretty good about ourselves at dinner that night.

During that week, we looked at two case studies that I thought were really interesting. In fact, I would go on to use both of them for the rest of my career as I started, bought into, or consulted businesses. The first case study dealt with what was called "the rule of 10." It was about managing an independent salesforce where you are hiring salespeople who might have a book of up to 10 or 12 companies that they carried and sold to dealers throughout their territory. The rule of ten is if you hire 10 sales employees, the concept suggests that you would get two superstars, two misfits, and six that would do their jobs but never manage to move above average.

The strategy for managing this kind of salesforce is to reward the superstars, live with the average ones, and at the first hint that identifies the misfit, let them go. Often, managers ignore the warning signs or take too long to address the issue, and end up costing the company much more in the long run than was necessary.

The second case study was about how to price a product in order to make it easy to sell and contribute profits to the bottom line. One formula to use aligns with the three-tier distribution system, where there is the manufacturer, a distributor, and a retailer. For example, the basic formula is if you are producing a product for $3, it will be sold to a distributor for $5 and the distributor will sell it to a retailer for $6. The retailer sells it to the end customer for $10. This is a three-tier distribution system. The strategy is to do focus groups with the end consumer to find out how much they would feel comfortable paying for the product. If you can't work backwards to ensure that each tier gets the profit they need, you should not make the product.

Another formula focused on how often you need to turn inventory over in order to make a profit. In the sporting goods industry, the magic number is three times per year. In the food distribution business, the number is four or five times per month. So, the general rule in order to be successful is that you either have to have higher margins, or higher turns, or better yet, both.

I saw this principle in action one winter when I took a tour through my accounts in Idaho, Montana, and Washington. When I worked at Lange, I met

Rod Campbell, who worked at one of the Seattle ski shops as a shop guy and sales floor stand-in when they were busy. He wanted to learn what an equipment rep did so I invited him to join me on this account tour so he could see how other stores ran their business. I also knew he had never been skiing so I suggested we stop by Schweitzer Ski Resort in Idaho as part of our itinerary. Best case scenario, he would learn some things that would make him more effective at his job and he might really like skiing.

Our first day, we called on a dealer in Spokane, Washington and then drove to Sandpoint, Idaho. It was just starting to snow when we went to dinner and, by the time we came out to the car, it was covered in six inches of new snow.

The next morning, Rod and I arrived at Schweitzer to find over three feet of new snow and a lot of eager skiers chomping at the bit to get on that mountain. Schweitzer is a great mountain because it's somewhat isolated and, therefore, never crowded. It regularly draws skiers from Spokane, Washington, and British Columbia.

That much new snow is not the best way to learn a new sport, so I gave Rod a full immersion lesson. Rod was exceptionally fit and a really good athlete so we started off slowly and he caught on very quickly. The new snow had enough resistance that after lunch, he was making great turns on low angle slopes. By the end of the first day, he was skiing all over that mountain.

We went to dinner and had a fine discussion about how often ski shops should turn over their inventory during the ski season. When we went to dinner that night, he could hardly stay awake because he was so tired.

When we woke up and left for Kalispell, Montana, Rod could barely walk because he was so stiff and sore. When we got there, we went right to Sportsman's Ski Haus, which was managed by Mike Quasden. Mike was known for his management strategies and he volunteered to show us his shop. He explained every ski and why he chose that particular ski for that price point. I saw Rod's eyes light up and knew he totally got the idea.

The next day we went skiing at Big Mountain (now Whitefish) and got to ski on packed powder, which Rod found to be a little easier than 18 inches of unpacked powder. After skiing, we went into the ski shop and met with Martin Hale, who was known for his promotional prowess during his week-long ski packages that were loved by Seattleites—they could come by train to Whitefish and ski with instructors for a whole week at very competitive prices.

The next day we headed south to Butte, Montana to call on Bob and Yvonne Leipheimer's Ski Shop. Yes, they are the parents of Levi Leipheimer, who rode in ten Tour de France races and won a bronze medal at the 2008 Summer Olympic Games in Beijing, China. Bob shared that he was building a strong summer business by expanding his product mix into bicycles and backpacking.

As we started home to Seattle from Butte, Rod said he couldn't believe how the industry owners were so willing to share information. We had gained a lot of valuable inventory knowledge on our trip and Rod went back and helped his shop improve their sales.

Inventory management was one of the many business principles they covered at the mini-MBA program in Virginia. After we completed the week-long program, Mac and I came back to K2 with a lot of information and more confidence in our management styles. Jim asked us to write up a report on what we learned and we leveraged those plans over the next few years. Some of the highlights include:

- Starting to make ski boots
- Distributing Marker bindings
- Entering the water ski market
- Entering the cross-country ski market
- Starting to make skateboards for the Japanese market

Jim also made a great decision to send Bruce Kirschner, Bill's son, to the CEO program at the University of Virginia. It was gratifying to see that GGCON was investing in the future of the company. Bruce became President for K2 and then he and his father invested in a new company in the fly-fishing business. Bruce eventually left K2 to become President and CEO of Sage Fly Rod Company, based on Bainbridge Island, Washington.

K2 continued to thrive because of the efforts of leaders across the organization. I observed two managers who were highly skilled at their jobs and received very little credit for their role in making K2 a great place to work. They were polar opposites in terms of their personalities, but they worked well together and created lots of success.

The first was PJ Jennick, who ran the race competition department. His team managed the World Cup racing events as well as finding athletes at all levels to sponsor. He also hired the "racer chasers," the staff who work with our sponsored athletes, literally traveling with them to every race and being our contacts on the ground at every event. PJ was a bulldog when he wanted something done and he was a great practical jokester. He had a keen skill of finding people that were results driven and I was always at peace about how we were perceived among the other racing teams working on the World Cup circuit.

The second was Fred James. Her job was to control spending and feed the ski press with positive press releases of how we were doing. She'd share stories about the different ski events K2 was participating in and information about the various racing venues.

One funny situation that Fred had to manage happened in 1971 when a series of curious events led to K2 accidentally launching the first wet t-shirt contest. Remember, this was a highly chauvinistic time and this contest occurred at the Red Onion bar in Aspen, Colorado. One of the judges was Stein Eriksen, Olympic gold medalist, and it should have been kept to the locals in attendance. Unfortunately, an editor for *Playboy* magazine happened to be in the audience attending with Bobbie Burns, the original hot dog skier. He ended up writing a story about it and publishing it in the magazine, much to the horror of the conservative owners at Cummins Diesel Company. I have no doubt that it contributed to their decision to sell K2. Of course, by now, we were all grateful they had made that decision so it all worked out in the end.

Fred was highly respected because she was pleasant to deal with and always returned calls or inquiries about K2 and what we were doing. She had a keen sense of confidence and she really added to our marketing and sales team. If a regional rep came up with a great local promotion, Fred could be counted on to make sure they got the information and the materials they needed to look professional.

At that time, I had an office that overlooked the cubicle area. From my office, I could see PJ's and Fred's cubicles that had a common wall. Fred was about 6' tall and PJ was about 5'6" so they always looked like Mutt and Jeff when they were standing next to each other. Fred was married to John Kubiak, founder and owner of Serac Ski Clothing in Seattle.

Fred was pregnant and when she started to show, PJ decided to play a prank on her. One day, I noticed that after Fred dashed out to catch the ferry, PJ got up and moved his adjoining wall into Fred's space by an inch. He did this every day for a few weeks so that as Fred's belly was getting bigger, her work space was getting smaller and smaller. She finally figured out what was happening and I saw her walk over and tower over PJ, shaking her finger at him while she chewed him out. Everyone in the office was laughing and egging her on. She finally stopped for a second, took a deep breath, looked around, and started laughing as PJ hurriedly expanded her cubicle back to normal.

They were good friends and both of them were really good employees. There is no doubt that K2 was a better company because of all they did to contribute to K2's growth and success.

Barb and Mike at Alpine Meadows near Lake Tahoe, CA

Schweitzer Ski Resort
Sandpoint, Idaho

- Founded in 1963 by Jack Fowler, Schweitzer Mountain currently boasts 92 runs over 2,900 skiable acres in the Selkirk Mountains.
- There are 10 lifts and a vertical drop of 2,400 feet. The average snowfall is 300 inches and they have terrain parks, tubing, twilight skiing, and Nordic trails.
- They offer group and private lessons for both children and adults.
- Learn more at Schweitzer.com.

Chapter 18

1978-1979: Lake Placid

Lake Placid, New York
44.2795° N, 73.9799° W
Elevation: 1,801 Feet (549 M)

Unexpectedly, the 1980 Olympics were held in Lake Placid, New York and K2 was selected as the official ski of those Games. I want to share with you the amazing series of events that led to that unprecedented marketing opportunity.

Typically, the countries and cities hosting an Olympics are determined seven to eight years in advance. They submit their bid and the International Olympic Committee (IOC) chooses among the candidates, intentionally moving the Olympics around the different regions of the world.

In 1968, the United States had won the bid to host the 1976 Winter Olympic Games, with Denver, Colorado being the hosting city. But those games never happened due to citizen protests. One contingent was the environmentalists who had seen the damage done to other ecologies hosting the games. They organized into a group called Protect Our Mountain Environment (POME) and protested various event venues being established in their area. The Denver Olympic Organizing Committee (DOOC) kept trying to move events to new areas, only to be met by another group of local residents saying, "Not here."

Then Denver residents watched the 1972 Games in Sapporo, Japan unfold with its $70 million price tag that the Japanese government had to step in and cover. The winter games notoriously do not bring in the same revenue as the summer games because it draws only one-third of the countries and one-seventh the participants.

The Colorado Congressmen and Senators discovered that the U.S. government would not help out and costs would fall to the citizens. A referendum was placed on the ballot of the 1972 state election, and it overwhelmingly passed to stop funding for the Olympics. In November of that year, the DOOC served notice to the IOC that the city would be unable to host the games due to a lack of available funding. To this day, Denver is the only city to ever reject their bid.

Four months later, the IOC granted the bid to Innsbruck, Austria, which already possessed the venues and infrastructure from hosting the 1964 Games. However, the IOC President at that time, Avery Brundage, was American and he dearly wanted to have the U.S. host an Olympics on his watch. With his term ending in 1980, he was advocating for that to happen. This is where K2 started to get its big break.

K2's northeast rep happened to live in Lake Placid, New York, site of the 1932 Winter Olympics. Bill Witte heard that Lake Placid was trying to organize a bid using the argument that they had all the infrastructure in place from the 1932 Olympics. The ski jumping hill was already built, as were the skating venues, and the ski hill on Whiteface Mountain had one of the scariest downhills in North America at that time.

Bill called Dick McNamara, who knew all the players in the ski community. Dick jumped on the phone and set up a meeting with a couple of people he was sure would be on the Lake Placid Olympic Organizing Committee (LPOOC) if it was a serious effort. Dick went to Lake Placid and effectively became the point of the spear for K2's efforts to secure the license to be the Official Ski of the 1980 Olympics. Dick was and still is a shrewd negotiator and he was highly respected in the ski world, especially in the Northeastern ski racing community.

Olympic sponsorship has its own history and it helps fund the games. The local organizing committee (in this case, the LPOOC) has the right to sell the title of "official fill in the blank" of those Games, and grant use of the Lake Placid symbol, the raccoon mascot, and access to the Olympic venues. They can also secure donated merchandise like all the Simmons mattresses needed to house the 130 Olympic teams or all the Coca Cola and Minute Maid orange juice that participants could drink.

In contrast, the U.S. Olympic Committee controls the five-ring emblem and the wreath that symbolizes the U.S. Olympic Team. The Olympic Committee doesn't have any official products, but can offer its corporate backers the title of "suppliers to the U.S. Olympic Team" or "partners with the U.S. Olympic Team." For example, that year, Levi Strauss provided all the uniforms for the U.S. Team, including an entire wardrobe they wore off the field. At the time, the 1980 Olympics set the new world record for the highest level of corporate participation. If you want to read a funny take on it, look up the article "The Adman Funds the 1980 Olympics" by Jerry Knight in *The Washington Post*. I suspect it was pieces like this that later made Avery Brundage bullish on not allowing advertising on camera, but more on that later.

When I found out that LPOOC had chosen K2, I knew that this would be a major feather in our cap. What made K2 unique was that we were the *only* sponsor for which athletes would be using our product in competition. With the Mahre twins, Phil and Steve, starting to be a force on the World Cup tour, it seemed that they would have a great chance of medaling in an Olympics held in America while racing on an American-made ski.

The ramifications of that kind of event would really solidify K2 in the ski market here and abroad, as well as signal that we were a powerful and significant player in world skiing. At the time, I was functioning as Western Sales Manager and I doubted if it would affect me very much. One thing I was sure of was that Heckler Bowker would play a big role in the pre-planning and goal setting for the effort. Little did I know I would end up playing a key role in our efforts.

At this time, our Marketing Manager, Ned Post, got an opportunity to go to another firm and left K2, becoming CEO of Wilson Sporting Goods, and after that, President and CEO of Smith Goggle Company. Barry Gordinier promoted me to be National Marketing Manager and, eventually, Coordinator of the Olympic effort! It was decided that I would work with Gordon and we would develop a plan and execute it to make the program viable and affordable. Fortunately, we had what I thought was plenty of time.

I went to the first meeting for all of the official sponsors and, per my usual, I had a legal pad. As the meeting progressed and I listened to each member of the LPOOC speak (I believe there were 20 of them), I took notes and started guessing their occupations. I guessed correctly for all but two members, a minister and a schoolteacher—every other one had tipped their hands on how the Games were going to affect their businesses. This became useful information in anticipating their priorities and votes on critical matters.

Some of the other official sponsor reps suggested we get together and talk about what we had learned and also see how we might cooperate to make each of us more effective come February of 1980. I got to know the reps from Coca Cola, Canon, Dannon Yogurt, and a whole host of others.

The official film was Kodak and, in a casual conversation with their rep, he mentioned that they planned to give out so much film that it equated to three times K2's annual gross. We already had planned to film the 1979 World Cup event, which effectively serves as a dress rehearsal for the Olympic alpine events. He offered to supply our film and I agreed to share the images we'd capture of the athletes in action.

By the end of the meeting, I knew that we had an advantage. Because athletes would be competing on our products, we'd be a critical partner to other sponsors who would have needs they could not solve without our help.

When I got back to K2, I met with Gordon and shared with him these two facts: 1) The LPOOC was severely disorganized and, recognizing that, we could likely create advantages for our product, and 2) Cooperation with the other sponsors would allow us to recuperate expenses by selling the imagery they would need to maximize their efforts.

I also realized that we were already behind schedule and I needed to create a sense of urgency to the upper management at K2. Gordon really lit a fire with a letter he sent to Barry and we quickly got the support and resources we needed.

I was able to use my staff members and assign them parts of the plan to manage. I also hired a friend of Brian Snelsons and put him in charge of securing uniforms for the K2 people going to Lake Placid. Gary Woodruff was the perfect guy for the job and he became my right-hand man. We put together a cohesive accessories plan including gloves, shirts, hats, belt buckles and trading pins. That was the start of a program we later parlayed into a worldwide accessories department selling more products to our distributors.

The other thing that really worked in my favor was Bill Witte, Lake Placid-based K2 rep who had let Dick know that they were making the bid to host. Bill was very entrepreneurial and created a plan that benefitted K2 and himself, too. We needed a large footprint in Lake Placid, so Bill became my captain of real estate. He bought two houses and secured the Favor Smith Law Office, which was across the street from the ice-skating venue. That became K2's headquarters for both the World Cup in 1979 and the Olympic Games in 1980. We were right in the heart of town where all the action was.

He leased Favor's personal home to house our executives—we called it the Chief's House. He also leased an 18-room boarding house to hold all the K2 staff, which we named Animal House. For the Olympics, the state of New York passed a law stating that anyone renting or leasing housing did not have to pay income taxes on that rental income. Bill later told me that his two houses were paid for by the rental income they generated. He really made a huge difference for me when he took that job.

The 1979 World Cup happened in February and gave us critical information that helped us be more successful in the Olympics. I attended along with Gordon, our racer chasers, and our film crew.

During the two-week event, three things happened that we knew were potentially problematic for us at the Olympic Games. The first was climatic. The morning after we arrived, a cold front moved in and the temperature dropped to -6° Fahrenheit. The "lake effect" added to the coldness as the dampness arrived. One of the first events we filmed was the ski jumping and our cameras froze up in the cold weather. We sent someone down to New York City who bought blankets and battery packs that were rechargeable. I was helping at the events, wearing everything I owned and was still freezing. I called Gary Woodruff and told him to add a down vest to our uniforms for 1980.

The second thing happened at the slalom hill on Whiteface Mountain. Texas Instruments (TI) sponsored the Olympics by supplying the racing bibs for the Alpine race events. I had met their rep at that earlier meeting in Lake Placid and we had chatted about supporting each other. When TI ordered the bibs, the back side had the racer's number on it and the front had the racer's number plus the TI logo boldly printed in color.

As I arrived, the TI rep grabbed me and said, "I am going to get fired!" I asked what was going on and he said that Avery Brundage had requested that all the racers wear the bibs backwards, essentially denying TI of any media coverage since the camera crews filmed them as they came down. I told him I would do what I could and I found Ed "Sleez" Chase, K2's racer chaser assigned to the Mahre twins. I told him that we needed them to wear the bibs with the logo on the front and he said he'd take care of it.

When the race started, I noticed all the racers were wearing the bibs with the logo on the front. Later, Ed told me that when the other racer chasers saw what the Mahres were doing, they told their racers who elected to join them. I knew that our access to athletes was our super power, making us a partner that everyone wanted to work with. In fact, we were able to sell our footage and images to other sponsors for around $200,000, helping us recoup a good portion of our costs.

The final and most troubling thing that happened was that in the second run of the slalom, Phil Mahre hit the bamboo pole absolutely dead center on the tip of his ski and broke his ankle. The original diagnosis was it was probably career-ending for a skier. We were all in shock. On the way home, we learned that Phil was on his way to Vail to see the legendary Dr. J. Richard Steadman, founder of the Steadman Clinic that treats U.S. Team members in all kinds of sports. Apparently, the way the ski stopped and the release of all that energy broke the bone that the tibia and fibula attach to, but there was no damage to the two main bones and minimal damage to the ligaments in his foot. Steadman worked his magic and Phil was able to have a spectacular career, including the 1980 Olympics.

My friend at TI called me to thank me for what happened there. Every single photo from that race was an ad for TI and, of course, the most used shot was of Phil approaching the gate that got him. I told him it was Ed Chase who pulled it off. He asked how many people were on my staff and I counted and said, "20 people including the racer chasers." He said, "You will be getting a box in a couple of days." When I opened it up, there were 25 Texas Instrument wrist watches in the box, valued each at $280.

Needless to say, our staff were thrilled to get new watches. But most importantly, we were clued into the fact that Brundage would try to keep commercial logos off TV screens for his last Olympics. Knowing this, we had time to make critical changes in our ski graphics and plan a way to get TV coverage for our athletes and the K2 brand.

Phil and Steve Mahre in a pre-Olympics ad for K2 Skis

© Whiteface Mountain Ski Resort

Whiteface Mountain Ski Resort
Wilmington, New York

- Founded in 1958 by Averell Harriman, Whiteface Mountain Ski Resort currently boasts 87 runs over 53 skiable acres in the Adirondack Mountains National Forest.
- There are 12 lifts and a vertical drop of 3,430 feet. The average snowfall is 138 inches and includes the longest single intermediate run in the Northeast, the 2.1 mile-long Wilmington Trail.
- They offer private, adaptive, kids, adults, and teens lessons.
- Learn more at Whiteface.com.

Chapter 19

1980: The XIII Olympic Games

Whiteface Mountain, New York
44.3659° N, 73.9026° W
Base Elevation: 1,220 Feet (372 M)
Peak Elevation: 4,867 Feet (1,483 M)

Just after Christmas, as we got ready to leave Vashon for Lake Placid, we felt like we were prepared to execute the complex and logistical nightmare of having an Olympics in a 5,000-person town at the end of a one-way road that would bring 50,000 people in and out each day for 21 days.

January 11th, I was on my way to the final sponsor meeting in Lake Placid. I got into Albany, but it was snowing, so I grabbed a motel room, called Barb, and went to bed. I was awakened at 5:30 am by a call from Barb; my dad had called with the sad news that my mom had passed away during the night. She had been suffering from emphysema, but it was still a surprise. I told Barb to meet me in Denver, booked a flight there, and went to the airport.

I called the LPOOC and explained why I wouldn't be at the meeting. Then I called Barry and said I would be back as soon as I could. I was overwhelmed by my staff's reaction and the kind things that K2 and Heckler Bowker did to support us. We also received amazing support from all my colleagues and friends from the ski industry. I met Barb in Denver and we drove to Salida and organized the funeral. I felt terrible for not being able to stay longer, but we had to get to Lake Placid to take care of the final details before the Games began.

The Games opened on February 13th and closed on the 24th. In that Olympics, there were 38 events over ten sports. Alpine skiing included six events—downhill, slalom, and giant slalom for both men and women. The Games also had biathlon, bobsledding, cross-country skiing, figure skating, ice hockey, luge, nordic combined, ski jumping, and speed skating. Athletes from 37 countries participated; the U.S. had the largest team with 101 athletes.

We had set up the K2 Headquarters (K2HQ) at the Favor Smith Law Office in the heart of downtown. Because we would be hosting K2 dealers and other special guests, we had created a reception space. We had nine televisions in that area and, during the day, we tuned into Canadian Television because they were broadcasting live all day, while ABC only broadcast during prime time.

Over the past year, the disorganization of the LPOOC had been a hindrance at first but, as the sponsors grew more savvy, it became a blessing because it allowed us to free wheel when we were dealing with the town of Lake Placid and the quirks of small-town politics. Luckily for us, Bill Witte had been working with both and we secured everything we wanted in the end.

One of the key things in our plan was to have the K2 logo prominently displayed from every camera angle we could think of when the Olympics began. If you watched, you might remember this image of the huge American flag (it was 40 feet by 60 feet) with the smaller K2 flag beneath it.

It was especially visible when the ski jumpers were in the air, but it was a prominent image in many shots during all three weeks of the Games. Let me tell you about how we pulled off that marketing bonanza. The town of Lake Placid had put in place height restrictions of 80 feet. We had always planned to buy a 100-foot flagpole and have it installed in front of K2HQ so we could fly those flags. Every American would want to snap a shot of the U.S. flag, as would every media outlet, and there would be K2's logo in every single one.

We had applied for a variance of the 80 feet height restriction but they wouldn't budge, so we bought a 60-foot two-piece flagpole and, in the months before the Games, installed it in front of our reception center at K2HQ. But behind the scenes, we also ordered our 100-foot three-piece flagpole to be delivered the first week in February. Up it went and immediately, so did the arms of the town council. They notified us to take it down or face a fine of $50. Best $50 any marketer ever spent!

They also told us it had to be removed within 30 days or we'd face steeper consequences. "No problem!" we said. The Olympic Games ended on February 25th and we shipped that 100-foot flagpole back to Vashon.

When we were at the Olympics, the following couples were staying in the four-bedroom apartment above K2HQ: Barry and Ann Gordinier, Dick and Maryann McNamara, Bruce and Karen Kirschner, and Barbara and I. The one thing we had not planned for appropriately was just how many people would end up visiting our Headquarters during the Olympics. Barbara picked up on that the minute we arrived and took the lead on solving the crisis. She—along with Karen, Ann, and Maryann—became K2's Olympic heroes!

Every morning at 4:20 am, they would have Gary Woodruff take the K2 van and drive around the five-mile one-way road, picking up pastries and sandwiches from local vendors while the Olympic Sponsors—Dannon Yogurt, Coca Cola, Minute Maid, etc.—delivered products for us to give away during the day. It was another example of how we all helped each other out.

A funny story about Coca Cola—they ended up providing heat to the freezing masses throughout the month. Before the Games began, they had installed Coke machines all over town, each designed to keep their product at the perfect temperature of 38° Fahrenheit. However, the weather was often near or below zero; those machines were working hard to keep their product from freezing. Every machine had lots of people huddled up against it, staying warm.

During the Games, we were entertaining K2 dealers, some of whom had won sales contests. As sponsors, we were given tons of tickets to the venues and we would use them as gifts and rewards. When we didn't have dealers, we would send Gary out into downtown Lake Placid and he would sell the tickets at discount prices so they wouldn't go to waste.

The hardest event to sell was Luge and I still don't know why. One night, our whole group went to the Luge event and it was spectacular. We were standing on one of the curves where we were close enough to touch the athletes if we wanted to. You could hear them coming and, as they got into the curve, you could hear them gasping for breath because of the G-forces they were absorbing. It was really a great time for us and exciting to see up close and personal.

Here is another funny coincidence that I discovered years later when I met my daughter, Britt. In 1980, she was 15 years old and had become a competitive ice skater. She trained in Colorado at the same rink as Scotty Hamilton, who won the Gold in Lake Placid. Just after the Olympics ended, she moved to Lake Placid and trained with Gus Lussi, the coach to Olympic gold medalists Dorothy Hamill and Dick Button. She lived just a couple blocks from K2HQ.

On another night, Gary and I pulled off a great move that we still laugh about today. There was a snow fort in downtown Lake Placid and, as we were passing by, a guy in a Lapland fur hat hollered, "Hey! K2 Guys!" We turned around and they waved us over. They were with Finlandia Vodka and were giving away free icy shots. Neither Gary nor I are drinkers so we didn't partake, but the Lapland hat guy asked if we had K2 pins to trade, which we did, so we swapped pins. He then asked us what it would take to get two pairs of K2 skis. I asked, "What do you have to trade?" He laughed and said, "When this ends, we do not want to take our inventory back to the distributor. I can give you 30 cases." Being the negotiator that I am, I countered 35 and the Lap hat. He said, "We have a deal!" and shook our hands.

Gary and I thought each case contained four bottles, but it turned out it was eight! The K2 Board of Directors and staff had vodka for the next year and the Lap hat is in my home along with my extensive pin collection from the Lake Placid Olympics.

Pin trading is a huge tradition at every Olympic Games dating as far back as the 1896 Games in Athens, Greece. There are six types of Olympic pins—Sponsor, National Olympic Committee (for each team), Media, Bid (countries vying to be hosts), Security (local police, fire, etc.) and Commemorative (sold through retail outlets). Because only a certain number are made each Olympics, they quickly become valuable collector's items. Pin trading is such a big deal that there is an IOC-recognized organization, the Olympin, which spans 30 countries and has over 500 members. At every Olympics, there are always some pins that are more difficult to get and become the targeted prize for that Games.

At K2, we were trying to get pins from every team that participated in the Alpine events at Lake Placid. Most were easy, but the USSR countries were difficult because they wouldn't let their athletes go anywhere without chaperones for fear of defections. Near the end of the Games, when we were getting down to the last few days of opportunities, Gary came to me and told me he knew where the athletes from Bulgaria, Hungary, Czechoslovakia, and East Germany were going to be between 12:00 and 1:30 pm. I knew this was probably my last chance, so I said, "Let's go!"

We jumped in the K2 van and I realized that we were headed out to the Olympic Village, which had extremely high security. It had only been eight short years since the tragic event at the 1972 Summer Games in Munich where 11 Israeli athletes and one German policeman had been killed during a hostage crisis. The Olympic Village had been built with security in mind and, after the Lake Placid Games, the village became one of New York's high security prisons, now called FCI Ray Brook. It's located halfway between Lake Placid and Saranac Lake in Essex County.

We drove up to the gate and the guard stepped out and said, "Hello, Gary." Clearly, he had been working on this and Gary introduced me to the guard who was at least 6'5" tall and a New York State Trooper. The guard told us we could go in, but not stay too long. Gary gave him some of the K2 swag and in we went. In the first building was a McDonalds and it was full of eastern bloc athletes. We joined them and I ended up getting every pin I was missing. As we were leaving, we stopped and I asked the guard what it would take to get a trooper's badge. He laughed and said, "That would be a stretch, but for two pairs of gloves, I'll give you my trooper belt buckle." It still sits in my pin collection. The power of sports swag is impressive.

Some of my favorite pins from the 1980 Olympics in Lake Placid

One of the things we had done was offer gifts to the LPOOC for their volunteers. The Olympics cannot run without hundreds of volunteers working in various roles across all the events. We had provided every volunteer with a set of K2 skis, poles, and Marker bindings, which K2 now distributed for that German company. The volunteers loved the gear and it was gratifying to see our products everywhere. But we really needed to be seen at the alpine events.

With all our swag success, we still needed to overcome Avery Brundage's zeal to not show ski logos in the alpine events. He had ruled that, unlike all previous games, skiers would not be allowed to hold their skis while waiting for their results. Volunteers would take their equipment from the athletes so they wouldn't have the chance to hold up their skis and give that moment of press to the brand they skied on.

But we hatched a plan to make sure that Steve and Phil Mahre had access to a pair of the 1980 Official Ski of the Lake Placid Olympic Games. Heckler Bowker had done a lot of research and had determined that the most visible color against snow, regardless of the light conditions, was school bus yellow. They were gaudy looking but the graphic was certainly visible even while they were racing. Both twins had a good chance of medaling and we were hungering for that moment of an American winning in an American Olympics while racing on an American ski.

When the slalom was scheduled to be the first alpine event, we were ready. Barb and I went to the slalom hill on Whiteface Mountain—we were excited and hoping for a good day. We had a pair of the skis hidden in a white canvas bag and, with our Sponsor Credentials, we were in the finish area of the race. Steve was the first brother on the course, but had bad luck and skied out of the course in the first run. We anxiously waited for Phil who won the first run, barely beating the Swedish racer, Ingemar Stenmark. As soon as he finished, the skis were captured and set aside so he couldn't be filmed with them.

Phil and Steve walked to the end of the ski corral and were trying to avoid the press asking questions because they were about to execute "the plan." As we were watching, they exchanged team jackets and Steve (in Phil's jacket) went to the press area and started answering questions. In the meantime, Phil (in Steve's jacket) wandered over to us and got right up to the fence where ABC Television was filming. Gary unbagged our skis and handed them to Phil, who turned around, faced the camera and kissed the front of the ski.

The volunteer in our area started to freak out so Gary retrieved the skis and bagged them up. Phil took off Steve's jacket and handed it to Steve's wife who was standing with us. Phil went over to go up for his second run and grabbed his actual skis from that volunteer and got on the lift. Stenmark had an amazing run, but we now knew Phil was going to medal as long as he finished the race. He skied his second run and missed the gold by .07 of a second. Phil became the only American to medal in an alpine event that year and the first ever U.S. ski racer to win an Olympic medal skiing on an American-made ski. We were euphoric!

My Life in Winters

Phil Mahre after his Olympic triumph on the shoulders of Ed Chase

We went back to the village and started to celebrate. We could all now relax so we decided to see some events. That afternoon, we went to the speed skating venue and watched Eric Heiden fall in the 10K event, get up, and still set one of his four world records of those Games. He also won five individual gold medals.

Gary had been working his tail off, so I decided to give him a reward and scored us two tickets to the Russian American Hockey Game. Just before the Olympics, the Russian team beat the American team in pre-Olympic competition with a score of ten to two so everyone expected the Americans to lose. As we were entering the building, a scalper offered us $500 each for our tickets. I said to Gary, "This is your call." He said, "We are going to the game." Little did we know that we would be part of the 2,300 people who saw "THE MIRACLE ON ICE HOCKEY GAME!" The U.S. went on to win the Gold medal.

To this day, every time February 22nd comes around, I get a call from Gary that always begins with, "Do you remember where we were at this time in 1980?" Yes I do, Gary. And I always will.

White Pass Ski Area
Naches, Washington

- Founded in 1951 by the Yakima Valley Ski Club, White Pass Ski Area currently boasts 45 runs over 1,402 skiable acres in the Cascade Mountain Range.
- There are 8 lifts and a vertical drop of 2,050 feet. The average snowfall is 400 inches and they also have a tubing hill and Nordic trail area.
- They offer private and group lessons for children and adults. You can even take a lesson with Andy Mahre, Steve Mahre's son.
- Learn more at SkiWhitepass.com.

Chapter 20

Women in Skiing

St. Moritz–Corviglia, Switzerland
46.4908° N, 9.8355° E
Base Elevation: 5,676 Feet (1,730 M)
Peak Elevation: 10,837 Feet (3,303 M)

Women have played a pivotal role in making snow sports and the industry great. I personally have worked with amazing women who have shaped skiing as well as my life and career. In this chapter, I want to highlight some interesting facts about women in skiing as well as feature some rock stars that you should know more about.

In ski racing, American women have outperformed their male teammates and that goes from the beginning of the Winter Olympics until today. Did you know that the first five U.S. athletes to win Olympic medals in alpine skiing were all women? It began in the 1948 Olympics in St. Moritz, Switzerland when Gretchen Fraser won three medals. She won gold in the Women's Slalom event and silver in the Women's Alpine Combined. While newspapers referred to her as a "skier-housewife," she was not only the first American to win skiing medals, she was the first person to bring any medals home to the western side of the Atlantic. Gretchen went on to become a coach, training the next U.S. medalist, Andrea Mead Lawrence.

Andrea first competed alongside Gretchen in the 1948 games but she medaled in the 1952 Olympics in Oslo, Norway. She won gold medals in both the Slalom and Giant Slalom events. She actually fell during the slalom but got back up so quickly that she still won, a rarity in the sport. Over the next three years, Andrea had three children, won the U.S. Nationals title in both Slalom and Downhill, and placed fourth in the 1956 Olympics in Cortina D'Ampezzo in Italy. After skiing, she became an environmental activist and a mountain was named after her in 2011.

The 1960 Olympics at Squaw Valley, California saw Penelope "Penny" Pitou win a silver medal in Downhill and Betsy Snite win a silver medal in Slalom. Again, no U.S. men made the podium, but that would change at the 1964 Olympic Games in Innsbruck, Austria when Billy Kidd and Jimmie Heuga won silver and bronze, respectively, in Men's Slalom. However, their races occurred after Jean Saubert won the bronze medal in Slalom and silver in Giant Slalom, making women the pioneers for U.S. alpine medals at the Olympics, with a total of nine between them!

Women started off strong in Olympic skiing and the tradition continues today. In fact, through to the 2022 Olympic Games in Beijing, China, women have won 29 medals compared to 19 won by men.

Event	Women	Men
Downhill	8	3
Super-G	3	6
Giant Slalom	8	2
Slalom	6	5
Combined	4	3

The most recent Olympic superstars are Julia Mancuso, Lindsey Vonn, and Mikaela Shiffrin.

Julia Mancuso

Julia has the most Olympic medals of any female American alpine skier. She won gold in Giant Slalom at the 2006 Olympic Games in Turin, Italy, silver in both Downhill and Alpine Combined at the 2010 Games in Vancouver, Canada, and bronze in Combined at the 2014 Games in Sochi, Russia. In addition, she has won five World Championship medals and seven races in the World Cup.

Lindsey Vonn

At the 2010 Olympics in Vancouver, Lindsey became the first American woman to win gold in Downhill—she also won bronze in Super-G. She went on to claim the bronze in Downhill at the 2018 Games in PyeongChang, South Korea. Lindsey has also won four World Cup overall championships, second only to Annemarie Moser-Pröll of Austria, another powerhouse woman and Olympic gold medalist. Vonn is one of six women who have won World Cup races in all five alpine disciplines. In June 2022, both Lindsey Vonn and Gretchen Fraser were inducted to the U.S. Olympic Hall of Fame.

Mikaela Shiffrin

Mikaela became the youngest Olympic Slalom champion in history when she won gold at the 2014 Games in Sochi. She won two more Olympic medals at the 2018 Games in PyeongChang, winning gold in Giant Slalom and silver in Combined. With eleven medals (six are gold), she is the most decorated U.S. skier in the alpine World Championships. She is the second most winning female alpine skier with 74 World Cup race wins. At the 2019 World Championships, she became the first Alpine skier (male or female) to win gold in the same discipline (slalom) across four consecutive championships.

The good news for these amazing women and others like them is that skiing is one of the few sports where women enjoy near pay equity with their male counterparts. Part of this due to the fact that ski racing is one of 35 professional sports where it's mandated that prize money be equal between the genders. According to the Federation International du Ski (FIS), the past three years have seen female alpine athletes out-earn their male counterparts.

Mikaela Shiffrin winning the Super-G at Lake Louise in 2018—photo by Paul Bussi

Brooke Shalam and Ben Falk did a great analysis of the factors that contribute to pay equity in ski racing. The first is the individual nature of the sport—in general, individual athletes experience better pay equity than team sports. Second, the sport of skiing occurs in mainly developed countries where gender equality and equity is a general goal, although it may not be a full reality. This also correlates with national/sovereign wealth and the money available to invest in female athletes.

I suspect that the European teams are supported financially by their governments. In Austria, as an example, the Olympic winners are routinely given a pension at their home ski area, essentially setting them up in a business for life. In America, until the late 1950's, the U.S. Ski Team was supported by the ski industry and many athletes still enjoy sponsorships by equipment companies.

Finally, Shalam and Falk found that sports where women appear graceful tend to have better pay equity. In other words, sports where aggression and physical effort are more visible to the audience, the pay gap is greater, the theory being that people still default to the stereotype that aggression and sweat are too masculine and, therefore, negative.

As that last point illustrates, women in skiing have also suffered from sexism and misogyny in the sport. For example, when Arnold Lunn created the Alpine Ski Club in 1908 in Switzerland, he originally denied membership to women. He only later changed his mind when he realized that ladies would "look attractive" doing this graceful sport and then he created an all ladies club in 1923.

I've noticed in my own career that female ski instructors are often relegated to teaching children in the beginning of their careers, which have notably lower tipping rates than adult lessons.

But women continue to hold critical leadership roles in all areas of the sport. Throughout the snow sports business, I am seeing more and more supervisors, directors, and upper management positions filled by very accomplished women. Perhaps this is happening because of the demand for better management and better results in our sport. Hopefully, this is a trend that will continue on the upswing.

Here is a list of women leaders whom I have either worked with directly and/or greatly admire their contributions to the sport and industry:

- Edna Dercum, Owner of Ski Tip Ranch and Co-Founder of Keystone Ski Resort
- Donna Nagel, Owner Crystal Mountain Ski Shop and Crystal Mountain Ski School
- Georgene Dunn Burton, Owner and Founder of Pooh Vail, the first daycare and ski school at Vail
- Renie Gorsuch, Owner of Gorsuch Ski and Sports Shop, probably the best and most successful retail shop in the ski industry
- Ursula Howland, ski instructor at Big Sky Mountain Sports and my personal ski guru
- Eliza Kuntz, Chair of the Board of Directors for the PSIA
- Jeanette Johnson, first female ski instructor at Sun Valley, Idaho
- Carol Kane, skier at Monarch who taught me how to ski fast
- Skeeter Werner, U.S. Ski Team member and Founder of Steamboat Springs Ski School
- Megan Larson, former Executive Director for the PSIA, Northern Rocky Mountain Division
- Peggy Hiller, CEO of PSIA-ASSI
- Dana Forbes, Executive Director for PSIA, Rocky Mountain Division
- Stephanie Cox, Executive Director for National Ski Patrol
- Kirsten Lynch, CEO of Vail Resorts
- Christine Baker, Vice President, Big Sky Mountain Sports at Big Sky Resort, Montana
- Julie Rust, Director of Ski Patrol at Vail Resort in Vail, Colorado
- Bonnie Hickey, Director of Sustainability at Bridger Bowl Ski Area in Bozeman, Montana.
- Robin Barnes, Ski School Director at Heavenly Valley Ski Area in California and also Portillo, Chile
- Bev Ogilvie, Ski School Director at Monarch Mountain in 1960

There are three other American women skiers I want to highlight because of their contributions to the sport and industry.

Marilyn Cochran, U.S. Ski Team, 1967-1974

Marilyn is a member of the skiing Cochran family, which has had several members on the U.S. Ski Team. Barbara Cochran, Marilyn's sister, won gold in Slalom at the 1972 Olympic Games in Sapporo, Japan. Barbara's son, Ryan Cochran-Siegle, won silver in Slalom at the 2022 Olympics in Beijing, China.

Marilyn skied for K2 Skis throughout her racing career and she won the Giant Slalom Championship Globe for the Winter of 1968-1969. She became the first American to win that event on an American-made ski.

When Marilyn started skiing for K2, we were supporting the Mahre twins and Ed Chase was their racer chaser. K2 knew that we would have to support Marilyn in the same way, but with someone she would trust and who could handle the ups and downs of ski racing. Fortunately, Jim Bombard filled that bill—he had a great pedigree from his NCAA racing career, had served as a K2 sales rep, and helped design the cross-country skis K2 was producing.

Marilyn and Jim quickly became a great team—she was getting great results, her confidence was growing, and she knew she was competitive in every race, especially in the giant slalom. The FIS World Cup series occurs over the whole winter season and it is designed to reward consistency. Every race is critical because the higher you finish the more points you accrue. At the last event of the season, the overall skier with the most points wins the Globe.

During that winter, Marilyn hit a rough patch and had a couple of races where she skied out of the course and got zero points. Jim discovered that she was losing confidence and he started to think what he could do to get her out of the funk. He came up with a very clever trick to get her going again. He worked on her skis that night, removing the bindings and setting them an inch further back. Then he undid his work, moving them back to their original/correct position and filled the holes.

The next morning was a training day. When they got to the practice hill, he told her how sorry he was that he had mounted her skis incorrectly, but now they were right. She skied like the devil that day so he told her these were now her training skis and he would mount up her new racing skis using the "new/correct" placement. Her confidence restored, she won the next race, stayed in the top 10 for the rest of season, and won the Globe.

Marilyn learned to ski at her family's ski hill in Vermont. Read more about Cochran's Ski Area in Chapter 30—they are still producing great skiers and racers today.

Suzy Chaffee, U.S. Ski Team, 1965-1968

Another woman who changed skiing significantly is Suzy Chaffee. Both Suzy and her brother, Rick, were members of the U.S. Ski Team and they hailed from Rutland, Vermont.

After her alpine racing career ended, she switched to freestyle, which was in its infancy. Of all the freestyle athletes, Suzy is probably the most well-known woman. She is a tall, athletic blonde with a bright smile. She was a great promoter and she hit it big time when she did commercials for Chapstick lip gloss. Her nickname became Suzy Chapstick. She was a spectacular freestyle skier, winning three World Championships in 1971, 1972, and 1973.

She probably monetized her skiing better than any skier of that era. She starred in several movies and promoted a range of products. More importantly, she became involved in politics and was one of the leaders and promoters of Title Nine, which changed athletics for women forever. She has stayed involved and is still working hard to improve life for underserved men and women. She helped pass the Amateur Sports Act of 1978 and was the first woman to serve on the board of the U.S. Olympic Committee. She was inducted to the Ski Hall of Fame in 1988.

In 2008, she ran for a seat on the Sedona, Arizona city council and lost. She is unstoppable; I would not be surprised if she succeeds on her next try. My regret is that at K2, we were so focused on alpine racing that we missed our chance to get her on our skis. If we had, history tells me that we would have dominated the freestyle segment with her and Wayne Wong both on K2s.

Debbie Armstrong, U.S. Ski Team, 1983-1988

The third woman I want to highlight is Debbie Armstrong. She was another skier I really wished we had been able to get on K2 skis. Debbie won a gold medal in Giant Slalom at the 1984 Olympic Games in Sarajevo, Yugoslavia. This is the same Olympics where the Mahre twins took gold and silver. That year, all five of the U.S. alpine medalists were from the Northwest (the others being Christin Cooper who won silver in Giant Slalom and Bill Johnson who won gold in Downhill).

Debbie's gold broke a twelve year streak for female gold medalists, hers becoming the first win since Barbara Cochran (Marilyn's sister) won gold at the 1972 Games in Sapporo, Japan.

Debbie was born in Salem, Oregon and grew up in Seattle. She learned to ski at Alpental Ski Area, which is now part of the Summit at Snoqualmie Pass. At Alpental, the trail "Debbie's Gold" and the chairlift "Armstrong's Express" are both named after her. She was inducted to the Ski Hall of Fame in 1984.

Since returning from racing, Debbie has been involved in many humanitarian efforts, including the Ski For All Foundation to help open skiing events to the disabled and Global ReLeaf Sarajevo, which reforests Sarajevo after the environmental devastation of the Bosnian war.

Debbie is the only Olympic gold medalist to serve a term on the Professional Ski Instructors of America (PSIA) Alpine Demo Team. It is made up of the top instructors in the U.S. Every four years, 30 men and women are chosen and are responsible for promoting and supporting the development of educational programs and activities at all levels in skiing and snowboarding.

Debbie is part of a long list of female Olympic medalists from the U.S.

Alpine

Gretchen Fraser (1948, gold, silver)
Andrea Mead Lawrence (1952, gold, gold)
Betsy Snite (1960, silver)
Penelop Pitou (1960, silver; 1964, silver)
Jean Saubert (1964, silver, bronze)
Barbara Cochran (1972, gold)
Susan Corrock (1972, bronze)
Cindy Nelson (1976, bronze)
Christin Cooper (1984, silver)
Debbie Armstrong (1984, gold)
Hilary Lindh (1992, silver)
Picabo Street (1994, silver; 1998, gold)
Dianne Roffe (1992, silver; 1994, gold)
Julia Mancuso (2006, gold;
2010, silver, silver; 2014, bronze)
Lindsey Vonn (2010, gold, bronze; 2018, bronze)
Mikaela Shiffrin (2014, gold; 2018, gold, silver)

Freestyle

Megan Nick (2022, bronze)
Jaelin Kauf (2022, silver)
Brita Sigourney (2018, bronze)
Devin Logan (2014, silver)
Maddie Bowman (2014, gold)
Hannah Kearney (2010, gold;
2014, bronze)
Shannon Bahrke (2002, silver;
2010, bronze)
Nikki Stone (1998, gold)
Elizabeth McIntyre (1994, silver)
Donna Weinbrecht (1992, gold)

In addition, Debbie is part of the prestigious PSIA Demo Team. Here is a list of talented women who have served in this important role over the years.

Carol Levine, 1980-1988
Ellen Post Foster, 1980-1988
Nancy Fiddle, 1984-1988
Suzanne Rueck, 1988-1992
Shawn Smith, 1988-2004
Whitney Thurlow, 1988-1992
Jane Mauser, 1988-1996
Kerrie Hannon, 1988-1996
Diana Golden, 1988-1992
Mariam Sodergren, 1992-1996
Alexandra Smith Boucher, 1992-1996
Marie Russell Shaw, 1992-2000
Nancy Oakes, 1992-1996
Alison Clayton, 1992-2000
Dee Byrne, 1992-1996

Amy Zahm, 1996-2000
Belenda Melschmidt, 1996-2000
Katie Harvey-Fry, 1996-2012
Megan Harvey, 1996-2008
Mermer Blakeslee, 1996-2000
Deb (Ackerman) Willits, 1996-2004
Jill Sickels Matlock, 2000-2004
Shaun Cattanach, 2000-2004
Debbie Armstrong, 2004-2008
(Olympic Gold)
Jennifer Simpson, 2008-2012
Robin Barnes, 2008-2012
Heidi Ettlinger, 2016-2020
Brenna Kelleher, 2018-2026
Zoe Mavis, 2022-2026

To me, it's important that we name women who have contributed to skiing and the industry. I have done my best to capture names but, if any are missing, please email us at Orders@7thMindPublishing.com and we will include them in the next printing of this book.

This past winter, Big Sky Mountain Sports expanded and a great group of new supervisors and instructors joined our locker room. I am really impressed by these young women and their strong skills and confidence. I can see that the ski industry will be in good hands with this next generation of capable leaders, accomplished instructors, supervisors, and managers. I'm proud that skiing has supported and valued women over the years–investing in women always yields great returns and it's my hope that more industries will follow suit.

© Summit at Snoqualmie

Alpental Ski Resort (Summit at Snoqualmie)
Snoqualmie Pass, Washington

- The Snoqualmie Summit was founded in 1937 but Alpental was built in 1967 by Bob Mickelson and James Griffin.
- The Summit at Snoqualmie includes four unique mountains with a total of nearly 2,000 skiable acres, 25 lifts, and the most night skiing in America.
- Alpental currently boasts 24 runs over 825 skiable acres in the Snoqualmie National Forest.
- At Alpental, there are 5 lifts and a vertical drop of 2,280 feet. The average snowfall is 434 inches and Warren Miller filmed the first time the founders explored the mountain.
- All of the mountains offer private and group lessons for children and adults.
- Learn more at SummitAtSnoqualmie.com.

Chapter 21

The 1980's: Warren Miller Goes Big

Deer Valley, Utah
40.6374° N, 111.4783° W
Base Elevation: 6,570 Feet (2,003 M)
Summit Elevation: 9,570 Feet (2,917 M)

After the 1980 Olympics in Lake Placid, things changed for both me and the sport. While I had planned to be at K2 for a long time, the leadership changed the compensation package right after the Olympics, which caused several of us to look elsewhere. I had been watching trends in other sports like tennis, cycling, and running, and ended up joining the team at Le Coq Sportif, a subsidiary of Adidas. But because of my deep connections in the ski industry, I stayed actively involved. Here's an overview of significant moments for the sport and the industry.

The Athletes

The Mahre twins went on to another spectacular performance at the 1984 Olympic Games in Sarajevo. By that time, I was a partner in a successful business in Jackson Hole, Wyoming and happened to be skiing on the day of the slalom race. As I was getting off a lift, I saw that the staff had written on a white board "Mahres Win Gold and Silver Medals in Slalom!" It took my breath away and I was in tears because I was so thrilled for them both. I had gotten to know them well during the past decade—I had a hand in getting them sponsored by Lange Boots, K2 Skis, and Marker Bindings, so I knew what this meant for them and their families.

I went home and watched the race on TV and cried again. I later heard that on the second run there was a trick gate that almost dumped Steve. When he got to the bottom, he grabbed a radio and talked to Phil at the top of the course. Phil was the last person standing between Steve and a gold medal, but family was more important. Ed Chase later told me that Steve very calmly described the trick gate and stood looking up at the course as Phil cleanly skied that gate and won the Gold. Later in life, I heard Steve say, "I was born two minutes after Phil and I have spent my life trying to catch up. At Sarajevo I got within .03 seconds of getting there."

At Sarajevo, other Americans did well, too. William Johnson took gold in Men's Downhill. Debbie Armstrong and Christin Cooper won gold and silver respectively in the Women's Giant Slalom event. Christin had grown up in Ketchum, Idaho and learned to ski at Sun Valley. Debbie got her start at the Alpental Ski Area at Snoqualmie Pass in Washington.

My experience watching all these racers led me to believe that it is impossible for American skiers to get any return on investment for all it takes for them to get to that elite status. The Mahres had a spectacular career that spanned 1970 to 1984 and resulted in them winning Olympic medals and multiple FIS World Cup races. When they were in Europe, like downtown Paris or Vienna, they would be signing autographs for hours. And yet, they were hardly noticed in the United States.

In the 1988 Olympics in Calgary, Canada new events were added including Alpine Combined and Super-G. Unfortunately, no American won a medal that year and Switzerland dominated, winning 11 of the 30 medals awarded.

The sport was beginning to change and a new type of athlete was emerging. Up to the mid-1970's, skiing was measured in seconds. You raced and the stop watches were the final arbiters as who was best. Faster was better. Fastest was best. There was a clear winner in every race.

But as freestyle began to grow in popularity, it drew former racers who enjoyed speed and also the creativity that freestyle allowed. The FIS recognized freestyle as an official sport in 1979, but this brought more regimentation. The mogul competitions were just about speed, but now judging was introduced, with skiers evaluated on how well they were able to ski moguls in a precise and controlled manner.

Freestyle debuted as a demonstration event at the 1988 Games in Calgary, Canada where spectators were able to watch moguls, aerials, and ski ballet. Moguls were the first to win approval for Olympic competition and would debut in the 1992 Games in Albertville, France.

During this time, Warren Miller's ski films were gaining in popularity. By the end of the 1970's, he was producing one per year and had gone from filming funny scenes of people falling off chairlifts to epic and inspirational films about the sport and landscape.

Warren's films both featured and made ski legends. Some were athletes that people had seen on their televisions and others were radical groundbreakers who were redefining the sport in every movie. It's still one of the honors of my life that I was in one of his films. In the 1980's, Warren released one film each year. Here is a list of the 10 titles:

1980	*Ski People*	1985	*Steep and Deep*
1981	*Ski in the Sun*	1986	*Beyond the Edge*
1982	*Snowonder*	1987	*White Winter Heat*
1983	*Ski Time*	1988	*Escape to Ski*
1984	*Ski Country*	1989	*White Magic*

Warren Miller was an iconic figure in the world of skiing. His films became the unofficial beginning of the ski season as they'd come out every fall, featuring what he filmed the previous winter. The audience was always so amped up that the local ski shops would start selling ski gear like crazy. In bigger cities, the predominant ski shop almost always sponsored the Warren Miller road show.

Warren had a great vision and a wicked sense of humor so his movies were always sold out. A Warren Miller film season became a place where the most talented and aggressive skiers would get sponsorships from ski and clothing manufacturers.

Please read Dan Egan's book, *30 Years in a White Haze*, and learn about Dan and his brother's adventures skiing all over the world with Warren. Dan is still skiing and you can sign up for his Steeps Camps at Big Sky Mountain Sports.

The Industry

After a very successful Olympic Games in Lake Placid, the K2 company was poised to dominate skiing, both in traditional alpine racing and the ever growing field of freestyling. K2 had already built a Demo Team and they'd send out these great skiers to the major ski areas. The goal was to show that skiing should be fun and all of them were spectacular fun seekers. Seeing them on a hill in their red, white, and blue uniforms (supplied by Roffe and Demetre) continued to emphasize K2's "made in America" message.

In the 1980's, we started seeing companies like Look Bindings consolidating with Rossignol to present packages that included skis, bindings and poles sold together. K2 partnered with Marker to build their own version of the package. But the king of this strategy was Salomon; they created a super package of skis, bindings, and boots. It was designed to capture more business from each account and, to date, I think Salomon has had the most successful strategy and brand loyalty.

The 1980's also saw the beginning of exit strategies for the 10th Mountain generation as their kids started graduating from college. Consolidation of ski shops was happening as the business became more lucrative and shops like Stan's for Sports sold out to Oshman's Sporting Goods in California, who eventually ended up with about 100 outlets. Most of the manufacturers were buying out small businesses to expand their product lines. Several businesses expanded from one shop to five in larger markets.

In the 1970's, the K2 territory I managed for Northern California and Northern Nevada had 141 dealers. In 2000, the K2 rep who had this same territory was servicing 17 accounts, and I imagine it's even smaller now. The average ski price from K2 in 1976 was approximately $150 a pair. In 2000, the average pair was $850. Also notable was Anthony Industries purchasing K2 in 1985 and K2 producing 2,000 snowboards.

On the retail side, another shift was beginning. The ideal retail model had been a great shop providing great customer service and enjoying the benefits of loyal customers—to a model where the shop with the cheapest price would dominate that market area.

In the early days of the industry, there was a lot of collegiality between the manufacturers, distributors, and retailers. After all, they might have been a foxhole buddy from the 10th Mountain Division. As a result, the various parts of this tiered system worked together to create success for all and very rarely did someone get stiffed on payments. The way the ski industry had originally started was disappearing quite rapidly and approaching the era of bottom-line decisions dictating the level of service.

The Ski Areas

While the 1950's and 1960's had seen a great expansion of ski areas and resorts, the pace slowed down dramatically in the 1980's. According to the National Association of Ski Areas (NSAA), these are the number of new ski areas founded or started by decade:

1950's	1960's	1970's	1980's	1990's	2000's	2010-21
67	109	43	23	10	8	11

In Chapter 28, I'll share my adventure of skiing all of the ski areas in Montana. Sadly, it was actually doable because now there are only 16 compared to the 81 that had been in operation in 1980.

There are several causes for this decline. First, the big resorts are capturing more and more of the ski dollars available from the general public. This makes it harder for smaller areas to be financially viable so there is less interest in taking the risk to open a new one or keep an existing one open.

But perhaps the most important challenge is climate change. Global warming has dramatically changed the snowline and many skis areas that used to get sufficient snow now struggle. Many cannot afford to install expensive snow making machinery and, even if they did, many ski areas are seeing temperatures too warm to keep their efforts from melting and then refreezing overnight to create horrible skiing conditions.

But the good news is that the 1980's did bring us 22 new ski areas in the following states: Alaska (1), California (1), Colorado (2), Indiana (1), Illinois (1), Michigan (1), Minnesota (2), Missouri (2), New Mexico (1), New York (1), Pennsylvania (3), Utah (1), Washington (1), West Virginia (2), and Wisconsin (2). Some notable additions include Beaver Creek in Colorado and Deer Valley in Utah. Which ones have you skied?

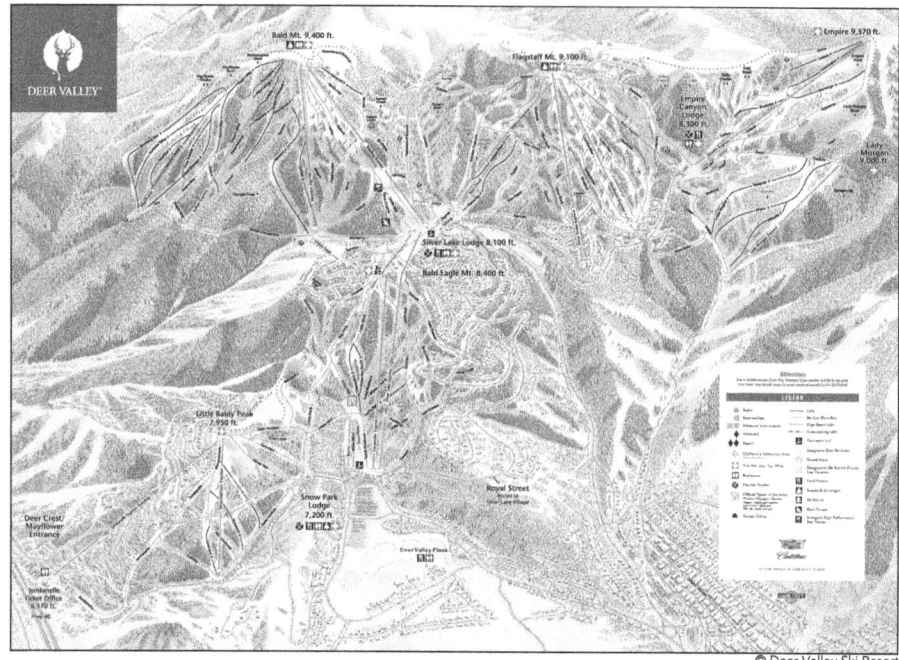

© Deer Valley Ski Resort

Deer Valley Ski Resort
Park City, Utah

- Deer Valley Resort was founded in 1981 by Edgar Stern.
- Deer Valley currently boasts 103 runs over 2,026 skiable acres in the Sierra National Forest.
- There are 21 lifts and a vertical drop of 3,000 feet. The average snowfall is 300 inches and they offer a winter program called "Ski with an Olympic Athlete."
- All of the mountains offer private and group lessons for children and adults.
- Learn more at DeerValley.com.

IV. RETURN TO THE MOUNTAIN

"Skis are not just pieces of wood, steel, and fiberglass. They are tools for escape, a medium for personal expression, a way to challenge fears, push limits and share incredible experiences with your friends."

Unknown, but clearly a skier

Chapter 22

The 1990's: Freestyle Goes to the Olympics

Bozeman, Montana
45.6770° N, 111.0429° W
Elevation: 4,793 Feet (1,461 M)

The 1990's continued some of the shifts started in the 1980's and added some more. In the meantime, Barb and I moved to Bozeman, Montana where we still live. I was still working in the outdoor sports business and helped co-found Simms Fly-fishing company and launch the Croakie eye strap product. In the 1990's, I worked as the Vice President of Marketing for R.L. Winston Fly Rod Company based in Twin Bridges, Montana.

But my love of skiing never ceases so I continued to actively ski and stay in touch with my colleagues across the industry. Here are some of the major events of this decade in skiing.

The Athletes

Skiing in the 1990's was shaped by the 1992 Games in Albertville, France. This was the first time freestyle skiing athletes competed at an Olympics and it was its own category, not a subset of the alpine events. There was one discipline, moguls, which still had an element of racing—it brought a fun and exciting edge to the sport as well as the challenges of subjective judging. The medalists that year were as follows:

Medal	Men's Moguls	Women's Moguls
Gold	Edgar Grospiron, France	Donna Weinbrecht, U.S.A.
Silver	Olliver Allamand, France	Yelizaveta Kozhevnikova, ROC
Bronze	Nelson Carmichael, U.S.A.	Stine Lise Hattestad, Norway

Nelson learned to ski at Steamboat Resort in Colorado and Donna grew up on the Hidden Valley Mountain in New Jersey.

The following alpine events were held—Alpine Combined, Downhill, Giant Slalom, Slalom, and Super-G. Americans won two medals—Diann Roffe won silver in the Women's Giant Slalom and Hilary Lindh won silver in

Women's Downhill. Diann got her start at Brantling Ski Center near Rochester, New York and Hilary learned to ski at Eaglecrest Ski Area on Douglas Island in Alaska.

The 1990's also saw the Winter Olympics split off the same four-year cycle as the Summer Games so this decade saw three Winter Games. Next was the 1994 Olympics in Lillehammer, Norway where aerial events were added to the official roster, giving freestyle two events. The first-ever Olympics medalists in that event were:

Medal	Men's Aerials	Women's Aerials
Gold	Andreas Schönbächler, Switzerland	Lina Cheryazova, Uzbekistan
Silver	Philippe LaRoche, Canada	Marie Lindgren, Sweden
Bronze	Lloyd Langlois, Canada	Hilde Synnøve Lid, Norway

In Women's Moguls, Elizabeth (Liz) McIntyre won silver for Team U.S.A.—she had learned to ski on the slopes of the Dartmouth Skiway in New Hampshire. The alpine events stayed the same as previous Games. Tommy Moe won gold for Men's Downhill and silver in Men's Super-G—showing that his start at Whitefish Mountain Resort in Montana set him up for success. Diann Roffe won gold in Women's Super-G, and Picabo Street won silver in Women's Downhill. Picabo had learned to ski at Sun Valley in Idaho.

The 1998 Winter Olympic Games were held in Nagano, Japan. These Games debuted the inclusion of snowboarding events, the first time a new sport was added without having demonstrations at previous Games. While snowboarding is an amazing sport, the focus of this book is skiing so I'll only share the skiing results. But we can all agree that Shaun White, who has won three Olympic gold medals, and other snowboarding athletes have made great contributions to snow sports and Team U.S.A. over their careers.

In Japan, all of the skiing sports stayed the same, but the Americans did very well in freestyle, claiming three of the four gold medals with a gold medal sweep in the aerial events. One memorable event was Eric Bergoust's win after a hard crash in practice. Despite his injury, he won with a world-record score. Eric learned to ski at the Missoula Snow Bowl in Montana.

Nikki Stone won gold in Women's Aerials after nearly retiring after Nagano. She got her start at Park City, Utah while Jonny Mosely, gold medalist in Men's Moguls, learned at Squaw Valley in California. He is the first person born in Puerto Rico to join the U.S. Ski Team. In alpine, the events stayed the same and Picabo Street brought home the only medal for U.S.A.—but it was gold, which she won in the Women's Super-G event.

Separate from the Olympic Games, Warren Miller continued his domination of the winter sport film business and put out these films over the decade. In 1999, he celebrated 50 years of the sport with a compilation movie of highlights.

1990 *Extreme Winter*
1991 *Born to Ski*
1992 *Steeper and Deeper*
1993 *Black Diamond Rush*
1994 *Vertical Reality*
1995 *Endless Winter*
1996 *Snowriders*
1997 *Snowriders 2*
1998 *Freeriders*
1999 *Fifty: Celebrating 50 Years of Winter Sports*

The Ski Areas

The 1990's brought a dramatic decrease in the creation of new ski areas—only 10 were added over this entire decade. The states who opened new ski areas were Iowa (2), Montana (2), New York (2), North Dakota (1), Pennsylvania (2), and Utah (1). Utah opened their Olympic Park in 1993 in preparation for hosting the 2002 Winter Olympic Games.

In addition, 52 ski areas closed their doors during this decade. Many were forced to close because they did not get enough snow to operate from Thanksgiving to Christmas, their prime income window, so they couldn't pay for their liability insurance. In some cases, owners just walked away from their forest service leases.

In the Lake Tahoe region alone, there are six ski areas that have closed—Plavada, Powder Bowl, Tannenbaum, Edelweiss, Echo Summit, and Iron Mountain. An ecologist, Jennifer Burt, has been studying how well those forest environments recover. She discovered a sharp difference between trails that were cleared by sawing down the trees and those that were bulldozed. The areas that cut trees are showing much faster and greater reforestation and healthier ecosystems overall. This photo of side-by-side trails at a Nevada ski area shows the impact of both methods in sharp contrast.

Ski trails created by bulldozing (left) versus chainsawing (right)—photo by Jennifer Burt

Kevin Morton manages the "Lost Ski Areas and Ski History of CA" Facebook page and says that the closed areas often still contain lift pylons, cables, and collapsed buildings. Some of these areas closed to the recessions that hit the U.S. economy in the late 1980's and early 1990's. In addition, global warming continued to take its toll with a particularly bad series of winters on the east coast. Many resorts make the bulk of their annual income over the holidays and when they can't open, the financial toll is devastating.

Another significant moment of this decade is that Apollo Global, a private equity firm, bought Vail Resorts in 1992 and launched their plan for massive expansion. Within five years, Vail Resorts became a publicly-traded company and started a buying spree that continues to this day.

In 1997, Vail Resorts purchased Breckenridge and Keystone from pet food company Ralston Purina. The original deal also included Arapahoe Basin but it was excluded by the U.S. Department of Justice for violating antitrust laws. Before the deal, Vail properties made up 12% of all skier days in Colorado but that would have tripled if A-Basin had stayed in the $310 million package.

Clearly, the 10th Mountain veterans had been hugely successful in launching the American ski industry. And it has now become the play area for investment firms and multi-national conglomerates.

The Industry

On the industry side, there seemed to be a lack of exit strategies for the mom-and-pop businesses, both in retail and manufacturing. In many cases, it was the success of the business that precluded their kids from taking over the business. Several of my friends in the ski business had earned enough wealth that their offspring were able to go to medical school or law school or join the fast growing world of technology.

One of our friend's son graduated from the University of Washington and went to work for a startup tech company that paid minimum wage, but matched that wage with a stock equivalent. This allowed him to make a living and also gain wealth as the company prospered. Not too long ago, I asked my friend what his son was doing. He said, "He's now managing his portfolio of properties." It turns out he was one of the first 10 employees at Amazon and, at the time they went public, he sold his stock for $38 million after taxes.

Some of the mom-and-pop sold their businesses and some were just sold for the real estate value. In retail, the consolidation continued and today most of the giants from the 1960's have been absorbed into Dick's Sporting Good stores. Only the best shops in each town survived the consolidation.

The resorts continued to do the most business because they learned how to become year-round destinations. With the advent of mountain biking, zip lining, and guide-led hiking trips, ski areas were able to make money at least ten months of the year. Add to that, fly-fishing and river rafting and the outdoor sports business expanded to cover a wide range of interests and enthusiasts.

You will find many ski patrol and ski instructors leading those businesses as well, because we had to find work every summer. Those positions are only needed five months of the year (November to March) so many of your favorite ski instructors could also be your favorite fly-fishing guides if you came back in the summer. I certainly did both for many years.

In the 1990's, I had two clients in the fly-fishing world that could not afford to hire a full-time sales and marketing manager, so I signed on to manage those areas for them. I earned $1,000 a month from each and 5% of sales over their previous year's income. They paid my expenses for calling on their accounts and rep salesforces. On my first trip back east, I asked one of the principal partners, who called on Orvis and LL Bean, to accompany me to make a sales call on those accounts.

He told me he was too busy to take the time. I guess he thought I would not get into those big accounts, but he clearly did not understand that I had previous contacts in the industry from my days at Simms. I got into LL Bean and called the buyer of fishing suspenders and accessories.

I about fell over when I walked into his office because on his desk was a photo of himself at Aspen in 1956 while he was on spring break from Colorado University. I laughed and told him, "I have the exact same photo in my scrapbook. Where did you stay that week?" And he said, "Ed's Beds." We laughed as we shared stories of the meal deals we found at the Jerome Hotel and Pinocchio's Pizza.

By the time I left, he had confided in me that he did not like the principal of the rep group and preferred to have his local salesman call on him. I guaranteed him that I would make sure that happened. Needless to say, I was pleased when I was able to tell the owner that I had tripled his sales in one visit!

In the 1990's, the manufacturers were also expanding their lineups and searching for products that could be sold in the off season. TaylorMade Golf had purchased Salomon Skis during the previous decade; their year-around cashflow and similar technology made a near perfect fit.

K2 introduced a bike in their product line that did okay, but they hit a home run with inline skates that were easy for their reps to sell because they were a great way to improve the customers' skiing fitness and balance skills. In this decade, K2 released the Extreme ski, the Velocity (with the most radical sidecut of any ski), Four, Xplorer, and Big Kahuna, one of the first fat powder skis. K2 also purchased two snowboard companies (Morrow and Ride), becoming the number two snowboard maker in the world.

K2 had previously acquired JanSport Mountaineering—in the 1990's, they sold JanSport to a company in Wisconsin who dropped the mountaineering part and created their brand of school backpacks for kids that have dominated that market for over 20 years. My granddaughter, Kiana, gets one every year.

That brings me to the best part of the 1990's for Barb and me. In December of 1997, my daughter contacted me for the first time. We both knew of each other's existence but each had not wanted to bother the other, figuring they'd reach out if they wanted to. We were thrilled to hear from her.

Britt was 32, living in California, and about to graduate with her Ph.D. from UC Santa Barbara. We decided to meet in San Francisco and our planes arrived about the same time. Britt asked a stranger to take photos of our first meeting and we both have that same photo framed in our homes.

I took her to dinner at Sam's and that was the beginning of us reclaiming our relationship. Barb and I attended her graduation ceremony that June and we have been together ever since. I taught her how to fly-fish, which we do together every summer, and we also have skied together many winters. More on that in future chapters.

Keystone Ski Resort
Keystone, Colorado

- Founded in 1970 by Max and Edna Dercum, Keystone currently
- boasts 130 runs over 3,149 skiable acres. Keystone was also shaped by Bill and Jane Bergman, for whom Bergman Bowl is named.
- Keystone incudes three mountains and five bowls and features night skiing. It's located along the Snake River in the White River National Forest.
- There are 20 lifts and a vertical drop of 3,128 feet. The average snowfall is 235 inches.
- They offer private and group lessons for children and adults.
- Learn more at KeystoneResort.com.

Chapter 23

The 2000's: Epic vs. Ikon

Salt Lake City, Utah
40.7608° N, 111.8910° W
Elevation: 4,226 Feet (1,288 M)

The 2000's brought many drastic changes to the sport of skiing and the industry at large. Some key moments are still felt today. Again, let's look at the athletes, the ski areas, and the industry.

The Athletes

In 2002, the Winter Olympics returned to U.S. soil, hosted by Salt Lake City, Utah and its surrounding areas. The Alpine and Freestyle events stayed the same and Americans won five medals. In Alpine, Bode Miller took gold in the Alpine Combined, and silver in the Giant Slalom. Bode had started his skiing career at Cannon Mountain in New Hampshire.

For Freestyle, Shannon Bahrke and Travis Mayer both won silver in Moguls and Joe Pack won silver in Aerials. They learned to ski at Lake Tahoe in California, Holiday Valley, and Lake Placid in New York, respectively. Joe started off as a ski jumper and learned to ski on the Olympic venue in Lake Placid.

The 2006 Olympic Games occurred in Torino, Italy. In Alpine events, Ted Ligety won gold in the Alpine Combined, getting his start at Park City, Utah. Julia Mancuso brought home gold in the Giant Slalom after learning at Squaw Valley in California.

In Freestyle, Toby Dawson earned bronze in Men's Moguls. Toby was born in South Korea but disappeared at the age of three at a crowded market. While his parents searched in all the orphanages, they never found him and he was subsequently adopted by a couple from Vail, Colorado, both of whom were ski instructors there. The Olympic media coverage led to Toby being recognized and eventually reunited with his birth parents.

The 2010 Games in Vancouver, Canada included 2,566 athletes representing 82 teams competing in 86 events. The U.S. team included 120 men and 92 women, and collectively, won 37 medals; nine gold, 15 silver, and 13 bronze.

In skiing, the Vancouver Games featured the debut of a new freestyle sport, ski cross. Here are the winners of this new Olympic sport:

Medal	Men's Ski Cross	Women's Ski Cross
Gold	Mike Schmid, Switzerland	Ashleigh McIvor, Canada
Silver	Andreas Matt, Austria	Hedda Bernsten, Norway
Bronze	Audun Groenvold, Norway	Marion Josserand, France

In Women's Moguls, Hannah Kearney won gold, Shannon Bahrke won bronze, as did Bryon Wilson. Hannah hails from Norwich, Vermont, which has several nearby ski areas and Bryon learned to ski near Butte, Montana.

In Alpine, the U.S. Team did exceptionally well, earning a total of eight medals. Bode Miller captured three medals—gold in Alpine Combined, silver in Super-G, and bronze in Downhill. He was joined on the Super-G podium by Andrew Weibrecht who won bronze and got his start at Whiteface Mountain, the home of the 1980 Olympic events.

Julia Mancuso and Lindsey Vonn each won two medals—Julia won silvers in both Alpine Combined and Downhill and Lindsey took home the gold in Downhill and bronze in Super-G. Lindsey learned to ski at Buck Hill in Minnesota. Currently, Julia has the most Olympic medals (four) of any U.S. women's alpine racer.

The rise of freestyle was not yet over. The 2014 Games in Sochi, Russia would debut two freestyle events, Slopestyle and Halfpipe. The newly crowned Olympians were as follows—notice that Team U.S.A. did well with six medals.

Medal	Men's Ski Slopestyle	Women's Ski Slopestyle
Gold	Joss Christensen, U.S.A.	Dara Howell, Canada
Silver	Gus Kenworthy, U.S.A.	Devin Logan, U.S.A.
Bronze	Nicholas Goepper, U.S.A.	Kim Lamarre, Canada

Medal	Men's Ski Halfpipe	Women's Ski Halfpipe
Gold	David Wise, U.S.A.	Maddie Bowman, U.S.A.
Silver	Mike Riddle, Canada	Marie Martinod, France
Bronze	Kevin Rolland, France	Ayana Onozuka, Japan

Hannah Kearney also medaled in Freestyle, with a bronze in Moguls. But who was missing from the podium was Canadian skier Sarah Burke, who had lobbied very hard to have the Halfpipe included in the Olympics. She died tragically during a training accident in 2012. At the Sochi Games, Sarah's coach scattered some of her ashes on the halfpipe in a special ceremony in her honor.

In the Alpine events, the U.S.A. saw familiar names on the podium. Julia Mancuso won bronze in the Alpine Combined. Ted Ligety won gold in the Giant Slalom and Mikaela Shiffrin made her Olympic debut, winning gold in Slalom. Andrew Weinbrecht won silver in Super-G and in an Alpine rarity, Bode Miller won bronze in a dead tie with Jan Hudec of Canada, both with a time of 1:18.67!

For you film buffs, Warren Miller created ten more fantastic ski films in the 2000's, all of which sold out theaters in ski towns and larger cities all over North America and beyond.

2000	*Ride*	2005	*Higher Ground*
2001	*Cold Fusion*	2006	*Off the Grid*
2002	*Storm*	2007	*Playground*
2003	*Journey*	2008	*Children of Winter*
2004	*Impact*	2009	*Dynasty*

The Ski Areas

The shrinking of the ski area catalog continued in the 2000's, going from 503 to 471 resorts, even with the addition of eight new areas in Colorado (2), Idaho (1), Michigan (1), New Hampshire (2), Vermont (1), and Virginia (1).

The biggest trend in the 2000's was Vail's continued expansion, now going beyond Colorado's state lines. In 2002, they paid $102 million to acquire Heavenly Ski Resort in Lake Tahoe, California. In hindsight, this was all preparation for Vail's launch of the Epic Pass in 2008. They were buying (and continue to buy) small regional areas that had a large, local base of season pass holders. This became a boom for Vail as they sold Epic Passes to the newly acquired area customers that gave them unlimited skiing at their home area and then three days at any other Vail Resorts property as well as seven days at Vail itself.

At that time, passholders paid $579 for access to any of the five Vail Resorts properties. This strategy created two positive effects for Vail. First, they were able to secure a good portion of their winter income upfront because October was the purchase deadline. Second, they brought a bevy of new skiers to Vail who had previously avoided the resort because of cost. Now, they were getting seven free days so many people booked trips to Vail along with other pass areas.

For example, one of my teaching clients regularly skied 50+ days a year at their home ski area of Afton Alps Resort in Minnesota. But they wanted to take advantage of their pass so they rented a vacation home in Dillon, Colorado. They skied Vail for seven days and then added on Breckenridge for three days and Keystone for two more. Just like an amusement park, the money that tourists drop on hotels, meals, and souvenirs far outweighs the price of admission.

Vail Resorts has continued to expand and now owns ski areas in every region of the United States, many properties in Canada, and now Europe, Japan, and Australia. I couldn't find data on how many Epic Passes were sold that first 2008 season, but in 2015-16, they sold 500,000 passes. In 2021-22, they sold 2.1 million and they've just announced that the price for 2022-23 will be $841 per person. This pass gives you access to 70 ski areas around the world.

In 2018, the Alterra Mountain Company launched their own version, called the Ikon Pass. It now includes 59 ski areas around the U.S., Europe, Australia, New Zealand, Chile, and CMH Heli-Skiing in Canada (yes, the company started by Hans Gmoser in the Bugaboos). The website, EpicOrIkon.com, helps people choose which is better for their particular needs.

The resort I teach at in Montana has an association with the Ikon Pass. It has allowed us to grow our business exponentially. Even in the height of the Covid-19 Pandemic, we have been able to maintain a growth curve and accelerate our infrastructure buildout. The guaranteed income early in the season gives resorts more ability to plan and expand. Here are the most recent locations:

EPIC PASS 2022-23	IKON PASS 2022-23
West—Heavenly, Kirkwood, Northstar, and Stevens Pass	**West**—June Mountain, Mammoth, Big Bear, Palisades Tahoe, Crystal Mountain, Summit at Snoqualmie, Mt. Bachelor, Schweitzer, and Sun Valley
Rockies—Beaver Creek, Breckenridge, Crested Butte, Keystone, Park City, Telluride, and Vail	**Rockies**—Alta, Arapahoe Basin, Aspen Snowmass, Big Sky, Brighton, Copper Mountain, Deer Valley, Eldora Mountain, Jackson Hole, Solitude, Snowbasin, Snowbird, Steamboat, Taos Ski Valley, and Winter Park
Midwest—Afton Alps, Alpine Valley, Boston Mills, Brandywine, Hidden Valley, Mad River Mountain, Mt. Brighton, Paoli Peaks, Snow Creek, and Wilmot	**Midwest**—Boyne Highlands and Boyne Mountain
East—Attitash, Big Boulder, Crotched Mountain, Hidden Valley, Hunter Mountain, Jack Frost, Laurel Mountain, Liberty Mountain, Mount Snow, Mount Sunapee, Okemo, Roundtop Mountain Resort, Seven Springs, Whitetail, and Wildcat	**East**—Killington, Loon Mountain, Snowshoe, Stratton, Sugarbush, Sugarloaf, Sunday River, and Windham Mountain
Canada—Whistler Blackcomb, Fernie Alpine Resort, Kicking Horse Mountain, Kimberley Alpine, Mont-Sainte Anne, Nakiska, and Stoneham	**Canada**—Ski Big 3, Revelstoke, Cypress Mountain, Red Mountain, Blue Mountain, and Tremblant
Europe—Les 3 Vallées, France; Skirama Dolomiti, Italy; 4 Vallées, Switzerland; and Ski Arlberg, Austria	**Europe**—Chamonix Mont Blanc, France; Zermatt-Matterhorn, Switzerland; Kitzbuhel, Austria; and Dolomiti Superski, Italy
Japan—Hakuba Valley and Rusutsu	**Japan**—Niseko
Australia—Falls Creek, Hotham, and Perisher	**Australia**—Thredbo and Mount Buller
	New Zealand—Coronet Peak, Mt. Hutt, and The Remarkables
	South America—Valle Nevado, Chile

But I'm afraid that skiing has become a sport that very few can afford anymore. I was recently watching a talk show and the guest mentioned he had just gotten back from skiing at Aspen. The host laughed and said, "You must be really rich!" It's a far cry from the start when surplus 10th Mountain Division equipment was handed out to help people try the sport of skiing.

The Industry

In the ski industry, the 2000's brought the consolidation of companies and their product lines. Companies like Salomon, Nordica, and the Marker/Volkl/Technica group added a clothing component into their product mix. K2 started this decade acquiring snowshoe brands and signing Steve Mahre's son, Andy, to their freestyle team.

In 2006, K2 moved to Seattle and purchased Line Ski Company. The next year, Jarden Corporation bought K2. Sadly, K2 had lost market share when they separated their brand from the racing model that had been super successful for us during the Mahre era.

When K2 made that decision, they effectively gave up the European market. With the rise of extreme skiing, not having a race ski in their line meant there was nothing to pique interest in their products. One person who helped them stay relevant was Rich Green, who designed their graphics. While the skis were now being made in China, the graphics were still all-American. Rich actually brought back graphics from the 1970's and 1980's and those retro looks gave K2 a boost with nostalgic skiers.

The 2000's also saw a change in the teaching side of skiing. As people watched the interesting ski shapes on the World Cup circuit, they wanted to try them. The radical side cuts of modern skis do help people turn, but the reality is that very few leisure skiers can sustain that turn through a terrain change or an interruption that makes them have to shorten or change their line.

The PSIA concluded that our clientele is rarely athletic enough to master that technique. Most of my clients ski seven to ten days per year—enough to have fun but not enough to tackle highly athletic or technical maneuvers. Many are also comeback skiers who paused their skiing when they had children and all that comes with busy parenthood. The good news is that modern skis and boots have design elements built in that really do make it easier and much more comfortable to ski. Read more about ski equipment in Chapter 16.

In addition, today's skiers now come to their lessons with specific goals. For example, my clients now tell me they would like a lesson that helps them learn to carve better while also getting a tour of the mountain. The lesson becomes a combination of picking the terrain that creates a sense of discovery, mixed with focused lessons on technique. Some clients come in and want to go through the progression from wedge turns to dynamic parallel skiing.

But mostly what I hear is, "Can you teach me to have more control so I can gain more confidence?" My answer is always the same, "Yes!" But I know that I must first gain their trust so that they will try some of the things that I explain and demonstrate. Good instructors can help you improve, often quite dramatically, even in as little as one lesson. Some of my clients have been coming every year and it's great fun to watch them improve each season.

The biggest challenge that most skiers face is that they are almost always skiing with others, like family or friends. The weaker skier in the group feels a lot of pressure to keep up and often pushes themselves beyond their ability, or gets exhausted because when they finally catch up to the group, everyone takes off again, never giving them the same amount of rest.

The reality is that it's rare for someone who started to ski as an adult to catch up with a spouse or friend who has skied since childhood. However, I always tell them that while they might not be able to ski with their fast-skiing friend, that person can always ski with them. This means that the other person needs to ski the terrain/speed of the less advanced skier. Part of my job as an instructor is to give them the words and confidence to make that request.

As we were exiting the 2000's, the ski teaching world was awakening to the fact that, if your client is smiling and having fun, they will improve faster than someone who is stressed. The better instructors are almost always gregarious and remember that the lesson they are teaching is always about the client and not their own priorities.

On a personal note, Barb and I continued to live in Bozeman, Montana. We'd regularly ski with friends at Bridger and Big Sky. We'd also take trips to visit friends in Washington and Colorado, often skiing our old haunts.

My daughter got married in 2003 and we were there to celebrate. Britt and her husband, Chris, came out to visit us every year and we got him into fly-fishing and he's now quite good. He's a snowboarder, but we still like him.

Buck Hill Resort
Burnsville, Minnesota

- Founded in 1954 by Charles Stone, Jr. and Nancy Campbell, Buck Hill currently boasts 15 runs over 45 skiable acres.
- There are 11 lifts and a vertical drop of 310 feet. The average snowfall is 60 inches and they also have a tubing hill and night skiing.
- Under the guidance of coach Erich Sailer, four Olympic skiers learned to ski at Buck Hill: Cory Carlson, Kristina Koznick, Tasha Nelson, and Lindsey Vonn. He also coached 15 U.S. Ski Team members, ranging from 1980 to 2022.
- They offer private and group lessons for children and adults.
- Learn more at BuckHill.com.

Chapter 24

2010-11: Return to Teaching

Big Sky, Montana
45.2857° N, 111.4012° W
Base Elevation: 6,800 Feet (2,073 M)
Peak Elevation: 11,166 Feet (3,403 M)

Since I left K2 in 1980, I had been working in several different sporting businesses—sometimes in sales, sometimes as an equity partner, and sometimes as a consultant. I had been skiing less and less because of pain in my knees. I had tried cortisone shots, chiropractic, etc. but, as much as I loved to ski, the pain had made those trips to the mountain unbearable.

In the Winter of 2008-09, I had my right knee replaced with a new titanium and plastic knee. I spent that winter rehabbing and working with a physical therapist to get ready to ski again. By spring, I was on the hill and skiing pain free for the first time in 10+ years. I was amazed at how I had been compromised by the pain. I also got to remember just how much I love the sport.

That summer, my recent consulting job was wrapping up and I decided to officially retire on September 30, 2010. On October 3rd, I called Big Sky Mountain Sports and asked if they needed instructors. I was hired over the phone. At last! I had created a retirement with a fun part-time job doing what I love more than anything!

Being a member of the Professional Ski Instructors of America (PSIA), I was obligated to do six hours of clinics before teaching and I was really looking forward to them. The day before the clinic started, I went up to Big Sky, made a couple of runs, and was astounded with the performance of the artificial knee. There was no pain and it was really stable even in the high pressure turns. It confirmed what I was told going into the surgery—that I really should have done it 10 years earlier.

When the clinic started, I requested to be in a moderate group—I didn't feel quite ready to ski high speeds or off-piste, which means on non-groomed trails or glades. I was really surprised when our clinician showed up and I knew him. J.B. Carroll is one of the hard-core, ex-racer clinicians in our ski school. We all asked if we were in the wrong class and he chuckled and said, "Relax. I am here because I wanted a couple of easy days before I get serious about the season."

He was really fun to ski with and as a group we were pleasantly surprised by how laid back he was. The two days we skied together were fun and full of laughs as we got ready for the season. It confirmed what I have known–that I love the camaraderie of a mountain team.

Big Sky Mountain Sports Ski School is the perfect place for me. They now have a team of 300+ instructors and 60 ski patrollers. They offer private and group lessons for every level of skier and snowboarder. At Big Sky, we offer clients clear guidance about skiing and boarding levels so they can pick the right level of lesson. We also assess them at the beginning of the lesson so we can adjust as needed.

Skiing Levels	Snowboarding Levels
1. First time on skis	1. First time on a snowboard
2. Can glide in a wedge | Stops evenly in a wedge | Links wedge turns | Controls speed with turn shape | Can stop by turning	2. J-Turns | Heel edge skidding with speed control | Standing on heel edge
	3. Edge control with directional change | Starting to link S-turns
3. Controls speed by turning | Can adjust wedge size mid-turn | Skies green easy runs confidently	4. Traverse across the slope on both edges | Linking S-turns on easy green runs
4. Starts turn in wedge | Consistently matches skis between turns	5. Can vary turn size & shape to control speed | Rides cat tracks safely
5. Consistently parallel on green runs | Use pole touch to trigger parallel matching on easy blue runs	6. Confidently riding blue runs dynamically | Riding with independent suspension | Maintain speed in moguls and powder
6. Can vary parallel turn size and shape on any groomed blue run	7. Confidently riding easy black runs | Flexion initiation vs. extension initiation | riding fakie on easy blue terrain
7. Links parallel turns in blue bumps | Links parallel turns in blue powder	8. Riding zipper lines through bumps | Maintains speed on all black terrain
8. Skis easy blacks safely and dynamically	
9. Dynamically carves turns | dynamically skis all lines in the bumps	9. Steep chutes and trees | highly technical terrain

Next up was the fall clinic for new and returning instructors in the Big Sky Mountain Sports Ski School. The first day, I was assigned to a group of Level 3 instructors, some of whom I knew. But there were a couple of instructors in our group who were new to Big Sky. Our clinician, Brenna Kelleher, was one of the trainers in our Adult Alpine school. She is a really good skier and we all had a fun day.

Level 3 is where you convert a wedge turner to an open parallel skier and take them from green runs to blue runs. Personally, this is my favorite lesson because it gives students a real sense of control over their skis, which gives them confidence.

As part of our training, Brenna asked us to plan a scenario to teach for about 15 minutes and then the group would critique the lesson and ask questions about the plan of progression for those hypothetical students. It was really interesting to watch and listen to the group in general, but the newbies provided the most entertainment because they were nervous, and you could tell they were trying to make a big impression.

The three of them talked themselves into a hole and, the more they tried to get out, the more they became flustered. Our trainer took over and asked them to ride the lift with her. The three of us who went up behind them assumed they were getting a tongue lashing but, when we got off the chair ride, we were surprised to see them laughing. Brenna had done a great job of getting them calm and focused.

We all went to the next trail where she had us share our scenarios and progressions. Next, she split us into two-person teams—the rest of the day we went about teaching and then trading partners. I recognized that she had set up a team building and mentoring situation to show the newbies that their peers can be a great source of knowledge going forward the rest of the season. Brenna is still at Big Sky and is a two-term member of the PSIA Demo Team.

The adult ski instructors at Big Sky Resort in 2021-22

At the next clinic, we switched to new groups where we had Level 1, Level 2, and Level 3 instructor groups and a clinician to facilitate our discussions for various scenarios. This is my favorite clinic for teaching—it really moves the lower level instructors from drills and tasks to doing movement analysis and constructing lesson plans and achievable goals on the fly.

It also introduces the critical shift from seeing the symptom to identifying the root cause. One of the best times in a lesson is when you see what's going on with your clients and then do a drill that works. The students can't help but smile as they FEEL the difference the shift is making in their skiing. One of the best times in teaching is the "aha moment!" when the student breaks through and starts feeling rather than thinking.

Once clinics finished, I spent that season teaching many fun lessons. That first year back to teaching was so much fun as I got to know the whole crew at Big Sky and then started to build a client list.

The Adult School supervisor recognized my skill set and started using me to correct what we call "broken lessons." When a student and instructor don't fit, Big Sky has a "customer first" attitude and offers a free lesson to get things back on track. I am one of a limited number of instructors trusted to turn the situation around.

Because of my background and experience, I have been given drills and tricks from hundreds of really clever and innovative instructors. Combined with the knowledge I accumulated while working in the ski industry, I can also assess and fix equipment issues, which is more likely the source of the problem than you might imagine. Finally, I've lived a great life and have good stories to tell.

My strategy is to always make sure the lesson is safe, fun, and generates forward progress. I use my entertaining stories to get the students to relax and then they quickly realize they are making headway.

One of the really fun parts about being an older instructor is to listen to the locker room chatter at lunch or after the day ends. I love hearing the instructors talk about their lessons and students. The children's teachers have the best stories because they hear everything about their family, pets, siblings, and school. We are often laughing at the great things that kids say.

It's also a hoot for me to hear the instructors plan for a free run when they get done teaching; it almost always contains a pretty high level of risk. Sometimes I want to intervene and tell them to not do that, but I realize at that same age, I was doing exactly what they are contemplating, and I wouldn't have listened to an "old guy." Sometimes I see them all scuffed up from a fall but, more often than not, I hear them planning their next extreme run.

As that first year back was ending, I thought I might teach for a year or two. I now know that what I thought was going to be a short-term stay at Big Sky has turned into a series of fun experiences and meaningful friendships.

That season reinforced that I really like teaching better than skiing, but the combination of both equals a perfect life. This coming 2022-23 will be my 16th season at Big Sky and I am excited to see what it brings.

Big Sky Resort
Big Sky, Montana

- Founded in 1968 by Chet Huntley (of NBC), Big Sky currently boasts 300 named runs over 5,850 skiable acres in the Gallatin National Forest.
- With 300 degrees of skiing off of Lone Peak, Big Sky is known as the biggest skiing in North America.
- There are 39 lifts and a vertical drop of 4,350 feet. The average snowfall is 400 inches and they also feature five terrain parks with progressing difficulty and headlamp night skiing.
- They offer private and group lessons for children and adults.
- Learn more at BigSkyResort.com.

Chapter 25

Transformation of Ski Lifts

Jackson Hole, Wyoming
43.5875° N, 110.8279° W
Base Elevation: 6,311 Feet (1,924 M)
Peak Elevation: 10,450 Feet (3,185 M)

Skiing was primarily and initially a way to move quickly over the snow. But when gravity took hold, people discovered that going downhill was and is the fun part of skiing. The part that has vexed generations is how to get up that hill so you could ski down it. In my lifetime, I have seen uphill transport change so much it boggles my mind at the sophistication that we see in uphill conveyances in 2022. They fall into two main categories: surface lifts and aerial lifts. Surface lifts transport skiers along the surface of the snow while aerial lifts raise the skier above the snow and bring them back down again at their destination.

Surface Lifts

In 1951-1952, I learned to ski after being towed uphill by a T-Bar. T-Bars are a type of surface lift, where the skier is moved along the surface of the snow by some kind of powered conveyance. The early versions were animal-powered by horses or ox with people holding on to a cable or rope.

Prior to the T-Bar, rope tows were common at ski areas and were powered by Model-A Ford engines that circulated the rope. People stepped up to the rope, grabbed onto it, and were pulled uphill to the other end. As you can imagine, people would often lose their grip, burn out their arm muscles, or fall, often sliding back down the hill, and taking other skiers with them.

The T-Bar and Poma lift attempted to solve this problem. Poma lifts carried single riders and used a circular disc attached to a stiff bar that was attached to the rope. The skier would put the disc between their legs so it rested up against their butt and they would hold on to the bar as the powered rope pulled them along. But if they bent their knees or tried to sit down, the Poma would snap back out and they would need to get out of the way of the next skier in the line or start creating a pileup of skiers and skis.

The Poma lift, which was made in the 1960's by a company named Pomagalski, was also called a "platter" lift. When I was in high school and college, I loved the Poma lift at Arapahoe Basin. It was on a six-foot-high platform, which made a perfect launch pad if you timed the moment right. As it started pulling you up, you could get about a 60-foot assisted jump, which was one of the most fun things a teenage boy could do.

The T-Bar was built for two riders, each with an arm of the T behind their butts. But as I learned with Paul Sakry at Cooper, a difference in height created quite a problem. And again, it was easy for riders to lose their balance or cross skis or poles with their neighbor. But since the alternative to all of these was to walk up the hill, we all made it work.

Another type of surface lift, the funicular or cable railway, grew out of the mining industry and was essentially a mine ore car moving on a set of tracks. At most early ski areas, all innovations were regional and almost every one was made from spare or abandoned equipment designed to transport a product of some kind from point A to point B.

Snowcats are another form of surface lift. Snowcats are the over-snow vehicle that groom the ski trails by raking the snow and packing it down. But many are outfitted with internal seats and can transport skiers over rough terrain and long distances to remote or backcountry skiing. Today, some are quite fancy with heaters and even bar service!

I'm pleased to say that the newest version of surface lifts is great for beginner skiers, especially children. It's called a Magic Carpet and essentially a moving sidewalk installed on the snow. Skiers step on and just stand in a relaxed position as they are moved up the hill. At Big Sky, ours is covered so that skiers stay protected from the elements. My granddaughter, Kiana, loved the Magic Carpet so much, she still talks about it. For her and many other kids, skiing down was the method to get back to the cool thing that took you up!

Aerial Lifts

It was only a matter of time before new methods of moving skiers uphill were invented. The earliest chairlift was fashioned at Sun Valley Resort, Idaho in 1936. The Harriman family, who owned the resort, wanted to increase visitors for both summer and winter vacations so they hired a Union Pacific engineer to solve this problem. James Curran had previously worked in Costa Rica where he had seen a conveyance to get bananas from the dock onto the ships. He modeled the first single chair after it, lifting the skier off the ground and carrying them to the top of the ski hill. In addition to moving more people up the mountain, it created an unexpected leap forward in safety because it gave skiers a chance to rest between runs.

Original designs either had the chair attached to the cable by prying the cable open and putting the attachment through so the cable held it in place. Or it involved a clamp mechanism, which meant that the chair had to be bolted onto the cable. Neither system made me personally comfortable because I am more than a little acrophobic, so being off the ground was not my favorite thing.

Of course, given my love for skiing, I had to overcome my fear to do my job. Chairlifts have always been prone to wind shutdowns because the way they can start to sway. The good news is that all chairlifts have a laser system, or something equivalent, that automatically shuts down the lift if they are getting out of perfect alignment.

I had two events on chairlifts that really stuck with me. The first was when I was the Assistant Director of the Vail Ski Patrol and I was riding the lift from Mid-Vail to the summit. The electric motor stopped, and they couldn't get it started, so the ski patrol had to evacuate the chair. My chair partner, a secretary from the marketing department, and I were at the highest point on that lift, just under the cliff below the summit. I had trained all our patrolmen how to do the evac, so I should have been confident in their hands. The secretary was freaking out and I was trying to stay calm and reassuring. When they got to us, we dropped our skis and poles to the ground and they hoisted the evac bag up to our chair. The bag has a steel band around the top of the bag and the bag itself has three layers of ripstop nylon and all kinds of strapping sewn on for security.

My chairmate refused to scooch off the chair into the bag, so in the end, I had to push her into the bag and the patrol belayed her down. I believe she must have passed out because she didn't make a sound when they got her out of the bag and put her skis on. They brought the bag up to me and I dropped into the bag. Of course, because "the boss" was in the bag, they let me free fall for about 40 feet. I did not pass out, but it scared the hell out of me. But I got even—the two patrolmen who played the joke on me got the worst opening routes and sweeps for at least two weeks.

The second chairlift event happened in the 1970's at Squaw Valley, California. The racing season in Europe was over and the Mahre Twins had returned to the states. My good friend and client, Martin Sulser, who owned the Swiss Ski Sports shop in downtown San Francisco, asked if there was any way I could arrange a demo day at Squaw to preview next year's K2 line up. The Mahres had just finished a fabulous year on the World Cup tour and they were building their brand, so I invited them to come and meet the staff at Swiss Ski and to Squaw for a public appearance. They agreed and I know they had a great time. It also sealed the K2 deal for Martin and his racer-oriented ski shop.

A little after lunch, Phil and Steve suggested that we ski off the KT22 peak, the steepest run on the mountain. We got on the chair to take us up there; I sent Martin up with Phil and Steve while I got on the chair right behind them. On that chair, there is a place where it is over 300 feet above the ground. My acrophobia was really in high gear so, as we approached the high point, I had my head down and my eyes closed. Something about the size of a quarter but heavier hit me on my right thigh. I was so afraid that I couldn't look up. When I unloaded, Steve asked me, "Are you sick or something? You are really pale." I explained what had happened and how I am acrophobic. He and Phil both were watching me as I went out and looked down the chute we were about to ski, and he asked, "Does this scare you?" I explained, "No. I'm fine when I am not off the ground and I have no problem skiing steep stuff." And off we went.

Twenty years later, Barb and I were at the induction of Jack and Donna Nagel into the Northwest Ski Hall of Fame. Steve walked up to me, and I said, "Are you Steve or Phil?" He said, "If you have to ask, you don't need to know." I said, "Come on, Steve, I know the difference." And he replied, "Yes, but are you still afraid of chairlifts?" We both had a good laugh about that.

The next innovation in chairlifts happened in the 1980's, when high speed four- and six-person lifts were created. The mechanism changed from chairs being attached to the cable to a new system where the chair entered the terminal and the chair detached from the cable, allowing it to slow down significantly before being hooked back on again to leave the terminal. This allowed people to more easily get on and off the chair without feeling rushed or falling. Once the chair cleared the terminal, it picked up speed to zoom up the hill at a faster rate, making the overall ride up much shorter too.

These high-speed chairs not only moved a lot of people up the mountain, they also started adding features like a safety bar that keeps you from falling out and also offers a bar to rest your feet/skis on.

I work at Big Sky Resort now and we have three- and six-person chairlifts and one eight-person chair that serves our base area and moves people out of the bottom area at a very efficient pace. The new Swift Current lift is the fastest chairlift in North America! It has cut my ride time by almost 10 minutes with the comfort of heated seats and bubbles that keep the wind off you on the ride up. Last week, we had three days of -8° Fahrenheit weather and these lifts kept us operating.

The next five years will see us replace an old, slow two-person chairlift with a 12-person gondola that will allow us to have a separate safe beginner area. It will also meet up with the new 80-person tram to the top of Lone Peak. The cost of these new marvels is astronomical, but it will create the best premier skiing access ever in North America.

Gondolas are another popular form of aerial conveyances at ski areas. There are different types of gondolas, each distinguished by variations in the cable and tower configurations and how many people they can carry. They go by the names of trams, funifors, and funitels, but all include an enclosed car that passengers step into and either sit or stand as the car moves up the hill. Just like chairlifts, modern innovations allow for faster rides, more passengers, and smoother transitions to get on and get off.

If you want to take a deep dive into ski lifts in North America, check out the website LiftBlog.com. It's a labor of love by Peter Landsman who works in lift operations at Jackson Hole Mountain Resort in Wyoming. He started the blog in 2015 and details all the lifts in the United States and Canada. He keeps a running list of new lifts opened each year.

As I review my experiences with the ski industry, the changes in uphill conveyance are the most impressive. Now, ski areas can get more people up onto the hill and enjoying the sport and the mountain. Just like an amusement park, people measure the value of the ticket by the number of rides they get in during a day.

Interestingly, Troy Nedved, the General Manager at Big Sky, just returned from a trip to Disney World with his kids. He commented that Disney has done such a great job of entertaining people standing in line, by winding the line through ride-based scenes, that his kids had fun the whole time they waited to get on the actual ride. I could see the gleam in his eye as he was trying to figure out how to do that at ski resorts. I wouldn't be surprised if that becomes the next innovation in ski lifts.

Jackson Hole Mountain Resort
Teton Village, Wyoming

- Founded in 1963 by Paul McCollister, Alex Morley and Gordon Graham, Jackson Hole Mountain Resort currently boasts 133 runs over 2,500 skiable acres in the Bridger Teton National Forest.
- There are 16 lifts and a vertical drop of 4,139 feet. The average snowfall is 526 inches and they also have two terrain parks. The open backcountry gate system accesses 3,000+ acres.
- They offer private and group lessons for children and adults.
- Learn more at JacksonHole.com.

Chapter 26

2012-2015: Paying It Forward

Gallatin Gateway, Montana
45.5389° N, 111.1194° W
Elevation: 4,953 Feet (1,510 M)

When I decided to return to teaching at Big Sky after retiring from business, my long-time friend and ski guru, Ursula Howland, played a big part in my decision. She had gotten me back on skis after my first knee replacement surgery. She had encouraged me to try skiing for a day to see how I'd feel. She showed me all the new lifts and trails that had been added since I last skied Big Sky.

One of my concerns was that I did not want to be that person who is past their prime. The worst thing I could imagine was having someone tell me that I was no longer an effective instructor. She promised me that she would take on being the judge of that. And if I had dropped below an acceptable level, she would either fix me or tell me I was done. I knew I could trust her. Ursula is a Level 3 PSIA instructor and also certified by the German Sports Department. She has been on *Ski Magazine's* list of 100 best instructors many times.

My hope had been to commute to Big Sky with Ursula every day. She already had a commuter partner but she invited me to join them. I was a bit worried because I had never met or skied with him and spending two hours each day driving back and forth is a big commitment. The road to Big Sky is curvy and travels through Gallatin Gateway along the Gallatin River.

Ursula described Rich as a great skier and a really fun guy who was "a bit out of the box" in his teaching but had a big following of returning clients. Having returning clients says a lot about someone so I figured he'd be okay.

My introduction to Rich Noonan was our first commute when instructors get our passes and lockers. He was funny, had a wicked sense of humor, and an interesting life history, including being in Seattle the same time that Barb and I were. Rich grew up back east, learning to ski at Bousquet Mountain, where he started teaching professionally in 1970 and never looked back. We hit it off immediately and I couldn't wait to start fall clinics so we could ski together.

When we first skied together, he blew me away. He was one of the most fluid skiers I have ever seen and it was amazing to ski behind him. He changed directions so smoothly that I had trouble figuring out how he initiated his turns, something I can usually spot easily. We ended up in a clinic group and really had a great time, laughing and playing like teenagers.

On the commute home, the three of us started a routine that still exists today. We talk non-stop, sharing how we see things, and listening to each other. We deeply respect and like each other so those two hours just fly by.

Most of our conversations center on what happened to each of us on any given day. We'd share how our clients were skiing and the techniques we used to help them improve. It's so fun to take them from working hard to turn to having it happen effortlessly. But, lots of days we talked about what we were seeing and/or hearing in the locker rooms and what clients said that was funny or controversial.

We liked to make predictions, too. For example, one of our peer instructors often skied with their weight too far back, making the turns a lot more work than they needed to be. We predicted that if they didn't get their body more forward, their knees would be killing them by season's end. Sure enough, by spring, they were experiencing a lot of soreness and swelling. The three of us will happily give out pointers when asked, but most of our peers are younger and not necessarily seeking our input.

Sometimes, we'd share stories of being critiqued by our clinic trainers. Ursula told a story about having a discussion on a chair ride with a clinician about a paper he planned to release. He made a false statement, which Ursula pointed out to him. He became flustered and called her "Contra Ursula." Interestingly enough, when he released the document, he included the correction in verbiage that Ursula had suggested.

Rich shared his story about a trainer telling him that he would never be able to be a trainer. When he asked why, the trainer said he couldn't be trained. Yet he attends clinics and events and always comes back with some creative new twist to an old progression. We can understand the trainer's frustration; Rich doesn't conform nor adhere completely to the PSIA-AASI models but, when you listen closely, they are an integral part of his teaching foundation. We are thankful as we "car-clinic" together, and struggle to understand how such a nonconforming wealth of knowledge and experience, once again, can get so easily dismissed.

My story was about a time I was skiing in a training group and the trainer asked to ride the chair up with me. On the way up he said to me, "Just because you are getting good results, doesn't mean that you are doing the right things." To this day, I can't figure out exactly what he meant.

For three years, our commute was just the three of us. Then Ursula, one of the contributors and coaches for the EpicSki website, got noticed by TheSkiDiva.com website. The owner, Wendy Clinch, organized a Diva West outing to Big Sky and the group requested Ursula for their lesson. Laura Herr was in the group and she and Ursula became friends. Laura, who was retired, moved to Bozeman and was hired to teach at Big Sky in 2014. So we became a great group of four.

Between Rich, Ursula, and me, we have over 150 years of teaching experience. We're all Alpine Level 3 instructors with PSIA and Laura was a Level 1 at the time we started commuting. Laura said that the two-hour car ride was like a full immersion into the history and techniques of skiing. We were all learning from each other. I think these rides should have counted for training time. I know that over the years of that commute, I stole enough tips and technical discussions that I could write a book about skiing!

Laura took full advantage of that ride time. She'd listened to our conversations and, if she had a tough lesson that day, she'd ask us what we would have done with that student. We would tell her what we thought and ask her what she did. It really made us think and we watched her go from Ursula's student to a highly productive and respected member of the Big Sky Mountain Sports School.

We encouraged her to get her Level 2 PSIA certification, which she did. The examiners gave her really high marks including a note to work for her Level 3 because her teaching was already at that level.

Laura sync skiing with Ursula at Big Sky after her PSIA certification

On one of the rides home, I shared what happened with my lesson and it's still one of my favorite stories. When I saw the name on the lesson page, it seemed familiar but I couldn't place it. And when I met him, I knew I recognized him but wasn't sure where. I said as much, but he just smiled. I asked what he wanted to work on and he said he was coming back from a five-year hiatus. He had bought new skis and they were so different that he thought it would be a good idea to go with an instructor to speed up the adjustment process. We rode up the lift and I had him ski in front of me for 10 or 12 turns and then down to me for another batch of turns so I could get a good look at what he needed.

He skied up to me and I said, "You learned to ski in a French technique ski school." He laughed and said, "Wow, that's impressive. I was stationed in France and learned to ski there. How come you know how the French teach skiing?" I told him about my time with Jack Nagel at Crystal Mountain.

I explained to him that the new skis are meant to be turned from the ball of the foot and all we had to do was to get him out of the sitting position that the French used to make the famous Jet Turn of the Killy era. I showed him the posture he needed to be in to take advantage of his new skis. Then I showed him how to use his arms and upper body to stay forward on the skis without using his quads. He had previously told me that he was good for about 10 to 15 turns, then he had to stop because his thighs were burning. He was a good student and got it on the first try.

We finished at noon and he booked me for the next day. He asked me if I had figured out who he was and I said no. He smiled and said, "I am a columnist for the *Washington Post* and you've probably seen me on *MSNBC*."

That night at home, I picked up a book I wanted to read and my client's face was on the back cover. He was the author David Ignatius! I googled him and discovered he is the authority on Middle Eastern terrorism. I could hardly wait to see him the next morning.

We had another day of great skiing. He was easily doing 25 turns and not even puffing because he was letting gravity and the equipment do their jobs. As we said goodbye, he gave me a great tip, asked for my mailing address, and said he was going to send me some books. Sure enough, I received a box from him of several great books and a kind note wishing me luck.

On another ride home, Rich and I shared a story about one of our regular clients. I had started teaching a woman who had hired me for three days. We had a great time and then she sent her brother to learn from me a few weeks later. That started an annual tradition of the whole family, with spouses and kids, coming out to Big Sky. I brought Rich in and we'd take turns skiing with different combinations of the family. They are a blast and we have fun skiing with them at least once every season.

One of my favorite Ursula stories is when she taught my granddaughter how to ski! It was December of 2013 and Kiana was six years old. I asked Ursula to start her off so I would not be the overbearing grandpa that I typically see on the hill, getting emotional and setting the wrong tone. Unfortunately for us, it was a really cold day hovering between -8° and +6° but Ursula kept her warm on hot chocolate and enthusiasm.

I knew that Kiana was in great hands so while her dad, Chris, snowboarded, Britt and I went skiing and intentionally avoided running into them on the hill. We all stopped for a great lunch and afterwards we tailed Kiana and Ursula. I was pleasantly surprised, and very proud, at how well she was doing. Ursula left and Britt, Kiana, and I went up the Magic Carpet. I was feeling surreal about three generations of us skiing together.

Kiana at age 10 with her Grandpa Mike and Ursula Howland

Kiana skied again when she was 10 and is quite athletic. She picks up new sports very easily (she surfs, rides horses, etc.), but is also a very talented singer and the performing arts seems to be her preference. She is now 15 and in her high school's show choir—they have won a couple of international competitions and she also is in their musical theater productions.

Like most working parents, Britt and Chris are busy but they come to visit us every summer and we fly-fish together. I hope that Kiana will come back to skiing and maybe attend college in Bozeman because Montana State University has a fantastic music and film school. That's Grandpa's dream scenario. I know she is going to be successful at anything she chooses—she certainly comes from a line that sets goals and accomplishes what they set out to do.

Throughout our commute, we grew very close. Laura and Ursula shared their favorite stories too, but not all of them were about skiing. Laura was a really good sailor and had a boat on Chesapeake Bay, which she loved. Ursula is also a commercial pilot and would regale us with her adventures flying. I loved the camaraderie of our happy foursome.

Unfortunately, Laura was diagnosed with cancer and became a participant in a protocol treatment from Johns Hopkins Hospital. She came back to Big Sky with a chemo pump on her body, but she kept on teaching. Only a handful of the instructors at Big Sky knew what was happening. When she switched to oral chemo, she taught almost every day and, if she had a day off, she would come up and ski by herself or with good friends or former clients.

She underwent a dramatic surgery and, for awhile, was cancer-free. We thought she was in the clear but, unfortunately, the cancer returned.

We watched her lose weight and strength. Laura and her wife returned to Chesapeake Bay and sailed until she had to go into the hospital for a last ditch shot at recovering from her disease. But it became obvious that, despite her battling valiantly, she was declining rapidly.

Rich, Ursula, and I decided to do one last thing for our friend. I gave her my Level 3 PSIA pin and we gave her an Honorary Level 3 PSIA-NRM document signed by the three of us, which she received on the day she was released from the hospital. She clearly understood that she would be a Level 3 in our eyes and hearts forever. She passed away on June 1, 2020.

If you ski at Big Sky in the future, you might come upon a tree with a plaque in her honor and a pair of pink ski poles hanging on the branches. It's our way of memorializing her precious time at Big Sky Resort.

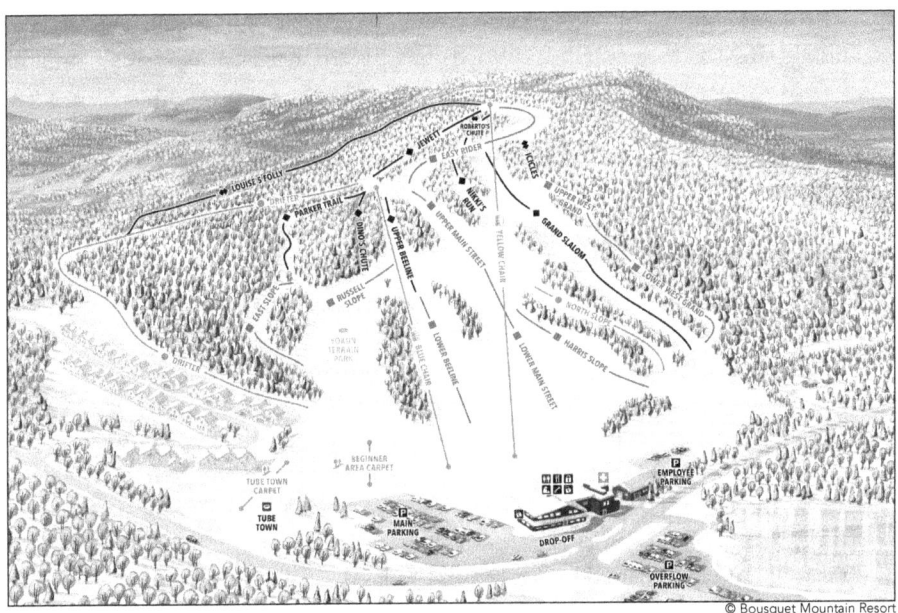

Bousquet Mountain Resort
Pittsfield, Massachusetts

- Founded in 1932 by Clarence Bousquet, Bousquet Mountain currently boasts 23 runs over 200 skiable acres in the Berkshire Hills.
- There are 6 lifts and a vertical drop of 750 feet. The average snowfall is 83 inches and they also offer a terrain park, tubing, and night skiing.
- They offer private and group lessons for children and adults.
- Learn more at BousquetMountain.com.

Chapter 27

History of the PSIA

Red Lodge, Montana
45.1908° N, 109.3364° W
Base Elevation: 7,433 Feet (2,266 M)
Peak Elevation: 9,416 Feet (2,870 M)

    The Professional Ski Instructors of America and American Association of Snowboard Instructors (PSIA-AASI) has played a pivotal role in skiing and snow sports in America. From the title, you can see that it evolved to reflect the needs of skiers and snowboarders. I want to share with you the history of this important organization and why learning from a PSIA-AASI certified instructor will help you improve faster.

    The PSIA was founded in 1961 and recently celebrated its 60th anniversary, adding AASI in 1997. Its purpose is to provide certification for instruction in the following six snow sports—alpine skiing, snowboarding, telemark skiing, cross-country skiing, freestyle skiing, and adaptive skiing.

    The PSIA-AASI has approximately 35,000 members and is organized into eight divisions serving different parts of the country—Central, Eastern, Intermountain, Northern Intermountain, Northern Rocky Mountain, Northwest, Rocky Mountain, and Western. I've served as President of the Northern Rocky Mountain Division.

    In the postwar era, most ski areas were leased from the federal government and typically were managed by one of the federal agencies, most likely the U.S. Forest Service. As skiing started to take off, more and more ski areas were created. The ski instruction component quickly became one of the biggest, and most lucrative, departments at any ski area or resort.

    The original organization of ski instruction was on a regional basis and the Forest Service watched as the Eastern Ski Instructors Association began, immediately followed by the Midwest Ski Instructor Association, Rocky Mountain, Northwest, and Western. As the baby boomers and their kids fell in love with skiing, ski areas realized that they could use ski schools as a good place to market their areas. But, from the Forest Service's perspective, the lack of a universal ski teaching system was becoming problematic.

Before the PSIA was founded, the instructors at each ski school taught the technique that their ski school director espoused. This usually came from the technique they were taught as a child and influenced by where they grew up. The three most common systems were the Austrian, French, and Swiss techniques because that is where the early immigrant ski instructors hailed from when they came to North America.

All three systems had minor but different variations on the basics. A good example is the beginning moves to get control in the early stages of instruction. Everyone was teaching the snowplow or wedge to increase friction so the skier slowed down and could control how fast they wanted to ski. In the turning phase, it was universal that to turn left you needed to add pressure to the leg opposite of the way you wanted to turn, i.e., the right/outside ski. But how that was accomplished varied among the systems. It's important to remember that we're talking about the barely-post-WWII-era when skis had no steel edges and a 5'10" skier would be skiing on a 210 centimeter ski (that's nearly seven feet long!) in ski boots that today would be the equivalent of a high-top pair of basketball shoes. It required a lot of muscle power to wedge and turn those skis.

While the three techniques had lots of similarities, it quickly became confusing for students; they might learn one technique at one ski area and then travel to another and be taught something else. For example, at the Squaw Valley Resort in California, the ski school used the French technique proponent. But at Badger Pass, their ski school director was an Austrian and used the Austrian technique. At my home area of Monarch Mountain in Colorado, our director was German, so I was taught the German technique. As a consumer, if you started learning in one system, then went where there was a different technique, your ski lesson could quickly become confusing and frustrating!

The Forest Service decided it was time to react because skiing was becoming such a big business. They made a plea to the various regional ski instructor associations asking them to develop a unified system. So, in the spring of 1958, a conference was held at Alta, Utah with leaders from the various associations. However, they could not find a solution that was acceptable to all involved.

In the Winter of 1960-1961, the U.S. Forest Service told the associations that something needed to happen, or it would be mandated that a unified instruction system would be part of the lease conditions when they came due for renewal. So, the various associations convened again at Big Mountain, Montana (now Whitefish) and worked out a way to create an American ski teaching system that would be standardized and used by all regions in the country. In addition, this body would provide certification for instructors to ensure quality and consistency. That became the founding of the non-profit organization, the Professional Ski Instructors of America (PSIA) in August of 1961.

The seven leaders who created the origins of the PSIA were:
- Bill Lash, Idaho was a Utah businessman and the first PSIA President
- Curt Chase, director of the ski school at Aspen, Colorado

- Max Dercum, founder of Arapahoe Basin and Keystone resorts in Colorado
- Doug Pfeifer, co-director of the ski school at Snow Summit in California
- Paul Valar, director of the ski school at Sunapee in New Hampshire
- Don Rhinehart, from the Sun Valley ski school in Idaho
- Jimmy Johnson, director of the ski school for the Minneapolis Park and Recreation program in Minnesota

An exciting moment happened for the PSIA demonstration team in 1965. Every three years, the international ski congress had an ongoing event, called Interski, that was a bit like the Olympics for ski instructors. It included some of the greatest skiers in the world from Austria, France, Germany, Italy and Switzerland. In 1965, Interski was held in Bad Gastein, Austria and the American team arrived. The team members were: Bill Lash, Toby Von Euw, Eric Windisch, Barry Bryant, Phil Jones, and Glen Young among a few others.

The event was known for wicked competition on the hill but relative segregation as teams stuck together at meals and off the mountain. Bill Lash decided to mix things up and hosted a party, inviting all the various teams. Everyone had a great time and broke through old barriers. In fact, that party set up the Americans to host the next Interski at Aspen, Colorado in 1968, the first time it had come to America. In 1975, ten years later, the PSIA debuted its newly created American Ski System at the Interski event in Czechoslovakia.

They were responsible for crafting the new American Teaching System. Skiing requires the use of four skills—balance, rotary motion, edging, and pressure. In addition, turning the ski is the main way a person makes it down a hill. There are four parts to every turn—initiation, control phase, completion, and blending into the next turn's initiation. Whether you are a beginner making your way down a gentle slope or an alpine racer competing in the Olympics, you're doing variations of these moves and faster speeds.

Today, the PSIA espouses these five fundamentals in skiing:
- Direct pressure to the outside ski
- Control edge angles with angulation and inclination
- Keep center mass over base of support
- Control the skis rotation with leg rotation
- Regulate the pressure created by the ski/snow interaction

As the PSIA continued its work, they created three levels of certification, which still hold today:

Level 1 is the designation of an instructor just starting to teach. Normally, Level 1 instructors do a three-to-five-day clinic before being tested and need to be able to do parallel turns. A very high percentage pass. The ones who do not pass must retake the clinic and get retested. Level 1 instructors teach beginning skiers, either adults or children.

Level 2 is an accomplished ski instructor who has the skills to ski up to and including dynamic parallel skiing on black diamond runs. Level 2 instructors usually have two or more years of teaching experience and hundreds of hours, either in clinics or shadowing instructors who most often are Level 3 instructors. In our ski school, we have a mentoring program where anyone who wants to can get advice and hands-on help while they work their way up the certification process. I earned this certification in 1965.

Level 3 is an expert instructor who is capable of skiing and teaching on all mountains and all ski conditions. I earned this certification in 1966 and recertified in 1992. Originally, you needed to be a Level 3 in order to be a director of a ski school.

In response to the rise of snowboarding, PSIA created the American Association of Snowboard Instructors (AASI) in 1997. AASI has become a critical part of snow sports schools and contributes to creating future generations of snowboarders.

I want to comment on two issues that can create some confusion for skiers. The first is that not all ski areas use instructors who are certified by the PSIA-AASI. Some of this is historical. At the time that PSIA was founded, it aligned with those ski areas that were leasing federal land. A high percentage of those ski areas became PSIA ski schools, requiring all their instructors to become PSIA certified. But many ski areas, particularly the smaller and/or newer ones, are on private land. As a result, some of them chose to create their own philosophy and system.

As a consumer, I encourage you to look at the ski school website and learn more about who you are being taught by and what experience and certification they have. It can still happen today that you learn one technique at one ski area, and then something else at another, if you are shifting between PSIA-AASI ski areas and those that are not.

What I love about the PSIA-AASI system is that it acknowledges the ecosystem between teaching skills, people skills, and technical skills, with the student at the heart of it.

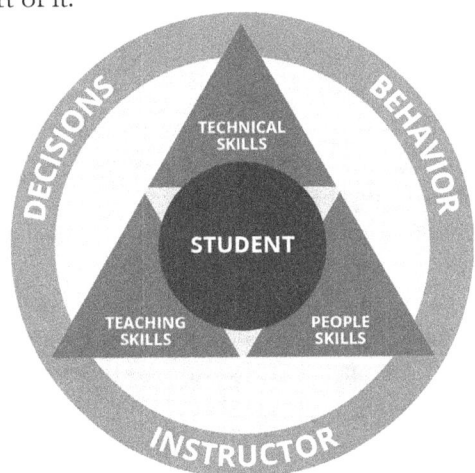

Learning Connection diagram courtesy of PSIA-AASI

The second area of confusion is how trail difficulty is assessed in the United States and Canada. If you have ever visited a ski area, you will see that all trails are coded with these symbols:

●	easiest	Green circles are the easiest runs on that mountain with a gentle slope and no obstacles.
●●	easy	
■	moderate	Blue squares are moderate runs on that mountain with a moderate slope and very few obstacles.
■■	more difficult	
◆	very difficult	Black diamonds are the most difficult runs on that mountain with very steep slope and potentially many obstacles.
◆◆	extremely difficult	
◆◆◆	dangerous	Skiing beyond your skill level can result in serious injury or even death.

The confusion comes from the fact that the color system is only for **that particular mountain** where you are currently skiing. For example, Afton Alps in Minnesota has green, blue, and black runs but the mountain only has a vertical drop of 400 feet. While Big Sky, Montana has a vertical drop of over 4,000 feet. A black diamond at Afton Alps will not compare at all to one at Big Sky and a newer skier can quickly find themselves in trouble.

Many resorts now use multiples of the symbols, so a double blue square is more difficult than a single blue square. At Big Sky, we use double black diamonds and triple black diamonds to indicate extremely difficult runs. These are generally what is referred to as "No Fall Zones," which means, if you fall, you will have a slide that has the potential to kill you. Most people skiing these runs are skiing with certified alpine guides and have to pass a rigorous pre-skiing test before they attempt the runs.

Several ski areas now offer a version of mountain guide lessons where Level 2 and Level 3 instructors will show you around the mountain. It is a great investment that will not only help you improve but will also keep you safe. Nothing ruins a vacation like a hospital stay.

I recently had the opportunity to ski with the Chair of PSIA's Board of Directors, Eliza Kuntz. As part of an article I was writing for the PSIA-AASI magazine, *32 Degrees*, I had decided to ski all of Montana's ski areas with my colleague and friend, Rich Noonan, a fellow Level 3 instructor. Read more about our adventures in Chapter 28.

We reached out to Eliza, who was the General Manager (and former ski school director) at Red Lodge, Montana. She invited us to come ski with their current ski school director and we made the two-hour drive from Bozeman.

Red Lodge, Montana is one of the most iconic ski areas in the west. It lies at the intersection of the Beartooth Mountains, which run east to west, and the Big Horn Mountains, which run north to south to Wyoming. This geological intersection results in one of the great snow patterns in the ski industry. It is not uncommon for storms passing through Montana to get hung up here and dump 36 to 48 inches of snow overnight. I can remember a storm that dropped eight inches of snow at Big Sky and 40 inches at Red Lodge the next day. Many Bozeman skiers took off to ski that epic snow at Red Lodge.

We arrived and met with Craig Beam, the Ski School Director. We were looking forward to skiing the mountain with him but we were in for a pleasant surprise when we were joined by most of their ski school staff! It was a light day and people were free so we enjoyed a great afternoon of camaraderie with our fellow PSIA-AASI instructors. Red Lodge has produced many fine instructors because Eliza instituted a groundbreaking apprentice instructor program that allows people the option of attending a very affordable three-day training clinic with an instructor. It was such a positive experience that many people were inspired to continue their growth and become certified instructors.

A great day skiing with members of the Ski School at Red Lodge Mountain, Montana

Eliza is now the Chair of the Board of Directors of PSIA and a long-time member of PSIA-NRM. She is one of the highest ranking women in the ski industry and a true north star for the modern client-based teaching system currently being implemented throughout the ski world. This new system will be showcased by the PSIA Demo Team at the 2023 Interski event in Finland.

The PSIA Demo Team is a big deal and the handful of instructors are chosen through a very competitive process. We are really proud of the fact that Big Sky has three PSIA Demo Team members on our ski school team!

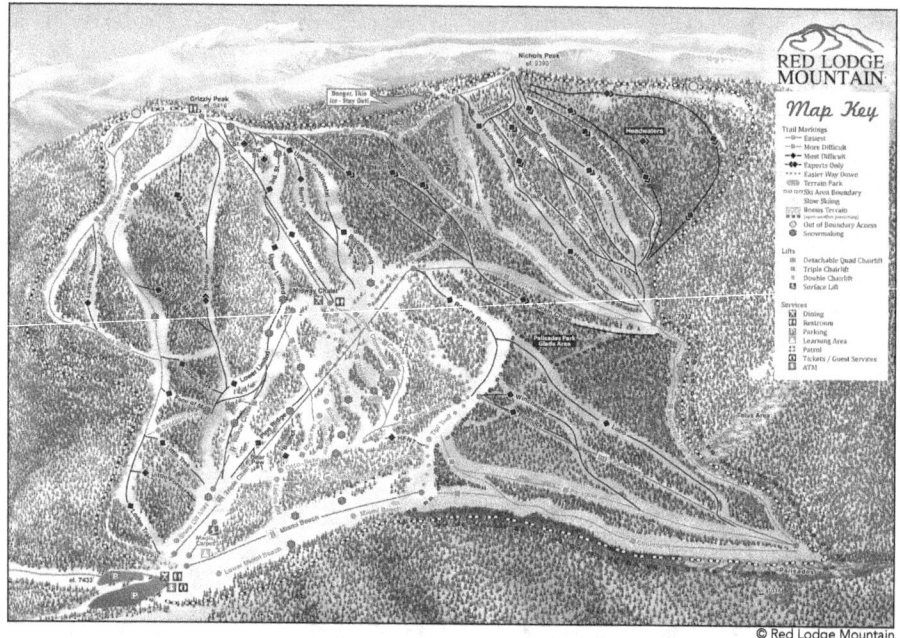

Red Lodge Mountain
Red Lodge, Montana

- Founded in 1960 by Grizzly Peak, Inc., a group of Montana skiing enthusiasts. With 1,635 skiable acres, it is located in the Custer Gallatin National Forest.
- There are 7 lifts, a vertical drop of 2,400 feet and an average annual snowfall of 250 inches. Red Lodge has two terrain parks for freestyle enthusiasts.
- They offer private and group lessons for children and adults.
- Learn more at RedLodgeMountain.com.

Chapter 28

2015-2016: Tour of Montana Ski Areas

Bozeman, Montana
45.6770° N, 111.0429° W
Elevation: 4,793 Feet (1,461 M)

In the fall of 2015, Rich and I decided to ski all the ski areas in Montana. And since I was the President of the Northern Rocky Mountain division of the PSIA-AASI, we thought we should visit all the member snow sports schools in the division as well. There are 16 ski areas in Montana; not all are member ski schools, but most are. Add to that the remaining five member snow sports schools in neighboring states and you can quickly see we had our work cut out for us. Oh, and one in Garmisch, Germany, but we didn't want to drive that far!

When we first started talking about skiing all of Montana's ski areas, it seemed so easy; we would be done within a month. We thought that with a focused itinerary, 30 days should be plenty of time to ski them all. We blocked out January from our teaching schedules and started planning. But the logistics quickly became a nightmare because most of these ski areas are not open every day of the week and our regular clients at Big Sky kept asking for lessons with us.

On Friday, January 8th, we started out by skiing Bridger Bowl, just 17 minutes from where we both live in Bozeman. Bridger is undoubtedly one of the best "town" ski areas in America. It is a not-for-profit area that has not only survived the last three recessions, but has thrived because it adopted a pay-as-you-go fiscal plan. If they have enough money to pay for a new lift, it gets built.

Bridger has some of the best low-angle tree skiing in Montana. Rich and I are both alumni of the Bridger Bowl Snowsports School, so we thought we really knew the mountain, but they've added several new lifts and the layout has changed dramatically. Thankfully, Rich's friend, Ric Blevins, joined us and pointed out all the new and spectacular things going on at this ski area. Some very clever glading has re-oriented the traffic pattern and makes for a great skier and boarder experience and some of the best powder snow available.

Next, we traveled to Discovery Basin Ski Area, which is owned by the third generation of the Pitcher family who also founded the mountain. It has one of the best beginner areas we have ever seen, separated from the rest of the mountain with its own lift. It has an incline that's easy for any level of beginner skier to manage. The best part is there are no high-speed skiers entering this area because there isn't any steeper terrain above it.

The backside of the mountain is blue and black terrain and is as challenging as any area we skied. When the snow conditions are good, it is a spectacular place to ski. One of the novel things about Discovery is that they are really committed to adaptive skiing and supporting those who need service animals. Also, the signage is awesome–they've repurposed snowboards and all are positioned to really help guide people around the mountain.

Next up was Showdown, in the Big Belts Mountain Range, near White Sulphur Springs. Driving into the parking lot on a Saturday morning is a lot like traveling in a time machine back to the 1960's. There is a group of people lined up and greeting the customers with, "Welcome to Showdown! We hope you have a great day!" Impressive, to say the least, but then you realize that this is the Snow Sports School staff. What a positive experience to arrive to such a warm welcome.

George Willet, the owner, spotted us and invited us to ski with him and some of his staff. We had an absolute blast with them. The highlight of our trip was witnessing the gifting of 200+ helmets by the Benefis Health System to kids who didn't have one. There were lots of smiles that day as those kids got the equipment they needed to enjoy the mountain safely.

When we returned from skiing Showdown, our quest was put on hold because our clients were requesting our presence for their ski vacations. We finally regained focus and laid out a plan to cover the other ski areas, accompanied by my old friend, Bob Shanks.

We stayed overnight in Kalispell on our way to ski Whitefish Mountain Resort. We arrived to 14 inches of new snow on a beautiful cold, clear day. Bob, who had skied Whitefish when he was in the U.S. Air Force and stationed at Spokane, was totally confused because he'd only ever skied it during "lake effect" foggy days. We skied like crazed people because of our tight schedule. We found really interesting pockets of un-skied, fantastic snow. We were sad to call it quits but we had to head for our next destination, which was a six-hour drive away.

Most of Montana's ski areas are closed some days of the week and the average distance between them is 180+ miles, making some days very long. We drove for six hours from Whitefish only to find out that Bear Paw Ski Bowl was not open for skiing that weekend (thanks Rich!). We made the decision to not let that stop us. In the morning, we drove the last hour and a half on a one-track road, pushing unplowed snow with the front bumper of my trusty Subaru Outback.

When we got there, it was just the three of us and 17 inches of new snow, but we knew we were being watched by the wolverine and mountain lion who had left their fresh prints in the snow. We hiked up and cut tracks on a fantastic day we'll never forget. We got in the car for the four-hour drive to the next area, giggling like teens the whole way. It still makes us giggle today.

Next up was Maverick Mountain Ski Resort in the Beaverhead-Deerlodge National Forest. Their terrain covers 255 acres and is equally split among beginner, intermediate, and advanced levels. Maverick still has that great "mom and pop" feel because they have eschewed big development or commercialization. We had a great morning of fun skiing, stopping at 1:00 pm because we decided to head to Helena to ski the Great Divide Ski Area. We really got excited because we saw that they were open for night skiing every Friday. Skiing two areas on the same day is a pretty big deal in a state the size of Montana.

Snow sculptures at the top of Maverick Mountain

We arrived and were on our skis by 4:00 pm. The day skiers were just leaving and the night skiers started to trickle in—the lights were on and we made our way up the hill. There was a lot of energy and the place was loaded with teenage skiers hitting the fantastic terrain parks. While skiing and riding the lift, Rich commented on the enthusiasm of the kids on the hill. In the meantime, in the day lodge there was live music and adult beverage entertainment.

One of the comments we heard on a chair ride was a teen girl yelling at her friend, "Jason, I hope you fall down and break your head off!" This was followed by a huge crashing sound on one of the terrain features. Rich and I were laughing so hard we could hardly ski down the ramp at the top of the chair. By 7:30 pm, the liquor factor was kicking in on the slopes so we left and drove to the Grubstake Restaurant for a great steak dinner before going to our hotel.

Our next adventure was at Lookout Pass Ski Area with the Idaho-Montana border running through the middle of their day lodge. Lookout is one of the oldest ski areas in the U.S. and has ties to the 10th Mountain Division, with a lovely tribute to the veterans in the lodge.

It was built by the Civilian Conservation Corps (CCC) and the area has always been known for its copious amounts of snow. It is not uncommon to get four-foot dumps overnight. Like a lot of the CCC built areas, the base is a little bit below the current snow line; it was actually raining on the lower mountain—more evidence of climate change. The owner, Phil, calls himself the "king of affordable skiing," and with good reason—they have all kinds of ski and snowboard programs that are innovative and affordable for kids, adults, and seniors alike.

The drive from Lookout Pass to Blacktail Mountain Ski Area was too daunting for an evening so we stayed in Bonners Ferry, Idaho and discovered a pub that was one of the best dinners on our trip. Driving into Blacktail is interesting because the parking lot is on top of the mountain. They have a new day lodge and all operations are from the "top down."

Bob Shanks, me, and Rich Noonan at Blacktail Mountain Ski Area

Sadly, we encountered another flat light day, only this time it was accompanied by howling winds at the top. Flat light happens on cloudy or snowy days when sunlight cannot reach the snow and cast shadows. It's those little shadows that help you read snow terrain well and give you a sense of depth perception. The website SeniorSkiing.com describes it as "skiing inside of a milk bottle."

The good news was that 60 yards down the hill it was relatively calm. This is a really great place to ski if you like scenery—the ski area overlooks Flathead Lake and has incredible views.

Next up was Turner Mountain Ski Area, which is 27 miles north of Libby, Montana. Turner was built in 1961 and, at that time, there was not a single tree on the entire mountain because of a catastrophic 1910 fire that burned almost all of Northern Montana and Idaho. This ski area exists because of the fierce commitment of a group of volunteers who refuse to let it go away—it is funded by lift ticket sales and donations.

The mountain itself can be the absolute best skiing in the state if you catch it on a one-foot-of-new-snow day. It has 2,100 vertical feet of a perfect blue pitch with tree skiing that is lovingly gladed by volunteers who come up in the summer and trim out trees that interfere with lines that they like to ski. That day, the upper two-thirds of the mountain was great skiing! But the bottom was plagued with the aftermath of a warm storm (rain) followed by a hard freeze, so we hit what we called "death cookies" welded down by ice with just enough new snow to hide them. Rich, Bob, and I skied into the day lodge area and burst out laughing because we had just run the gauntlet through them.

Our adventure took us next to Teton Pass Ski Resort. I had been in this area before on a fly-fishing expedition, but had forgotten how rugged this part of the Rocky Mountain range is. We arrived at the day lodge where we met Chuck, the General Manager, Nate, the Snow Sports Director, and his staff of two. They told us that the alternative school from Browning was coming with 50 kids. We were surprised and asked, "How do you handle 50 kids with three instructors?" As he was smiling, it dawned on us that they actually had five that day. So Rich and I jumped in to help.

In 30 minutes or so, they had moved all the beginners to the Magic Carpet and the Magic Carpet riders to the chairlift. By the one-hour mark, all but one was on the chairlift. Nate told us to go ski and check back later. It's always so amazing to be part of the community of instructors.

The coolest thing of our whole trip happened at lunch, when we sat and listened to a teenage girl tell her friend (who had quit) how much fun it was to learn to ski. The raw enthusiasm she had while describing her experience reminded us of what we actually do when we teach someone how to ski or ride. She closed out her talk and asked her friend, "Are you going to try again?" To which he replied, "Probably not." But her final comment was, "Well, I am going up on the chair and I sure wish you could come with me." As we were leaving, I went to the ski school to say goodbye and there he was with Nate, learning to stop with a wedge.

Next, we went to another legendary place, the Yellowstone Club—the only private ski resort in the world. The gate at Yellowstone Club is exactly like going into any private, gated community, except that you're entering a winter wonderland. Lone Peak towers over the complex and the fact that almost all of Yellowstone Club's runs are on a north aspect assures the quality of the snow.

Geoff Unger, their Ski School Director, invited us to speak to their staff and bring them up to speed on the direction of PSIA-AASI-NRM. Of course, we jumped at the chance to do that and have the opportunity to ski the club.

We were there after a storm that dropped 10 to 14 inches of snow, so we eagerly went out to check out the hill. Seven of their key people joined us—the skiing was fantastic and the discussions on the chairlift were lively and enlightening. One of the constants of our Montana Tour was the fact that we skied in a lot of flat light. That day was no exception, and we both had this feeling that we were going to get hammered sooner or later.

For me, it was sooner—I got caught in a compression and, just as I hit the low point in my range of motion, I hit another compression. Thank you, Heidi, for helping me out of the hole I created in your mountain. Rich got his in one of their north facing chutes when both his skis were ripped off in the middle of a turn. But the rest of the day was amazing. If you ever get the chance to ski Yellowstone Club, thank your lucky stars and run, don't walk.

We left early on Saturday and drove to Missoula to ski the Snow Bowl Ski Area, which has hosted the U.S. National Championships and the NCAA National Championships. It's built on two peaks and has a wide range of terrain from Paradise Trail (a three-mile long cruiser) to steep chutes and bowls off the peak.

We went up the mountain and headed to the western part of the ski area. We had phenomenal snow, but virtually no visibility. I wasn't worried, though, because Rich had lived in Missoula and I was confident that he knew the mountain. After getting lost for a second time that morning, I finally asked, "So how long has it been since you've skied here?" "1976!" he replied. So much for a local guide.

We were really getting cold from the wind so we headed to the mountaintop warming hut, which was stocked with firewood and has a great fireplace stove. We decided to head down the mountain, which was a great last run because of the wind deposition in the trees.

As we were leaving Missoula, we realized that we only had one ski area left in our quest. It was tempting to head up and ski it the next day, but we decided to go for the famous "Powder Thursday" experience. We left Bozeman at 6:00 am on March 3, 2016 to ski Lost Trail Ski Area in Sula, Montana.

We arrived at a mountain with eight inches of new snow. This is a great ski area that lies on the state border, between Missoula, Montana and Salmon, Idaho. The ski area was originally built in 1938 as a Boy Scout project with the help of the CCC and then went into private ownership—the Grasser family is its stewards today.

We went directly to the Snow Sports School looking for Stu Hoyt, but he was teaching a telemark clinic. Chris Miller, the Director, introduced us to Jerry Hinman, a lifetime member of NRM and we hustled out to ski a couple of runs before lineup. We arrived at the top and skied the south face in windblown, variable snow conditions. It was challenging and fun skiing.

Lost Trail has five chairlifts and three are running on Powder Thursdays. We got to ski their fantastic gladed terrain. They had a large beetle kill and the U.S. Forest Service came in and logged the dead trees out as part of a fire prevention project. I suspect Stu and Jerry, who are both retired foresters, had a hand in that. I am not quite ready to say that we saved the best for last, but I will say that I will be asking for Thursdays off in my teaching schedule for next year.

We put 4,500 miles on my Subaru and each one was well worth it. It was the best ski season we have ever experienced for a myriad of reasons—from the camaraderie with each other and people we met, to the joy of playing in the snow, to our re-connection to the variety of snow sports in America.

If you learned at a town area and are still skiing there, you are blessed, and we encourage you to expand your horizon; go to a destination resort just so you can see the power of your skills and knowledge. If you learned to ski at a big time resort, and that is the only place you ski, you need to go to a small, local ski area to immerse yourself in the regional vitality and passion.

Each area has its own flavor with a full complement of challenges for every level of skier. If you're lucky, and the weather cooperates with you, each one is capable of offering an epic ski day you will talk about for the rest of your life. We are so grateful for this wonderful adventure we shared together.

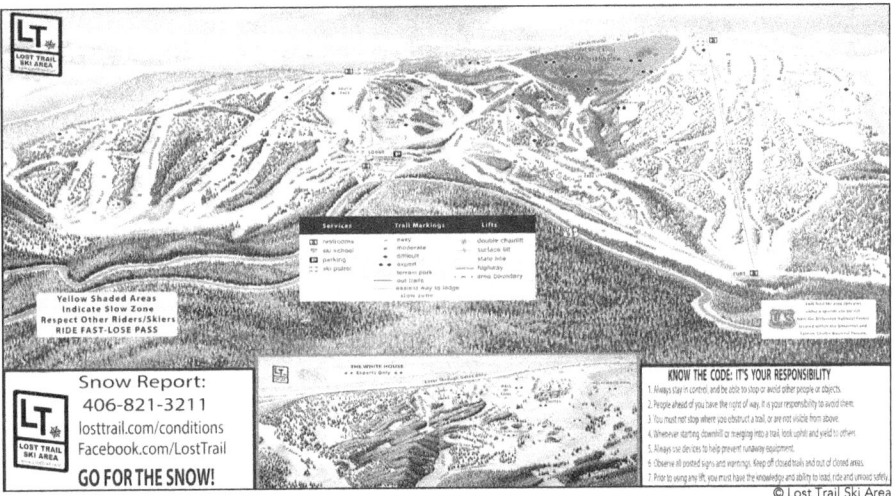

Lost Trail Ski Area
Sula, Montana

- Founded in 1938 and currently owned by the Grasser family, Lost Trail currently boasts 60 runs over 1,800 skiable acres in the Bitterroot Mountain Range on the Montana/Idaho border.
- There are 8 lifts and a vertical drop of 1,800 feet. The average snowfall is 325 inches and they are part of the rich history of Lewis and Clark's expedition.
- They offer private and group lessons for children and adults.
- Learn more at LostTrail.com.

Chapter 29

2019-2021: The Pandemic

Big Sky, Montana
45.2857° N, 111.4012° W
Base Elevation: 6,800 Feet (2,073 M)
Peak Elevation: 11,166 Feet (3,403 M)

The Winter of 2019-2020 began with a bang. Over the Halloween weekend, a storm came in and snowed for about 72 hours. We normally have a great Indian summer, but it never really warmed up and Big Sky opened on Thanksgiving Day with a great base of natural snow augmented by their extensive snow making. Our fall clinics were fun because we were skiing on our "good skis" instead of the normal "rock skis" we start the season with.

The snow sports instructors were excited because over the summer, our Manager, Troy Nedved, had been promoted to General Manager and Christine Baker, our longtime Children's Ski School Supervisor, was promoted to Vice President of Mountain Operations. They, in turn, hired a new Adult Ski School Supervisor to help manage the group lesson instructors. Paul Mannelin had worked for years as a ski coach and trainer in our ski school, so he was not thought of as "the new guy," but a trusted colleague. Paul had an extensive amount of project management in the construction business in Florida. He was a rock star and really great about placing clients into the correct groups.

Chris Jones, our Private Lessons Supervisor, was really good at recognizing the skill sets of the adult instructors and pairing up the assigned private lesson clients with the appropriate instructor. Things were running really well and we got through the winter holiday crush with hardly a hiccup.

We have a program at Big Sky called "Master the Mountain," which is a multi-week program for the locals who want to learn how to enjoy the complex mountain. Big Sky is the largest ski resort in North America with four mountains with 300 runs connected by 39 lifts. The mountain is nicely balanced with the terrain split among beginning (23%), intermediate (25%), advanced (34%), and expert/extreme (18%). Locals like this program because they can ski with an instructor and improve their skills, with their goals often being the ability to ski off-piste, in the glades, and onto the steeper pitches of Lone Peak, which has runs dropping from 300 degrees around the summit.

One of my clients from the previous year called me and asked, if she put together a group of six, would I lead their group. Very flattering to say the least. I said yes, but she needed to choose carefully, because ski ability and social interactions are diverse, and we had seen some of these groups blow up because someone in the group skied too slow or tried to dictate what they wanted over the desires of the group.

I was fortunate because my group was absolutely a great fit and we had the best time. All improved to the degree that they were skiing blue/intermediate runs at fast speeds and we skied several difficult/black diamond runs, including Moonlight and Midnight off the Challenger lift. At the end of the season, one of the groups hosted a dinner party for the members and their spouses. They all still ski together and I see them all the time out and about on the mountain.

My second group was what I call "The Cruisers." They just like to ski and get better but, for whatever reason, have no interest in really challenging themselves. I always take that group because they are funny, and it's fun to sneak in a few runs that they initially don't want to ski but have fun once they try. I had a former student in this group and she brought her husband, Paul, with her. She is French Canadian and goes by the name of Huggy. They are both full of fun and trickery.

Huggy skis about three levels above where she thinks she is and Paul is about two levels below where he thinks he is. We had a really snowy day and, as usual, I was not wearing a muffler on my face because I hardly ever get cold. We had stopped and Paul asked me why I was skiing with my face exposed and, before I could reply, he said, "Maybe it's because you're protected by the fat in your face." I burst out laughing and Huggy was horrified—she made Paul apologize and scolded him the rest of the day. He never heard the last about that because every time I saw them on the hill I would remind him he thought I had a fat face and it would set Huggy off busting his chops about his comment.

The Master the Mountain program is always in January, and it provides work during the traditionally slow part of the season. Well, that January had no slow season, because we had joined the Alterra Group, who created the Ikon Pass, their version to compete with Vail's Epic Pass. The Ikon Pass offers skiers a season pass at their home ski areas, and three to seven days at a menu of 30+ different ski areas. For example, people from Salt Lake City could get their annual pass to Brighton and get seven days at Big Sky, five days at Jackson Hole, and several other areas within driving distance of Salt Lake.

When the Ikon Pass launched at Big Sky, it was messy at first. With the influx of new skiers, parking lots got full and lines got long—the tram lines went from 45 minutes to two hours. Some locals started harassing Ikon Pass holders and there were anti-Ikon bumper stickers showing up on the safety bars on the chairlifts. One sticker even made it to the bar mirror in the base lodge restaurant and the barkeeper lost his job for it. The leadership team sent word to the Big Sky staff that the Ikon Pass was here to stay; the staff should be making sure all skiers were having a first rate experience at Big Sky.

Interestingly, the local businesses were thriving with the influx of new visitors, so their owners were really happy. But that would soon all come to an unexpected end. At the end of January, we began to hear more about the new flu-like virus that was killing people in assisted living places in the Seattle area. In a short time, it was on the news constantly and we were all struggling with what to do to keep ourselves and loved ones safe.

By the end of February, Barb and I were wearing face masks and not going out except to buy groceries. As we entered March, our busiest month for teaching, Barb and I talked about the risks versus rewards of my being exposed to so many people while teaching.

By March 13th, I made the decision that I was done for the year. One of the key reasons was that the state of Washington would be having spring break the next week, which would bring a deluge of younger visitors to the mountain who might not be as concerned or careful. I told my supervisors and they fully supported me. But just two days later, the Boyne Group (that owns Big Sky) and Vail Resorts decided to close for the season. Big Sky closed down on March 15, 2020. Little did any of us know the pandemic was just gearing up. It drove the cancellation of the remaining alpine World Cup skiing events and would go on to cause the postponement of the Summer Olympic Games in Tokyo, Japan.

Big Sky sent a message to all their employees outlining the plan going forward. I will say that the Boyne Group was very generous and most, if not all, of the employees received some form of severance—at Big Sky Mountain Sports, we received 100% of our private lesson pay that was on the books. They also alerted all the employees of programs and unemployment options available due to the Federal Pandemic Relief Act passed by the U.S. Congress.

The new management team in place at Big Sky and the "we take care of our employees" stance that came from Steven Kircher, President and CEO of Boyne Corporation, set the standard for the entire ski industry and many other areas followed this example. In addition, the leadership team was already planning for the next year and how to manage either a normal season or a worst-case scenario. Communications were very clear that Big Sky would be operational for 2020-2021. They put in place many measures to keep us and clients safe. For example, they would limit how much time we would spend in the locker room. Every instructor would have their temperature taken as they entered the building and face masks were in place in all the buildings and on all the lifts.

The lift lines would be set up to mandate social distancing. If you were exposed to or caught the virus, you had to go into a quarantine for 10 days and had to test negative before returning. Big Sky was very generous and would pay you for seven of the ten days. If people ask me how I would grade Big Sky's response to the pandemic, I unequivocally would give them an A+.

Because of our ages and compromised immune systems, Barb and I made the decision that I would not return unless one of the many vaccines being developed at the time became a reality. I sadly realized that it was a very real possibility that I might not return to ski teaching. But the supervisors at Big

Sky Mountain Sports made it clear to me that they wanted me back as soon as I could because I was a key person in the Ski School. When the vaccine became available, I was one of the first instructors vaccinated because of my age. I got my second shot on February 24, 2021, free skied on March 1st, and taught my first lesson of the winter on March 3rd.

My supervisor, Paul Mannelin, made it clear that he was willing to let me have a schedule that was not too exhausting, so I ended up doing a morning-only schedule for March and I taught 23 days. At my exit interview, Paul and Christine Baker told me that they wanted me to come back for the 2021-2022 season. They shared with me their plans to use the senior instructors to help the new hires learn about Big Sky culture and give clinics to help improve their skiing. They also wanted me to teach a clinic to share some of my tips and strategies. Needless to say, I was honored.

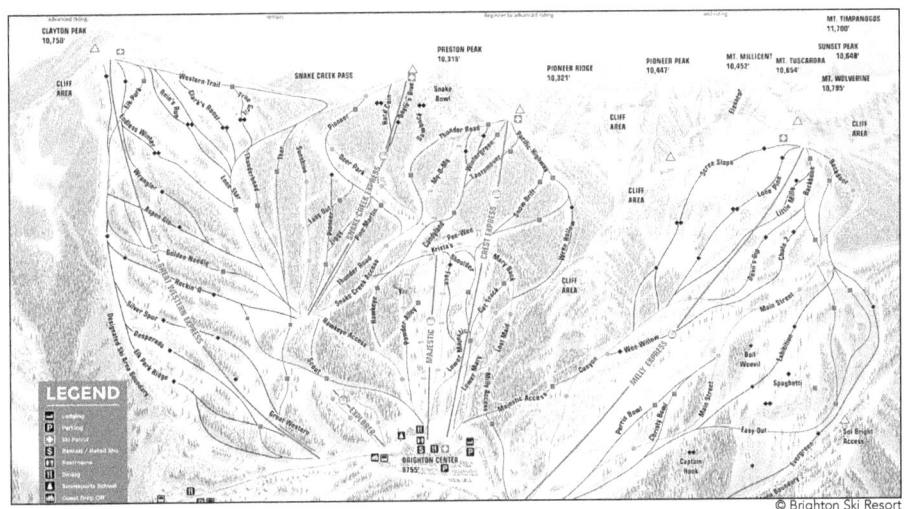

Brighton Ski Resort
Brighton, Utah

- Founded in 1936 when the Alpine Ski Club built the first rope tow, Brighton currently boasts 66 runs over 1,050 skiable acres in the Big Cottonwood Canyon. It's named after a Scottish settler, William Stuart Brighton, who purchased the land in 1871.
- There are 4 lifts and a vertical drop of 1,875 feet. The average snowfall is 500 inches.
- They also have terrain parks, night skiing, snow biking, and naturalist tours with a forest ranger.
- They offer private and group lessons for children and adults.
- Learn more at BrightonResort.com.

Chapter 30

2021-2022: Milestones and Medals

Santa Barbara, California
34.4208° N, 119.6982° W
Elevation: 49 Feet (15 M)

The Winter 2021-2022 season began with earning my 50-year pin. Ursula, Rich and I continued our commutes and we had a great launch to the season. The snow conditions were great and we all taught many lessons over the Thanksgiving and winter holidays.

In January of 2022, I celebrated my 80th birthday and the next day, I accomplished one of my bucket list items—teaching skiing into my 80's. It was with one of my longtime clients and we had a ball skiing on new snow.

Earlier in the morning, Ursula asked if I would make a run with her before lessons. We have been fast friends and ski colleagues since 1991 and when my bad habits sneak back in my skiing, she is the one who fixes me. We laugh now, because the correction is always the same thing she corrected back in the 90's. Even ski instructors need help with their form so never be shy about signing up for a lesson now and then. You'll be amazed at how much it will help you enjoy this wonderful sport.

We jumped on the Ram Charger lift and, when we got off, she asked, "Where should we go?" and I replied, "I don't care." She then said, "You choose." And we burst out laughing because we always say the same thing. We believe that every ski area should have a pair of runs named I DON'T CARE and YOU CHOOSE.

We took off and, as usual, she let me lead the first half and then she passed me to lead the second half. When we got to the bottom she stopped. As I skied up to her, she gave me a big hug and we both were a little emotional realizing that we had been waiting to take a run together for a long time. The absolute best part of skiing is to ski with cherished friends.

We went back to the Mountain Sports School and the word was out. The rest of the day, every ski and snowboard instructor went out of their way to wish me a Happy Birthday! It was a really great day.

As part of my 80th birthday celebration, my fellow instructor, Rich Noonan, and I decided to take off the last week in January to visit the two Colorado ski areas where I learned to ski—Ski Cooper and Monarch Mountain. As I mentioned in the introduction, we were joined by my dear friend, Bob Shanks, and my godson, Tom Hove. It felt full circle to ski on those two mountains where I first learned to ski and discovered something I would love my whole life.

Because Tom had not skied in several years, I asked Rich to give him some tips. Rich is one of the most creative instructors I have ever seen. He took Tom under his wing and, by the end of the trip, Tom was skiing better than ever.

When Tom was in his early 20's, he once asked me for the secret that allowed me to ski away from him and gain ground on every turn. I jokingly told him that was something he should ask when I was on my deathbed and I would tell him then. Well, the last run we skied at Monarch, I tried to ski away from him and couldn't do it. On the way home, I told Rich what had happened—he burst out laughing and I knew then what they had been working on. I replied, with a big smile on my face, "Damn you, Rich! I will never catch up to Tom now!"

After we got back, we settled into our teaching routine with lots of great lessons and clients. February 2022 brought the XXIV Olympic Games at Beijing, China, the first city in the world to host both a summer and winter Games. However, they didn't really have the natural snow or temperatures, which created problems in many events. Athletes from 91 countries competed in 109 events across seven sports with 15 disciplines.

I watched many of these ski events with my daughter, Britt, who had flown out to spend a week with Barb and me. We also spent time working on this book and going through my Olympic pin collection and photos from my career in skiing. It was a great time together—because we didn't meet until she was 32, we still are learning about each other and the lives we have led.

Sync skiing with my daughter, Britt Andreatta, at Big Sky

The International Olympic Committee (IOC) continued to add mixed team events and Beijing saw the debuts of mixed teams in freestyle skiing (in aerials), ski jumping, snowboard cross, and short track speed skating. At previous Games, they had added mixed teams in alpine skiing, parallel skiing, figure skating, biathlon, and curling. They also added women's events in sports that previously only had men's teams. This included Nordic skiing, monobob sled, and big air for freeskiers.

In the skiing events, the buzz about the U.S. Alpine Team was focused on Mikaela Shiffrin. She was expected to medal in more than one of her five events, but she did not finish (DNF) three of her five races. However, a month later in Courchevel, France, Mikaela won the overall World Cup title after winning silver in the Super-G at the Alpine World Cup Finals.

The course at Yanqing National Alpine Ski Centre became known as "Ice River" because the warmer temperatures were causing melts and refreezes. Mikaela was one among 20 or more athletes who slid off the downhill course in the Giant Slalom event. This issue plagued other alpine events throughout the Games.

However, American Ryan Cochran-Siegle won the silver medal in Super-G. Ryan is a member of the famous "Skiing Cochrans" family, which has had members on the U.S. Ski Team in the 1960's, 1970's, 2000's, 2010's, and 2020's. His mother, Barbara Cochran, won a gold medal in the Slalom during the 1972 Winter Olympics in Sapporo, Japan.

She taught Ryan how to ski at the family-owned Cochran's Ski Area in Richmond, Vermont. It was built by her parents (Ryan's grandparents) in 1961 when Mickey and Ginny built their own private ski hill to teach their four kids to ski. Mickey was another WWII veteran, serving with 84th Infantry Division before coming home to be part of launching the ski industry. They were very successful with all four of their kids (Barbara, Bob, Marilyn, and Lindy) skiing at the Olympics, representing the U.S. Team. Ryan is part of the next generation and is one of ten Cochrans who have been on the U.S. Ski Team.

The Cochran's Ski Area has now expanded to serve the local community in Vermont. It offers ski lessons, after school programs, and a ski club. It's a small ski area, but if you have been paying attention to my review of Olympic athletes, you'll notice that many get their start on small, local ski areas. I have no doubt that Cochran's Ski Area will produce more champions in the future, both in and outside of the Cochran family.

In Freestyle, the U.S. Team did exceptionally well, winning the gold in the first Mixed Team Aerials, followed by China (silver) and Canada (bronze). In addition, American athletes won seven more medals. Here are the athletes and also where they learned to ski.

- Colby Stevenson—silver in Men's Freeski Big Air (Park City, Utah)
- David Wise—silver in Men's Freeski Halfpipe (Sky Tavern Ski Area near Reno, Nevada)
- Alex Ferreira—bronze in Men's Freeski Halfpipe (Aspen, Colorado)

- Alexander Hall—gold in Men's Freeski Slopestyle (Zurich, Switzerland)
- Nicholas Goepper—silver in Men's Freeski Slopestyle (Perfect North Slopes, Indiana)
- Megan Nick—bronze in Women's Aerials (Whiteface, New York)
- Jaelin Kauf—silver in Women's Moguls (Vail, Colorado)

As March rolled around, we enjoyed more great winter storms and the spring break hustle as everyone tries to get their last runs in for the season. The season ended with Christine and Paul telling me that they want me back for as many seasons as I wish to ski. And that's what I plan to do. My new bucket list includes earning my 60 year PSIA pin and teaching on my 85th birthday. If you ever come to Big Sky, I hope you'll come find me and say hello.

As the snow melted and returned to the sea, I did too. I flew out to California to visit Britt, Chris, and Kiana in Santa Barbara. We spent a week together doing the final edits to this book and I got to see my Kiana perform in the spring concert for her high school's choir. As I was sitting there, I was so grateful for this precious time we have together. I think the pandemic taught all of us how important family is and that joy is in these moments that we all lost when we couldn't be together.

Working with Britt on the final edits to this book

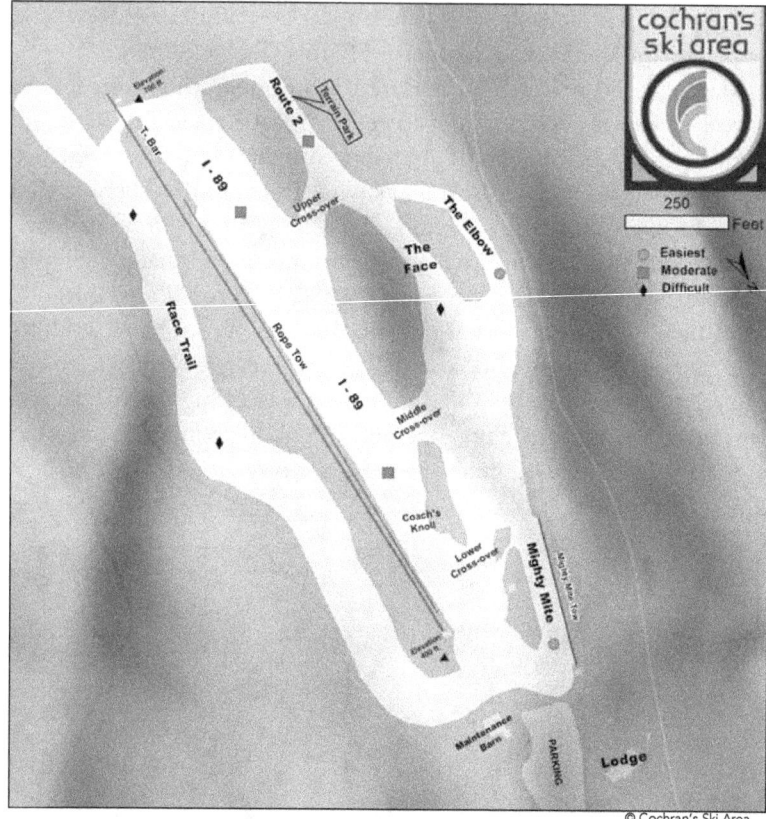

Cochran's Ski Area
Richmond, Vermont

- Founded in 1961 by Mickey and Ginny, Cochran's Ski Area currently offers 6 runs over 30 skiable acres near the Winooski River.
- There are 3 lifts and a vertical drop of 500 feet; the average snowfall is 150 inches.
- Ten of the family members have been on the U.S. Ski Team and six have skied in the Olympic Games—Barbara (1972), Marilyn (1972), Bob (1972), Lindy (1976), Jimmy (2006, 2010), and Ryan Cochran-Siegle (2022).
- Their mission is "No child will be denied the opportunity to ski or ride." Cochran's is a non-profit organization and they offer a series of affordable programs and scholarships. They provide training for eight local high schools and host weekly races.
- They offer private and group lessons for children and adults.
- Learn more at CochranSkiArea.com.

As I wrap up these stories, I realize how lucky I have been in my life and I am thankful for the health and skill set I still have after skiing for 70 years and teaching for 66 years. As I wrote this book, I realized that the most important part of this story is the family, friends, and colleagues I have had the privilege of getting to know and work with. Every adventure and experience I have had came about because of great people who did amazing things to create the ski industry. I was so lucky to meet and work with all of the people I have mentioned—they taught and mentored me, opened doors for me, and supported me every step of the way.

Most of all, I am thankful for Barb and her love. Without her, most of these amazing stories would not have happened and I wouldn't have had the joy of sharing them with my best friend and partner.

Barb and I celebrating our 55th wedding anniversary in 2022

I am grateful for this amazing life that skiing has given me and my family. I hope that you will give this amazing sport a try or find something that gives you as much joy as skiing has given me.

"Life is like skiing. Just like skiing, the goal is not to get to the bottom of the hill. It's to have a bunch of good runs before the sun sets."

Seth Godin,
American author and avid skier

ACKNOWLEDGEMENTS

There are many people that I wish to acknowledge, both for their support in writing this book and for the amazing life I have enjoyed in the ski industry.

First of all, to my family:

- My wife, Barb: Thanks for this life you have shared with me and your encouragement throughout the writing of this book.
- My daughter, Britt: Thank you for having the foresight that my ski industry experience might make a readable book. It looks like you might be right. Your skill set and accomplishments are extraordinary. Your work ethos and stamina are beyond compare. This project has been fun and has brought us so much closer.
- My granddaughter, Kiana: This book is for you so you can pass along the family lore to the next generations. Barb and I are so proud of you and confident that you're going to have a great life.
- My son-in-law, Chris: Your computer genius kept me in the game and I am forever grateful to you for being so helpful during the writing this book. But, most of all, I am grateful that you are such a good husband to our daughter and an exceptional father to Kiana.
- My cousin, Tom Eve: Your support and insistence that I should write this book is greatly appreciated and acknowledged. You and your Barb are dearly loved by us.

Next, to my Salida crew: Rick and Auralee Carroll, Lance and Sally Stapleton, Debbie Snow, Karen Decker, Julie Dines, Ben and Shirley Beauregard, Norm Ronald, Joann and John Ordaz, Lynn Funk, Leona Barrera Gil Gallegos, Clarence Bell, Dan Cady, Maggie Arguello, Maggie Martinez, and Mike Phillips. You all mean so much to me and I will be forever grateful that we grew up together.

To Marla and Tanner Cady: Dan was such a big influence on me and my skiing. I'm so glad I can express my love for Dan publicly through this book.

Next, to my ski patrol friends and mentors along the way: Bill Sears, Bob Shanks, Jim Garrick, Scott Stevenson, and Jim Clarke. You each made a big impression on me and patrolling with you was some of the best times in my well-lived ski life.

To my ski instructor colleagues who mentored me and helped my career along the way: Jerry Coffey and Tom Jacobson at Vail as well as Morrie Shepard the Director. Bev Ogilvie, Max Dercum, Jerry Muth, Jack Nagel, Rich Noonan, Ursula Howland, Jill Chumbley, Stu Chumbley, Zoe Mavis, Brenna Kelleher, Heidi Ettlinger, Christine Baker, Emily Nedved, Chris Ohlman, Paul Mannelin, Chris Jones, Connor Kelleher, AJ Oliver, Tony Brown, Morris Jaffee, Terry Schooley, Mike Hickey, Bonnie Hickey, Stu Hoyt, Eliza Kuntz, Andres Shackett, and Heidi Maier. (I am sure I will remember a lot more after this book is published and we'll add you to the next printing.) All of you have made contributions to the sport of skiing and I am positive that I use drills and tricks that I borrowed from you.

To my K2 crew, who make up a great part of my life and all have contributed to the writing of this book: Dick McNamara, Gary Woodruff, and Schultz Greenberg, who provided access to all things K2. Schultz, you are still the best "belly to belly" salesman I have ever seen!

To Jan DeCosse: Thank you for all the many hours you spent editing the manuscript and galleys. I am grateful for your expertise. Jan is a longtime friend. She worked at Montana State University in several capacities including the Dean's Office of the School of Arts and Architecture and the MSU Alumni Foundation, the fundraising arm of the University.

To my daughter, Britt Andreatta: Your project management, editing, and graphic design truly made this book awesome. I hope people will check out all the amazing things you do in your career as an author, speaker, and CEO of Brain Aware Training. Now, let's go skiing!

Dan Egan, author of *30 Years in a White Haze*, a must-read for anyone who skis the steeps. Along with his brother, they are the super stars of Warren Millers films of the high-risk skiing in the 70's and 80's. A friend and colleague who encouraged me to write.

Erik Sheckleton, former President of PSIA, and one of the few instructors certified at the highest level in three disciplines—Alpine, Telemark, and Snowboard. Erik is currently on the Board of Directors for INTERSKI, the international governing body for ski instruction around the world. The next Interski event will be in 2023 in Levi, Finland. I encourage all skiers to access the site and watch the best teachers in the world. Erik is a friend and colleague and always has a friendly word for all of us at Big Sky.

Phil Pugliese, owner of SkiTalk.com: Phil has been generous in sharing his photo archives. He ensures that the early history of skiing and the images of the sport and industry are accessible to authors and researchers. I encourage skiers to visit SkiTalk.com and see how much fun the last 70+ years have been.

Photo Credits:

Cover photo: Courtesy of Crystal Images at Big Sky Resort. Bigskyphotos.com
Section photo: Courtesy of Fletcher Manley, Jr. Fletchermanley.com
All trail maps are copyright of the respective ski areas—see websites for current versions.
Photos on these listed pages are credited to the named photographers or sources:
2 Rich Noonan; 4 Tom Hove; 8 Thelma Tancik; 13 Author; 16 Unknown; 22 Ski USA poster shared by Marla and Tanner Cady; 35 Jebbie Browne; 38 Fletcher Manley Jr.; 47 Jebbie Browne; 52 Fletcher Manley Jr.; 56 Doug Devin; 60 Barb Ewing; 61 Alan Lauba; 67 Author; 73 Dick Swan; 76 Danny Stoffel and CMH Heli-Skiing & Summer Adventures; 81 K2 images courtesy of Heckler Bowker Advertising Agency; 86 Phil Pugliese at SkiTalk.com; 101 John McIntosh; 106 K2 comps poster, photo by John Terence Turner; 107 & 114 K2 images courtesy of Heckler Bowker Advertising Agency; 118 Courtesy of Paul Bussi (2018) Idealphotography.com; 132 Jennifer Burt; 144 and 154 Crystal Images at Big Sky.com; 156 Britt Andreatta; 161 Diagram reprinted with permission from PSIA-AASI, June 2022; 163 and 167 Rich Noonan; 168 Author; 177 Crystal Images at Big Sky.com; 179 Chris Sneathen; 180 Author, 204 Rich Noonan

REFERENCES

Introduction
Investors. (n.d.) *Annual reports*. Vail Resorts. https://investors.vailresorts.com/annual-reports

Skistar. (n.d). *Our industry*. https://www.skistar.com/en/corporate/about-skistar/our-industry/

Colorado Ski Country. (2015, Dec. 9). *Economic study reveals ski industry's $4.8 billion annual impact to Colorado*. https://www.coloradoski.com/media_manager/mm_collections/view/183

International Skiing History Association. (n.d). *Ski resorts years they were founded*. https://www.skiinghistory.org/history/ski-resorts-years-they-were-founded

History of Skiing. (2022, 19 Mar.). In *Wikipedia*. https://en.wikipedia.org/wiki/History_of_skiing

The Steamboat Pilot. (1952, Mar. 6). *Steamboat Skiers Shine At Junior National Championships In Slalom And Downhill Held At Winter Park*. Colorado Historic Newspapers. https://www.coloradohistoricnewspapers.org/cgi-bin/colorado?a=d&d=STP19520306.2.23&e=-------en-20--1--img-txIN%7ctxCO%7ctxTA--------0------

Loveland Ski Area. (n.d). *Trail map*. https://skiloveland.com/the-mountain/trail-map-mountain-stats/

Loveland Ski Area. (n.d). *History*. Ski Loveland. https://skiloveland.com/history/

Chapter 1
Ski Cooper. (n.d). *Mountain stats*. https://www.skicooper.com/mountain-stats/

Ski Cooper. (n.d). *About Cooper*. https://www.skicooper.com/about-cooper/

Forest Service. (n.d). *Ski Cooper Alpine Ski Area*. https://www.fs.usda.gov/recarea/psicc/recarea/?recid=12526

Chapter 2
Isserman, M. (2019). *The Winter Army: The World War II odyssey of the 10th Mountain Division, America's elite alpine warriors*. Mariner Books.

Witte, D. (2015). *World War II at Camp Hale: Blazing a new trail in the Rockies*. History Press.

Fox, P. (2013). *Deep: The story of skiing and the future of snow*. Rink House Productions.

Dercum, E. (1981). *It's easy, Edna. It's downhill all the way*. Sirpos Press.

Uncover Colorado. (2022, Mar. 7). *The US Army's Tenth Mountain Division and Colorado*. https://www.uncovercolorado.com/10th-mountain-division-colorado/

Hart, M. (n.d). The 10th Mountain Division: The ski industry catalyst. *Mountain Town Magazine*. https://mtntownmagazine.com/the-10th-mountain-division-the-ski-industry-catalyst/

Vail Resorts. (n.d). *Building our iconic villages: Vail's history from small town to world-renowned*. https://www.vail.com/explore-the-resort/about-the-resort/about-vail/history.aspx

Warren, G. (Director). 2013. *Climb to glory* [Film]. Warren Miller Entertainment.

Gage, B. & G. (Directors). 1996. *Fire on the mountain* [Film]. Gage and Gage Productions.

Anthony, C. (Director). 2020. *Mission Mt. Mangart* [Film]. Chris Anthony.

SnowBrains. (2022, May 31). *The history of the legendary 10th Mountain Division, the men who started USA's ski industry*. Snow Brains. https://snowbrains.com/10th-mountain-division-history-fire-mountain/

The Storm King. (n.d.). *Winter Warriors: The 10th Mountain Division*. http://thestorm-king. com/Sierra_Stories/10th_Mtn_Division/10th_mtn_division.html
U.S. Army Center. (n.d.). *Po Valley 1945*. https://history.army.mil/brochures/po/72-33.htm
Camp Hale. (2022, April 13). In *Wikipedia*. https://en.wikipedia.org/wiki/Camp_Hale
McNamara, C. (n.d.). *Skiing in America popularized by Tenth Mountain Division WWII veterans*. Show & Tell. https://showandtellworks.com/2016/11/15/tenth-moun-tain-veterans-popularized-american-skiing/
Leonard, B. (2015, Jan. 20). Famous 10th Mountain Division veterans. *Adventure Journal*. https://www.adventure-journal.com/2015/01/the-aj-list-famous-10th-moun-tain-division-veterans/
Case, M. (2021, July 9). *Skiing, Sen. Bob Dole and the Von Trapp Brothers: 10 facts about the 10th Mountain Division*. USO. https://www.uso.org/stories/2396-skiing-sen-bob-dole-and-the-von-trapp-brothers-10-facts-a bout-the-10th-mountain-division
SnowBrains (2022, May 31). *The history of the legendary 10th Mountain Division, the men who started USA's ski industry*. Snow Brains. https://snowbrains.com/10th-mountain-di-vision-history-fire-mountain/
Ski Rose. (n.d.). *Our history above the ordinary*. https://skirose.com/history-of-mt-rose/

Chapter 3
Ski Monarch. (n.d.). *Mountain maps*. https://skimonarch.com/mountain-maps/

Chapter 4
Eagle Scout. (2022, Apr 26). In *Wikipedia*. https://en.wikipedia.org/wiki/Eagle_Scout
Wendell, B. (2018, Feb 8). Bryan on Scouting. *Scouting Magazine*. https://blog.scouting-magazine.org/2018/ 02/08/famous-former-scouts/
Aspen Snowmass. (n.d.). *Trail map*. Aspen Snowmass. www.aspensnowmass.com
Colorado Ski Country. (n.d.). *Aspen Mountain*. Colorado Ski. https://www.coloradoski.com/resorts/aspen-mountain
Town of Snowmass Village. (n.d.). *History*. https://www.tosv.com/253/History

Chapter 5
Colorado Ski History. (n.d.). *Hidden Valley*. http://www.coloradoskihistory.com/lost/ski estespark.html
Farnell, S. (2021, Oct. 4). *Ode to Hidden Valley, Rocky Mountain National Park's ghost town ski area*. https://www.visitestespark.com/blog/post/ode-to-hidden-valley-estes-parks-ghost-town-ski- resort/
National Ski Patrol. (n.d.). *History*. https://nspserves.org/history/

Chapter 6
Arapahoe Basin Colorado. (n.d.). *The mountain*. https://www.arapahoebasin.co m/the-mountain/winter-101/
Arapahoe Basin Colorado. (n.d.) *History of Arapahoe Basin ski area*. ttps://www.arapa-hoeba sin.com/history/
Pomerantz, A. (2020, Feb. 23). Summit County pioneers: Edna and Max Dercum. *Summit Daily*. https:// ww.summitdaily.com/news/summit-county-pioneers-ed-na-and-max-dercum/

Chapter 7
Vail Resorts. (n.d.) *Fact sheet*. https://news.vailresorts.com/mountain/vail/fact-sheet/
Vail Colorado. (2022, Apr 26). In *Wikipedia*. https://en.wikipedia.org/wiki/Vail_Colorado
Hauerman, D. (2002, Aug 24). Ski school from 10 instructors to 1500. *Vail Daily*. https://www.vaildaily.com/news/ski-school-from-10-instructors-to-1500/

Chapter 8
International Skiing History Association. (n.d.) *Ski resorts: Years they were founded*. https://www. skiinghistory.org/history/ski-resorts-years-they-were-founded

My Life in Winters 185

CHNC. (1952, Mar 6). *Steamboat Skiers Shine At Junior National Championships In Slalom And Downhill Held At Winter Park*. Colorado Historic Newspapers. https://www.coloradohistoricnewspapers.org/cgi-bin/colorado?a=d&d=STP19520306.2.23&e=-------en-20--1--img-txIN%7ctxCO%7ctxTA--------0------

Town of Winterpark. (n.d.) *Live, play, or visit*. https://wpgov.com/live-play-visit/

Winterpark Resort. *Home Page*. www.winterparkresort.com

Chapter 9

Yost, C.P. (n.d.). *Sports Safety. Accident Prevention and Injury Control in Physical Education, Athletics, and Recreation*. Ed.gov. https://files.eric.ed.gov/fulltext/ED079293.pdf

Stratton. (n.d.). *Mountain statistics*. https://www.stratton.com/the-mountain/mountain-statistics

Stratton. (2019, Jan 26). Stratton Mountain Resort. *New England Ski History*. https://www.newenglandskihistory.com/Vermont/strattonmtn.php

Chapter 10

Crystal Mountain Resort. (n.d.). *Home Page*. https://www.crystalmountainresort.com

Crystal Mountain Resort. (n.d.). *Winter map*. https://www.crystalmountainresort.com/-/media/crystal/images/2122-images/2122-maps/2122-winter-map-full.ashx

Dunleavy, B. (2019, Dec. 5). *Nearly 4,000 Americans per year injured while using cellphones, study finds*. UPI. https://www.upi.com/Health_News/2019/12/05/Nearly-4000-Americans-per-year-injured-while-using-cellphones-study-finds/7991575559289/

Lyons, G. (1990, April 24). Pickle-Ball—founders of game say paddle sport simply is a barrel of fun. *Seattle Times*. https://archive.seattletimes.com/archive/?date=19900824&slug=1089412

Chapter 11

United States Ski Team. (2022, Feb. 8). In *Wikipedia*. https://en.wikipedia.org/wiki/United_States_Ski_Team

International Olympic Committee. (n.d.). *International Ski Federation*. https://olympics.com/ioc/international-ski-federation

International Ski Federation (FIS). (n.d.). *About*. https://www.fis-ski.com/en/inside-fis/about-fis/general/facts-figures

Beijing 2022. (n.d.). *Beijing 2022 Paralympic Winter Games 04-13 March*. https://www.paralympic.org/beijing-2022/results/medalstandings

Palisades Tahoe. (n.d.). *History runs deep*. https://www.palisadestahoe.com/explore/our-history

Forest Service. (2017, Feb 23). *Forest Service releases videos featuring Julia Mancuso, highlighting Tahoe National Forest and upcoming World Cup at Squaw Valley*. https://www.fs.usda.gov/detail/tahoe/news-events/?cid=FSEPRD533349

Chapter 12

Obituary. (2022, Feb. 20). Yoshitada Nakagawa (Yosh). *The Seattle Times*. https://obituaries.seattletimes.com/obituary/yoshitada-nakagawa-1084461704

American Baptist Churches USA. (2022, Mar. 7). *American Baptist Churches USA celebrates life and ministry of Yosh Nakagawa*. https://www.abc-usa.org/2022/03/american-baptist-churches-usa-celebrates-life-and-ministry-of-yosh-nakagawa/

Billy Kidd. (2021, Nov. 30). In *Wikipedia*. https://en.wikipedia.org/wiki/Billy_Kidd

Phillips, A. (2003, Jan. 12). Werners became first family of Steamboat. *Steam Boat Pilot*. https://www.steamboatpilot.com/news/werners-became-first-family-of-steamboat/

Fetcher, B. (n.d.). *Steamboat Ski Area*. Colorado Ski History. http://www.coloradoskihistory.com/areahistory/steamboat.html

Chapter 13

Lange. (n.d.). *Home Page*. https://www.lange-boots.com/

CMH Bugaboos Lodge. (n.d.). Retrieved May 10, 2022 from https://www.google.com/maps/place/Bugaboos+Lodge/@50.7535439,-116.8369807,11z/data=!4m5!3m4!1s0x0:0x19fd042064365a32!8m2!3d50.7535439!4d-116.7056598

Hans Gmoser. (2022, Feb. 4). In *Wikipedia*. https://en.wikipedia.org/wiki/Hans_Gmoser

Chapter 14

International Skiing History Association. (2022, March 7). *The Legacy of Spider Sabich*. https://www.skiinghistory.org/news/legacy-spider-sabich

CBS News. (2014, Aug. 10). *25 years ago in Virginia, a very different Ebola outbreak*. https://www.cbsnews.com/news/25-years-ago-in-virginia-a-very-different-ebola-outbreak/

Masia, S. (2016, Nov. 18). *K2, Marker, Völkl brands in limbo*. Skiing History. https://www.skiinghistory.org/news/k2-marker-v%C3%B6lkl-brands-limbo

Ancient Skiers (n.d.). *A local ski company achieves global success*. http://www.ancientskiers.com/wp-content/uploads/2014/02/Summer-Newsletter-2015.pdf

VMSD Staff. (2012, July 23). *K2 Skis Booth Fashioning an award-winning booth to highlight the brand's 50-year history*. https://vmsd.com/k2-skis-booth/

Sun Valley. (n.d.). *Home Page*. https://www.sunvalley.com/

Preston, R. (1995). *The Hot Zone: The terrifying true story of the origina of the Ebola virus*. Anchor.

Chapter 15

Ross, B. (2012, Oct.). A Focus on fun: Celebrating 50 years of K2 skis. *Outdoor Japan*. https://www.outdoorjapan.com/regions-in-japan/kanto-region/a-focus-on-fun-celebrating-50-years-of-k2-skis/

SkiTalk.com. (n.d.). K2 Cheeseburger ski lineup. Retrieved June 1, 2022 from https://www.skitalk.com/threads/all-things-k2.1794/

Statista (n.d.). *Number of participants in kayaking in the U.S. 2006-2020*. https://www.statista.com/statistics/191249/participants-in-kayaking-in-the-us-since-2006/

Heavenly Lake Tahoe. (n.d.). *Home Page*. https://www.skiheavenly.com/

Sierra Nevada Geotourism. (n.d.). *Heavenly Mountain Resort Snow Sports Area*. https://sierranevadageotourism.org/entries/heavenly-mountain-resort/ad1bda69-618a-450f-a8d2-ef36bd9d389a

Chapter 16

Free the Powder. (n.d.). *History of skiing*. https://www.freethepowder.com/pages/history-of-skiing

Ski Essentials. (n.d.). *11 most influential skis of all time*. https://www.skiessentials.com/11-most-influential-skis-of-all-time

International Skiing History Association. (n.d.). *Evolution of ski shape*. https://skiinghistory.org/history/evolution-ski-shape

Bode Miller. (2022, March 27). In *Wikipedia*. https://en.wikipedia.org/wiki/Bode_Miller

Loon Mountain. (n.d.). Loon Mountain. https://www.loonmtn.com/

Chapter 17

Darden Executive Education & Lifelong Learning. (n.d.). *Certificate in Business Strategy*. https://www.darden.virginia.edu/executive-education/business-strategy-certificate

Dunfee, R. (2013, June 3). K2, Sun Valley, Aspen & the first wet t-shirt contest. *Curbed*. https://archive.curbed.com/2013/7/3/10223376/k2-sun-valley-aspen-the-first-wet-tshirt-contest

Hanson, M. (2014, Sep. 4). The soul gallery: Bobbie Burns. *Powder Magazine*. https://www.powder.com/stories/soul-gallery-bobbie-burns/

Mutt and Jeff. (2022, April 25). In *Wikipedia*. https://en.wikipedia.org/wiki/Mutt_and_Jeff

Schweitzer. (n.d.). *Trail map*. https://www.schweitzer.com/

Chapter 18

Bids for Olympic Games. (2022, Feb. 28). In *Wikipedia*. https://en.wikipedia.org/wiki/Bids_for_Olympic_Games#Olympic_Winter_Games

Moore, J. (2015, April 7). When Denver rejected the Olympics in favour of the environment and economics. *The Gaurdian*. https://www.theguardian.com/sport/blog/2015/apr/07/when-denver-rejected-the-olympics-in-favour-of-the-environment-and-economics

Olympics. (n.d.). *Lake Placid 1980*. Olympics. https://olympics.com/en/olympic-games/lake-placid-1980

1980 Winter Olympics. (2022, April 13). In *Wikipedia*. https://en.wikipedia.org/wiki/1980_Winter_Olympics#Organizing_Committee

Knight, J. (1979, Dec. 9). The Adman Funds the 1980 Olympics. *Washington Post*. https://www.washingtonpost.com/archive/politics/1979/12/09/the-adman-funds-the-1980-olympics/0bf223d6-d675-4d16-86bb-1f51dd3e8619/

Whiteface. (n.d.). *Home Page*. https://whiteface.com/

Chapter 19

Feeser, R. (2022, Feb. 18). The sport of Olympic pin trading. *CBS News*. https://www.cbsnews.com/news/the-sport-of-olympic-pin-trading/

Olympin. (n.d.). *The world's largest Olympic collectors club*. Olympin Club. https://www.olympinclub.com/

Bids for Olympic Games. (2022, Feb. 28). In *Wikipedia*. https://en.wikipedia.org/wiki/Bids_for_Olympic_Games#Olympic_Winter_Games

History.com Editors. (2021, Sep 1). *Massacre begins at Munich Olympics*. https://www.history.com/this-day-in-history/massacre-begins-at-munich-olympics

Olympics. (n.d.). *Lake Placid 1980*. Olympics. https://olympics.com/en/olympic-games/lake-placid-1980

1980 Winter Olympics. (2022, April 13). *In Wikipedia*. https://en.wikipedia.org/wiki/1980_Winter_Olympics#Organizing_Committee

List of Olympic medalists in figure skating (2022, May 23). In *Wikipedia*. https://en.wikipedia.org/wiki/List_of_Olympic_medalists_in_figure_skating

Alpine skiing at the 1980 Winter Olympics. (2022, March 21). *In Wikipedia*. https://en.wikipedia.org/wiki/Alpine_skiing_at_the_1980_Winter_Olympics

SkiTalk.com. (n.d.). Phil Mahre wins Olympic medal on K2 ski. Retrieved June 1, 2022 from https://www.skitalk.com/threads/all-things-k2.1794/page-2. Photo by K2 staff and originally printed in the October 1980 edition of *Skiing* magazine.

On the Snow. (n.d.). *White Pass Ski Resort*. On the Snow. https://www.onthesnow.com/washington/white-pass/ski-resort

Ski White Pass. (n.d.). *Home Page*. https://skiwhitepass.com/

Meyers, D. (2018, Jan. 25). A look back at history: White Pass opens for skiing. *The Chronicle*. https://www.chronline.com/stories/a-look-back-at-history-white-pass-opens-for-skiing,19937

Chapter 20

Winter Olympics. (n.d.). Olympics.com. Retrieved June 1, 2022 from https://olympics.com/en/olympic-games/

Walker, M. (Jan. 20, 2022). *Women of Winter Sports: The First U.S. Olympic Ski Medalists*. Retrieved June 1, 2022 from https://blogs.loc.gov/headlinesandheroes/2022/01/women-of-winter-sports-the-first-u-s-olympic-ski-medalists/

Wiegand, J. (2022, June 7) Lindsey Vonn Voted into U.S. Olympic & Paralympic Hall of Fame. *Ski Magazine*. https://www.skimag.com/news/lindsey-vonn-us-olympic-hall-of-fame/

Mikaela Shiffrin (2022, June 1). In *Wikipedia*. https://en.wikipedia.org/wiki/Mikaela_Shiffrin.

Olympic medalists in alpine skiing (Feb. 28, 2022). In *Wikipedia*. https://en.wikipedia.org/wiki/List_of_Olympic_medalists_in_alpine_skiing

Olympic medalists in freestyle skiing (April 16, 2022). In *Wikipedia*. https://en.wikipedia.org/wiki/List_of_Olympic_medalists_in_freestyle_skiing

Shalam, B. & Falk, B. (Sept. 27, 2021). *What we can learn from the female [trail]blazers of alpine skiing since 1924 through the present.* History of skiing and snowsports. https://scholarblogs.emory.edu/historyofskiing/2021/09/27/what-we-can-learn-from-the-female-trailblazers-of-alpine-skiing-since-1924-through-the-present/

Professional Ski Instructors of America (n.d.). *Alumni teams*. Retrieved June 1, 2022 from https://www.thesnowpros.org/who-we-are/teams/alumni-teams/

Chapter 21

National Ski Areas Association. (n.d.). *Industry Stats*. NSAA. https://www.nsaa.org/NSAA/Resources/Indust ry_Stats/NSAA/Media/Industry_Stats.aspx?h-key=8247ed3b-e20e-46d2-9c5d-36b92782c297

Tagliabue, J. (1984, Feb. 20). Mahre twins win slalom medals as the Olympics end in Sarajevo. *The New York Times*. https://www.nytimes.com/1984/02/20/sports/mahre-twins-win-sla lom-medals-as-the-olympics-end-in-sarajevo.html

Olympics. (n.d.). *Sarajevo 1984 Alpine Skiing Results*. Olympics. https://olympics.com/en/olympic-games/saraj evo-1984/results/alpine-skiing

Olympics. (n.d.). *Calgary 1988 Alpine Skiing Results*. Olympics. https://olympics.com/en/olympic-games/calga ry-1988/results/alpine-skiing

Debbie Armstrong. (2021, Dec. 7). In *Wikipedia*. https://en.wikipedia.org/wiki/Debbie_Armstrong

Egan, D. & Wilbur, E. (2021). *Thirty Years in a White Haze: Dan Egan's Story of Worldwide Adventure and the Evolution of Extreme Skiing*. Degan Media, Inc.

Warren Miller. (n.d.). *Film Archive*. https://warrenmiller.com/film-archive

The Summit at Snoqualmie. (n.d.) *Alpental*. https://summitatsnoqualmie.com/alpental

Griffin, James. (n.d.). *Alpental—The Beginning*. Summit at Snoqualmie. https://summitatsnoqualm ie.com/Documents/Summit/general/Alpentals-Story.pdf

On the Snow. (n.d.). *Alpental Ski Resort*. https://www.onthesnow.com/washington/alpental/ski-resort

Chapter 22

Olympics. (n.d.). *Albertville 1992*. https://olympics.com/en/olympic-games/albertville-1992

U.S. Ski and Snowboard Hall of Fame. (n.d.). *Hall of famers*. https://skihall.com/hall-of-famers/

Beijing 2022. (2022, Feb. 4). Freestyle skiing 101: Olympic history. *NBC Olympics*. https://www.nbcolympics.com /news/freestyle-skiing-101-olympic-history

Olympics. (n.d.). *Lillehammer 1994*. https://olympics.com/en/olympic-games/lillehammer-1994

Warren Miller. (n.d.). *Film Archive*. https://warrenmiller.com/film-archive

Olympics. (n.d.). *Nagano 1998 Freestyle Skiing Results*. https://olympics.com/en/olympic-games/nagano-1998/results/freestyle-skiing

Brown, J. (n.d.). The scars of skiing's past. *Tahoe Quarterly*. https://tahoequarterly.com/ski-ride-2018/scars-skiings-past

Isaac, A. S. (2021, Oct.). *U.S. ski resorts in operation during 2020/21 season*. National Ski Areas Assocation. https://nsaa.org /webdocs/Media_Public/IndustryStats/ski_areas_per_season_thru_2021.pdf

Pope, K. (2019, Aug. 15). A complete list of every mountain Vail Resorts has ever purchased. *5280 Denver's Mile High Magazine*. https://www.5280.com/2019/08/a-complete-list-of-every-mountain-vail-resorts-has-ever-purchased/

TaylorMade. (2022, March 4). In *Wikipedia*. https://en.wikipedia.org/wiki/TaylorMade

Chapter 23

Olympics. (n.d.). *Salt Lake City 2002 Results*. https://olympics.com/en/olympic-games/salt-lake-city-2002/results/

Warren Miller. (n.d.). *Film Archive*. Warren Miller. https://warrenmiller.com/film-archive

Pope, K. (2019, Aug. 15). A complete list of every mountain Vail Resorts has ever purchased. *5280 Denver's Mile High Magazine*. https://www.5280.com/2019/08/a-complete-list-of-every-mountain-vail-resorts-has-ever-purchased/

Beijing 2022. (2022, Feb. 4). Freestyle skiing 101: Olympic history. *NBC Olympics*. https://www.nbcolympics.com/news/freestyle-skiing-101-olympic-history

New Shoolers. (n.d.). *How Vail's EPIC pass changed the game*. New Schoolers. https://www.newschoolers.com/news/read/How-Vail-EPIC-Pass-Changed-Game

Parks & Trips. (n.d.). *Current & historic EPIC lift pass prices*. https://parksandtrips.com/current-historic-epic-lift-pass-prices/

Vail Resorts. (n.d.). *Annual reports*. https://investors.vailresorts.com/annual-reports

Epic or Icon. (n.d.). *Epic vs Ikon decide which pass is better for you*. https://epicorikon.com/

Buck Hill. (n.d.). *Home page*. https://www.buckhill.com/

Buck Hill. (n.d.). *Buck Hill history*. https://buckhill.com/buck-hill-history/

Brown, C.A. (2019, Jan. 3). *The coaching legacy of Buck Hill's Erich Sailer*. SkiRacing.com. https://skiracing.com/legend-of-the-flatlands-the-coaching-legacy-of-buck-hills-erich-sailer

Chapter 24

Big Sky Resort. (n.d.). *Our methodology*. https://bigskyresort.com/mountain-sports/our-methodology

Big Sky Resort. (n.d.). *Big Sky Resort historic timeline*. https://bigskyresort.com/2025/historic-timeline

Chapter 25

Ski lift. (2022, May 6). In *Wikipedia*. https://en.wikipedia.org/wiki/Ski_lift

Kuta, S. (2021, Feb. 2). The invention of the ski lift. *Smithsonian*. https://www.smithsonianmag.com/innovation/how-railroad-engineer-from-nebraska-invented-worlds-first-ski-chairlift-180976878/

Gondola life (May 26, 2022). In *Wikipedia*. https://en.wikipedia.org/wiki/Gondola_lift https://liftblog.com/about/

Jackson Hole. (n.d.). *Lift and trail status*. https://www.jacksonhole.com/maps/mountain-winter

Jackson Hole. (n.d.). *Jackson Hole history*. https://www.jacksonhole.com/history

Chapter 26

The Ski Diva. (n.d.). *If you're a woman who loves to ski, you've come to the right place!*. https://www.theskidiva.com/

The Ski Diva. (n.d.). *Forums*. https://www.theskidiva.com/forums/index.php?threads/congratulations-ursula.18815/

Clinch, W. (2017, April 25). *EpicSki is shutting down*. https://www.theskidiva.com/rest-in-peace-epicski-is-shutting-down/

Pugliese, P. (2017, April 24). *Remembering EpicSki.com*. https://www.skitalk.com/threads/remembering-epicski-com-1999-2017.4742/

Bousquet Mountain. (n.d.). *Home Page*. https://bousquetmountain.com/

New England Ski History. (n.d.). *Bousquet Mountain Ski Area*. https://www.newenglandskihistory.com/Massachusetts/bousquet.php

Chapter 27

Professional Ski Instructors of America (n.d.). *History*. https://www.thesnowpros.org/

Ski Museum (n.d.). *Doug Pfeiffer*. https://skimuseum.ca/honoured-members/doug-pfeiffer/

Ski Hall of Fame. (n.d.). *Paul Valar*. https://skihall.com/hall-of-famers/paul-valar/

Kray, P. (2011). *American Snow: The snowsports instruction revolution.* Professional Ski Instructors of America and American Association of Snowboard Instructors (PSIA-AASI)

Red Lodge Mountain. (n.d.). *The mountain.* https://www.redlodgemountain.com

Chapter 28

Bridger Bowl. (n.d.). *Home Page.* https://bridgerbowl.com/
Showdown. (n.d.). *Home Page.* https://www.showdownmontana.com/
Whitefish Mountain Resort. (n.d.). *Home Page.* https://skiwhitefish.com/
Visit Montant. (n.d.). *Bear Paw Ski Bowl.* Visit Mt. https://www.visitmt.com/listings/ski-area/downhill-ski-area/be ar-paw-ski-bowl
Maverick Mountain. (n.d.). *Home Page.* https://skimaverick.com/
Mount Helena City Park. (2021, March 19). In *Wikipedia.* https://en.wikipedia.org/wiki/Mount_Helena_City_P ark
Lookout Pass. (n.d.). *Home Page.* https://skilookout.com/
Blacktail Mountain Ski Area. (n.d.). *Home Page.* https://blacktailmountain.com/
Turner Mountain. (n.d.). *Home Page.* https://www.skiturner.com/
Teton Pass Resort. (n.d.). *Home Page.* https://www.skitetonmt.com/
Yellowstone Club. (n.d.). *Home Page.* https://yellowstoneclub.com/
Montana Snow Bowl. (n.d.). *Home Page.* https://www.montanasnowbowl.com/
Ski Discovery. (n.d.). *Home Page.* https://www.skidiscovery.com/
Lost Trail Ski Area. (n.d.). *Home Page.* https://losttrail.com/

Chapter 29

Big Sky Resort. (n.d.). *The Big Sky experience.* https://bigskyresort.com/the-big-sky-experience
Big Sky Resort. (n.d.). *Master the mountain.* https://bigskyresort.com/mountain-sports/local-programs/master-the-mountain
Brighton Resport. (n.d.). *Home Page.* https://brightonresort.com/
Murphy, M. (1996, July,). *Development of Brighton Resort.* https://historytogo.utah.gov/brighton-resort/

Chapter 30

Axon, R. (Feb. 17, 2022). IOC says this is the most gender equal Winter Olympics. But the Games are hardly equal and here's why. *USA Today.* https://www.usatoday.com/story/sports/olympics/beijing/2022/02/17/ioc-touts-gender-equity-mixed-team-events/6824508001/
Olympics. (n.d.). *Beijing 2022 Results.* https://olympics.com/en/olympic-games/beijing-2022/results/
Olympics (n.d.). *Mixed events enrich the Winter Games programme.* https://olympics.com/en/news/mixed-events-enrich-the-winter-games-programme
Poggi, A. (Feb. 19, 2022). *Mikaela Shiffrin leaves Beijing 2022 without a medal.* https://olympics.com/en/news/mikaela-shiffrin-leaves-beijing-2022-without-medal
U.S. Ski and Snowboard Team. (n.d.). *2022 U.S. Olympic Alpine Team.* Retrieved June 1, 2022 from https://usskiandsnowboard.org/alpine
U.S. Ski and Snowboard Team. (n.d.). *2022 U.S. Olympic Freestyle Team.* Retrieved June 1, 2022 from https://usskiandsnowboard.org/freestyle
Fenrich, H. (Feb. 18, 2022). Analysis: Plenty went wrong for U.S. Alpine Skiing at Olympics. *NBC Chicago.* https://www.nbcchicago.com/news/sports/beijing-winter-olympics/analysis-plenty-went-wrong-for-us-alpine-skiing-at-olympics/2763200/
Skiing Cochrans. (Feb. 16, 2022). In *Wikipedia.* https://en.wikipedia.org/wiki/Skiing_Cochrans
Cochran's Ski Area. (n.d.). *Home Page.* https://cochranskiarea.com/

Updated 9.1.23

INDEX

10th Mountain Division iv, 8-14, 24, 32, 34, 50, 65, 91, 93, 126, 127, 133, 139, 167
32 Degrees magazine 162
1896 Olympic Games 111
1948 Olympic Games 116, 122
1948 Olympic Games 116, 122
1952 Olympic Games 116, 122
1956 Olympic Games 41, 67, 116
1960 Olympic Games 67, 116, 122
1964 Olympic Games 116, 122
1968 Olympic Games 58
1972 Olympic Games 103, 120, 122, 180
1976 Olympic Games 103, 122
1980 Olympic Games 3, 103, 104, 107, 112, 124
1984 Olympic Games 121, 122, 124
1988 Olympic Games 125
1992 Olympic Games 122, 125, 130
1994 Olympic Games 122, 131
1998 Olympic Games 122, 131
2002 Olympic Games 122, 132
2006 Olympic Games 117, 122, 136
2010 Olympic Games 117, 122, 136
2014 Olympic Games 61, 117, 122, 137
2018 Olympic Games 61, 62, 122, 117
2022 Olympic Games iv, 58, 62, 93, 99, 103, 106, 109-117, 120-126, 131, 132, 136, 174, 177

A

ABC Television 113
Abu Garcia Company 75
Acrophobia 148, 149
Adam, Sherman 96
Adaptive skiing 158, 166
Adidas 124
Adirondack Mountains National Forest 108
Aerial ski lifts 147
Aerials 62, 125, 131, 136, 147, 150, 178
Afton Alps Resort 138, 139, 162
Agre, Peter 20
Air Force National Guard 39
Ajax Mountain 21, 22, 36
Akia toboggan 37
Alais, Emille 94
Alaska 20, 72, 127, 131
Alaska Airlines 20
Albertville, France 125, 130
Aldrin, Buzz 20
Allais, Émile 58
Allamand, Olliver 130
Almond, Don "Mother" 36
Alpental Ski Resort v, 121, 123, 125, 189
Alpine Combined 62, 116, 125, 130, 136, 137
Alpine skiing 4, 58, 62, 91, 109, 116, 122, 158, 178
Alps 32
Alta turns 46
Alta, Utah 46, 159

Alterra Mountain Company 138
Amateur Sports Act of 1978 121
Amazon 133
American 3, 15, 20, 48, 59, 61, 66-68, 81, 87, 103, 110, 113-117, 120, 125, 133, 140, 158-161, 178, 181
American Association of Snowboard Instructors (AASI) 158, 161, 190
American flag 110
American Teaching System 160
Anderson's Sporting Goods 75
Anderson, Tom 30
Andreatta, Britt ii, iii, 3, 44, 111, 135, 141, 155, 156, 177, 179, 182, 183
Apollo Global 133
Appleton, Wisconsin 134
Arapahoe Basin Ski Area iv, v, 11, 12, 17, 27, 30-34, 42, 50, 55, 56, 133, 148, 160
Arapaho National Forest 5, 44
Armstrong, Debbie 121, 122, 125, 189
Armstrong, Neil 20
Aspen Snowmass Ski Resort v, 11-13, 17, 21-23, 34, 36-39, 61, 78, 100, 134, 139, 159, 160, 178
Astronauts 20
Athens, Greece 111
Atomic Skis 95
A&T Ski Company iv, 3, 9, 48, 52, 64-69, 92
Australia 15, 138, 139
Austria 48, 66, 67, 82, 91, 103, 116-118, 137, 160
Austrian technique 48, 159
Avalanche 11, 26, 30, 32, 41, 46, 48, 51, 67
Average snowfall 5, 10, 14, 18, 33, 44, 50, 57, 70, 89, 96, 108, 115, 128, 135, 146, 151, 157, 171, 175, 180

B

Baby boomers 11, 45, 158
Backcountry skiing 94, 148
Bahrke, Shannon 122, 136, 137
Bainbridge Island, Washington 100
Baker, Christine 119, 172, 175, 179, 182
Baker-Snoqualmie National Forest 57
Bald Mountain Ski Area (aka Sun Valley) 82
Barnes, Robin 119, 122
Bartley, Riley and Hess 20
Beam, Craig 163
Bear Paw Ski Bowl 166, 190
Beartooth Mountains 163
Beattie, Bob 56, 75
Beattie, Jack 75
Beaver Creek Resort v, 40, 127, 139
Beaverhead-Deerlodge National Forest 167
Beconta 75
Beijing, China 60, 99, 117, 120, 177
Benedict, Fritz 13
Bergman, Bill and Jane 135
Bergoust, Eric 131
Bernsten, Hedda 137

Bicycles 88, 134
Big Belts Mountain Range 166
Big Horn Mountains 163
Big Mountain (aka Whitefish) 99, 159
Big Sky Resort, Montana 2, 3, 62, 142, 146, 162, 172
Big Sky Mountain Sports 2, 119, 122, 126, 142, 154, 174
Bill's Ski Shop 9
Birthday 3, 4, 24, 176, 179
Bitterroot Mountain Range 171
Black diamonds 162
Blacktail Mountain Ski Area 168, 191
Blakeslee, Mermer 122
Blevins, Ric 165
Blickensderfer, J.C. 5, 43
Blue squares 162
Bluford, Guilon 20
Boeing 94
Bombard, Jim 120
Borgerson, Mel 48, 53
Boucher, Alexandra Smith 122
Boulder, Colorado 51, 56
Bousquet, Clarence 157
Bousquet Mountain Resort 152, 157
Bowerman, Bill 11
Bowker, Gordon 53, 80
Bowman, Maddie 122, 137
Boyne Group 174
Boy Scouts 6, 15, 170
Bozeman, Montana 57, 119, 130, 141, 165
Bradley, Steve 42, 93
Brantling Ski Center 131
Breckenridge Ski Area 34, 133, 138, 139
Bridger Bowl Ski Area 63, 119, 141, 151, 165
Brighton Ski Resort 175
Brighton, Utah 175
British Columbia v, 71, 72, 76, 99
Bronze medal 99, 116, 117, 122, 130, 131, 136, 137, 178
Brosseau, Ben 2
Brower, David 11
Brown, Bill 40
Brundage, Avery 103, 104, 106, 107, 113
Bucket list 4, 176, 179
Buck Hill Resort v, 45, 61, 141, 190
Buena Vista, Colorado 16
Bugaboos, British Columbia, Canada v, 71
Bulgaria 112
Burke Mountain Ski Academy 62
Burke, Sarah 137
Burnsville, Minnesota 141
Burt, Jennifer 132, 183
Burton, Georgene Dunn 41-44, 47, 119
Bush, George W. 20
Busso, Paul ii, 118, 183
Butte, Montana 99, 137
Butterfield, Russ 65
Button, Dick 111
Byrne, Dee 122

C

Cady, Dan 17, 21-24, 30, 34, 37, 39
Cady, Jack and Jerry 17
Calgary, Canada 125
California ii, 58, 61, 62, 66, 72, 75, 78, 84, 89, 116, 119, 126, 127, 131, 135-138, 149, 159, 160, 176, 179
Campbell, Nancy 141
Campbell, Rod 99
Camp Hale, Colorado 7, 8, 11-13
Canada v, 24, 42, 44, 60, 71-76, 84, 93, 109, 117, 131, 136-138, 150, 162, 173, 178, 183

Canadian Mountain Holidays (CMH) 72, 76, 138, 183
Canadian Ski Team 60, 72
Cannon Mountain Ski Resort 61, 136
Canon Cameras 105
Carmichael, Nelson 130
Carroll, J.B. 142
Carter, Tim 72
Cascade Cement 46
Cascade Mountain Range 115
Cattanach, Shaun 122
Chafee, Rick 120, 182
Chaffee, Suzy 120
Chairlifts 121, 125, 148-150, 169-173, 190
Charlottesville, Virginia 97
Chase, Curt 159
Chase, Ed 107, 114, 120, 124
Cheeseburger ski iv, 83-86, 187
Cheryazova, Lina 131
Chesapeake Bay 156, 157
Chew K2 80, 81
Chile 119, 138, 139
China 4, 60, 99, 117, 120, 140, 177, 178
Chinook 64
Christensen, Joss 137
Civilian Conservation Corps (CCC) 91, 168
Civil Rights Leaders 20
Clark, Earl 12
Clarke, Jim "JC" 34, 41
Clayton, Alison 122
Climate change 43, 127, 133, 168
Clinton, Bill 20
CMH Heli-Skiing 72, 76, 138, 183
Coca Cola 104, 105, 110
Cochran, Barbara 120-122, 178, 180
Cochran family 178, 180
Cochran, Marilyn 53, 56, 66, 120, 121, 178, 180
Cochran-Siegle, Ryan 120, 178, 180
Cochran's Ski Area v, 120, 178, 180
Colgate Darden School of Business 97
Collins, Bob 69, 71
Colorado ii, 2-6, 10-12, 15-19, 21, 23-26, 28-34, 38, 40-48, 51, 56, 59, 62, 66, 70-75, 88, 100, 103, 111, 119, 127, 130-138, 141, 159, 160, 176, 178, 179
Colorado Conservation Corps 16
Colorado State University 24, 27, 30, 31, 50, 69
Continental Divide 43
Cooper, Christin 121, 122, 125
Copper, Bill and Mary Jo 9
Corrock, Susan 122
Cortina D'Ampezzo, Italy 116
Courchevel, France 178
Covid-19 139, 172, 174
Cox, Stephanie 119
Crested Butte Ski Area 139
Croakie eye strap 130
Cronkite, Walter 20
Cross-country skiing 58, 62, 67, 88, 90, 100, 109, 120, 158
Crystal Mountain Athletic Club (CMAC) 58, 61, 62
Crystal Mountain Ski Resort iv, v, 11, 45, 46, 48, 51-69, 81, 119, 155
Cub Scouts 6, 15
Cummins Diesel Company 100
Curran, James 148
Cushing, Alexander 63
Cussler, Clive 20
Custer Gallatin National Forest 164
Czechoslovakia 112, 160

My Life in Winters   193

D

Dannon Yogurt 105, 110
Dartmouth, New Hampshire 131
Dartmouth Skiway 131
Davingon, Al 94
Davis, Herb 2
Davis, Wilfred 12
Dawson, Toby 136
Dealers 75-79, 81-88, 98, 109, 111, 126
Deer Valley Ski Resort v, 128
Deer Valley, Utah v, 124, 127, 128, 139
Denver, Colorado 24, 32, 42, 43, 44, 56, 66, 68, 71, 75, 88, 103, 109
Dercum, Edna 14, 32, 119, 135
Dercum, Max 32, 135, 160, 182, 185
Dercum, Rolf 32, 56
Devin, Doug 48, 52
Devin, Grace 46, 53, 55, 56
Devin, Steve 58, 59
Dick's Sporting Good 133
Dillon, Colorado 30, 33, 138
DIN system 93
Discovery Basin Ski Area 165, 166, 191
Disney World 151
Dole, Charles Minot "Minnie" 12
Douglas Island, Alaska 131
Downhill skiing 14, 32, 58, 62, 67, 93, 94, 109, 116, 117, 122, 125, 130, 131, 137, 147, 178
Dunn, Georgene 41-44, 47, 119
Dynaglass Skis 88
Dynamic Skis 94
Dynastar Skis 68, 94

E

Eaglebrook School 4
Eaglecrest Ski Area 131
Eagle Scouts iv, 16, 19, 20, 185
Eastern Ski Instructors Association 158
East Germany 112
Eaton, Earl 12, 40
Eaton, Gordy 84
Echo Summit Ski Area 132
Ecologist 29, 116, 132
Ed Chase 107, 114, 120, 124
Edelweiss Ski Area 132
Ed's Beds in Aspen, CO 21, 134
Egan, Dan 126, 189
Eisel, Leo 31
Elan Skis 94
El Dorado-Toiyabe National Forest 89
Environmental activist 29, 116, 132
Epic Pass iv, 4, 136, 138, 173, 190
EpicSki website 153
Equipment companies
    Abu Garcia Company 75
    Adidas 124
    Atomic Skis 95
    A&T Ski Company iv, 3, 9, 48, 52, 64-69, 92
    Beconta Ski Company 75
    Cummins Diesel Company 100
    Dynaglass Skis 88
    Dynamic Skis 94
    Dynastar Skis 68
    Elan Skis 94
    Garmisch Ski Boots 9
    Gerry Mountain Sports 34, 69
    Haderer Ski Boots 48
    Head Skis 12, 32, 34, 68, 79, 80, 83, 85, 92
    JanSport 88, 134

Jarden Corporation 139
K2 Skis iv, 3, 39, 44, 65-68, 75, 78-88, 94, 97, 100-107, 109-113, 120-127, 134, 139-142, 149, 183
Killy Skis 58, 88, 155
Kneissl Skis 85
Lange Boots iv, 3, 55, 68-75, 85, 92, 93, 98, 124, 186
La Trappeur Ski Boots 66
Le Coq Sportif 124
Line Ski Company 139
LL Bean 134
Look Bindings 75, 85, 126
Marker Bindings 85, 92, 100, 113, 124, 126, 139, 187
Morrow Snowboards 134
Nike Corporation 11
Nordica Boots 74, 75, 93, 139
Olin Ski Company 95
Orvis 134
Pre Skis 88, 90, 91
Ride Snowboards 134, 138
Roffe and Demetre 126
Rossignol Skis 75, 78, 80-85, 94, 126
Sage Fly Rod Company 100
Salomon Bindings 66, 85, 92, 126, 134, 139
Schwinn Bicycles 88
Serac Ski Clothing 101
Simms Fly-fishing 130, 134, 204, 205
Smith Goggle Company 105
TaylorMade Golf 134
Technica Ski Boots 139
Volant Skis 94
Volkl Skis 75, 139

Eriksen, Stein 100
Estes Park, Colorado 24, 28
Ettlinger, Heidi 122, 182
Europe 24, 34, 65, 125, 138, 139, 149
Ewing, Barbara (Barb) iii, 52-57, 64-69, 101, 109, 113, 130, 134, 135, 141, 150, 152, 174, 177, 181-183
Ewing, Levon and Thelma 6
Exterminator trail 46

F

Fat powder skis 134
Federal Pandemic Relief Act 174
Federation International du Ski (FIS) 118
Ferreira, Alex 178
Ferries, Chuck 68, 80, 84, 87, 88
Fiddle, Nancy 122
Figure skating 109, 178, 188
Filming 94, 113, 125
Finlandia Vodka 111
Fisher, Roman 15, 20
FIS World Cup 58, 59, 120, 125
Flathead Lake 168
Flat light 168
Florida 172
Fly-fishing 100, 133, 134, 169
Forbes, Dana 119
Ford, Gerald 20
Forest Service 11, 41, 45, 65, 67, 158, 159, 170
Forever Trail 37
Fort Collins, Colorado 26, 31, 55, 69
Fort Drum, New York 13
Foster, Ellen Post 122
Fowler, Jack 102
Fox, Harvey 75
France 58, 68, 88, 91, 99, 125, 130, 137, 139, 155, 160, 178
Franko, Jurij 94
Fraser, Gretchen 116, 117, 122

Freeski Big Air 178
Freeski Halfpipe 178
Freeski Slopestyle 179
Freestyle skiing iv, 14, 40, 62, 84, 121-125, 130, 131, 136-139, 158, 164, 178
French technique 58, 88, 94, 155, 159, 173
Friends of the Earth 11
Fritz, Joel 35, 37
Funiculars 148
Funifors 150
Funitels 150

G

Gallatin Gateway, Montana 152
Gallatin National Forest 146, 164
Garmisch, Germany 165
Garmisch Ski Boots 9
Garrick, Jim 45
Garrison, Jim 86, 87, 97
Gart Brothers 88
Gart, Jerry 88
Gates, Bill 20, 60
Georgetown, Colorado 31
German Sports Department 152
German technique 159
Germany 8
Gerry Mountain Sports 34, 69
Giant slalom 58, 59, 62, 67, 94, 109, 116, 117, 120-125, 130, 136, 137, 178
Global warming 43, 127, 133, 168
Globe 120
Gmoser, Hans 72-76, 138, 186
Godin, Seth 181
Goepper, Nicholas 137, 179
Golden, Diana 122
Gold medal 1, 32, 41, 58, 71, 100, 111-117, 120-125, 130, 131, 136, 137, 178, 179
Gondola 34, 36, 42, 150
Gordinier, Barry 83, 105
Gorsuch, Renie 119
Gorsuch Ski and Sports Shop 119
Graham, Gordon 151
Grasser family, 171
Graves, Linus Oliver and Helen 44
Great Divide Ski Area 167
Green circles 162
Green, Ernest 20
Green Mountain National Forest 50
Grenoble, France 58, 88
Griffin, James 123
Groenvold, Audun 137
Grospiron, Edgar 130
Groswold, Thor 32
Gunbarrel 20, 21, 25

H

Haderer Ski Boots 48
Hahnenkamm Ski Race 67
Hall, Alexander 179
Hamill, Dorothy 111
Hamilton, Scotty 111
Hannes Schneider Arlberg technique 91
Hannon, Kerrie 122
Harriman, Averell 108
Harvard University 86, 87, 97
Harvey-Fry, Katie 122
Harvey, Megan 122
Hastings, Merrill 12
Hattestad, Stine Lise 130

Head, Howard 12, 92
Head Skis 12, 32, 34, 68, 79, 80, 83, 85, 92
Heavenly Ski Resort v, 89, 138
Heavenly Valley Ski Area 84, 85, 119
Heckler Bowker Advertising Agency 80, 81, 84, 87, 105, 109, 113
Heckler, Terry 80
Heiden, Eric 114
Helena, Montana 167, 191
Heli-skiing 72, 76, 138, 183
Helmets 90, 93, 166
Herr, Laura 153-157
Herschbach, Dudley R. 20
Heuga, Jimmie 66, 116
Hickey, Bonnie 119, 182
Hidden Valley Mountain 130
Hidden Valley Ski Area v, 27, 28, 30, 130, 185
Higbie, Harley 40
High Alpine Avalanche Research Station 11
High school 3, 9, 17, 18, 20, 26, 39, 49, 147, 156, 179, 180
Hiking 20, 133
Hiller, Peggy 119
Hinman, Jerry 170
Hockey game: U.S. vs. Russia 114
Holiday Valley Resort 136
Holland, Diana 13
Hove, Marilyn 56, 66
Hove, Tom 3, 4, 177, 183
Howell, Dara 137
Howelsen Hill Ski Area v, 4, 66, 67, 70, 119, 130,
Howland, Ursula 2, 119, 152-157, 176, 182
Hoyt, Stu 170, 182
Huber, Rupert 95
Humboldt-Toiyabe National Forest 14
Hungary 112
Huntley, Chet 146

I

Idaho 60, 62, 68, 72, 81, 82, 88, 98, 99, 102, 119, 125, 131, 138, 148, 159, 160, 167, 168, 169, 170, 171
Ignatius, David 155
Ikon Pass iv, 67, 136, 138, 139, 173, 190
Illinois 127
Indiana 127, 179
Indian Flats, Colorado 16, 19
Injuries 3, 37, 38, 42, 45, 49, 53, 92, 131
Inline skates 134
Inn Ferno 16, 17, 21
Innsbruck, Austria 66, 103, 116
International Olympic Committee (IOC) 103, 178
International Ski Federation (FIS) 62
Interski 160, 163, 183
Iowa 71, 132
Iron Mountain Ski Area 132
Italy 8, 116, 117, 136, 139, 160

J

Jack Nagel Ski School 53
Jackson Hole Mountain Resort v, 150, 151
Jackson Hole, Wyoming v, 124, 139, 147, 150, 151, 173
Jacobs, Dave 71
James, Fred 85, 100
JanSport 88, 134
Janss, Bill 23
Japan 8, 103, 120, 121, 131, 137-139, 174, 178, 187
Jarden Corporation 139
Jennick, PJ 100

My Life in Winters 195

Jerome Hotel in Aspen, CO 21, 134
Johns Hopkins Hospital 156
Johnson, Bill 121
Johnson, Jeanette 119
Johnson, Jimmy 160
Jones, Chris 172, 182
Josserand, Marion 137
Jump, Lawrence (Larry) 12, 32, 33
Junior National Ski Championships 41

K

K2 Skis iv, 3, 39, 44, 65-68, 75, 78-88, 94, 97, 100-107, 109-113, 120-127, 134, 139, 140, 142, 149, 183
Kalispell, Montana 99, 166
Kandahar binding 91
Kane, Carol 119
Kanonen Trail 20, 21
Kansas 26
Kashiwa, Bucky 94
Kauf, Jaelin 122, 179
Kearney, Hannah 122, 137
Kelleher, Brenna 122, 143, 182
Kelly, George 35
Kennedy, John F. 20
Kenworthy, Gus 137
Keystone, Colorado 135
Keystone Ski Resort v, 32, 119, 133, 135-139, 160
Kiana 134, 148, 155, 156, 179, 182
Kitzbühel, Austria 67
Kidd, Billy 66, 116, 186
Killy, Jean Claude 58, 88
Killy Skis 58, 88, 155
King, Jr., Martin Luther 20
Kircher, Steven 174
Kirkwood Ski Area 139
Kirschner, Bill 65, 79, 80, 84-88
Knee replacement 142
Kneissl Skis 85
Knott, Walter 94
Kodak Film Company 105
Kozhevnikova, Yelizaveta 130
Kuntz, Eliza 119, 162, 182

L

LaChapelle, Dolores 29
lake effect 13, 106, 166
Lake Placid, New York iv, 3, 61, 103-106, 109-113, 124, 126, 136
Lake Placid Olympic Organizing Committee (LPOOC) 104, 105, 109, 110, 113
Lake Tahoe, California 84, 89, 101, 132, 136, 138
Lamarre, Kim 137
Landsman, Peter 150
Langdon, Gub 72, 74
Lange, Bob 55, 72, 92
Lange Boots iv, 3, 55, 68-75, 85, 92, 93, 98, 124
Langlois, Lloyd 131
LaRoche, Philippe 131
Larson, Matt 62
Larson, Megan 119
Lash, Bill 159, 160
Las Vegas, Nevada 81, 85, 87
La Trappeur Ski Boots 66
Lauba, Alan 58, 61, 62
Lawrence, Andrea Mead 116, 122
Leadville, Colorado 6, 7, 9, 10, 15
Le Coq Sportif 124
Leipheimer's Ski Shop 99

Lessons 5, 10, 14, 18, 23, 33, 40, 44, 50, 57, 63, 64, 70, 72, 82, 89, 96, 102, 108, 115, 119, 123, 128, 135, 140, 141, 143, 145, 146, 151, 157, 162, 164, 165, 171, 175-178, 180
Level 1 PSIA 144, 154, 160
Level 2 PSIA 144, 154, 160, 162
Level 3 PSIA 143, 144, 152, 154, 157, 161, 162
Levine, Carol 122
Levi Strauss 104
Lewis and Clark's expedition 171
Libby, Montana 168
Lid, Hilde Synnøve 131
LiftBlog.com 150
Ligety, Ted 61, 136, 137
Lillehammer, Norway 131
Lincoln, New Hampshire 96
Lindgren, Marie 131
Lindh, Hilary 122, 130
Line Ski Company 139
Litchfield, John 12, 23
LL Bean 134
Logan, Devin 122, 137
Lone Peak ii, 146, 150, 169, 172
Long, Dewey 16
Longet, Claudine 78
Look Bindings 75, 85, 126
Lookout Pass Ski Area 167
Loon Mountain Resort v, 90, 96
Lost Trail Ski Area v, 170, 171, 191
Loveland Pass 5
Loveland Ski Area 2, 5, 11
Lynch, Kirsten 119

M

Magic Carpet 148, 169
Mahre, Andy 115, 139
Mahre, Phil 3, 104, 107, 113, 114, 124, 149, 150, 160, 168, 183, 188
Mahre, Steve 42, 56-59, 86, 93, 104, 107, 113, 115, 124, 139, 149, 150
Mahre twins 104, 106, 120-125, 149
Maine 61
Mancuso, Julia 61, 117, 122, 136, 137
Manley, Fletcher, Jr. ii, 183
Mannelin, Paul 7, 9, 11, 83, 148, 151, 160, 172-175, 179, 182
Marker Bindings 85, 92, 100, 113, 124, 126, 139
Marker, Hannes 92
Marketing 12, 105, 130
Marolt, Billy 45, 59
Marriott, Bill 20
Marriott Hotels 20
Martinod, Marie 137
Martinsen, Knut 65
Massachusetts 4
Master the Mountain 172, 173
Matlock, Jill Sickels 122
Matt, Andreas 137
Mauser, Jane 122
Maverick Mountain Ski Resort 167
Mavis, Zoe 122, 182
Mayer, Travis 136
Mazatlan, Mexico 39
McCollister, Paul 151
McDonalds 112
McIntyre, Elizabeth "Liz" 122, 131
Mcivor, Ashleigh 137
McNamara, Dick "Mac" 83
Meatto, Frank 95

Medals: see Bronze, Silver, and Gold
Medicine Bow-Routt National Forest 70
Melschmidt, Belenda 122
Michigan 127, 138
Mickelson, Bob 123
Microsoft 20, 60
Mid-Vail 35, 41, 149
Midwest Ski Instructor Association 158
Mighty Mites 47, 53, 59, 63, 64
Mikulich, Jim 2
Miller, Bode 61, 94, 136, 137, 187
Miller, Chris 170
Miller, Lee and Daisy 89
Miller, Warren iv, 14, 35, 36, 77, 123-126, 131, 138
Milt's Face trail 35, 37
Minnesota 45, 61, 127, 137, 138, 141, 160, 162
Minute Maid 104, 110
Missoula, Montana 131, 170
Missoula Snow Bowl 131
Missouri 127
MLB 20
Moe, Tommy 131
Moguls 30, 62, 125, 130, 131, 136, 143
Monarch Mountain iv, v, 3, 15-18, 24, 119, 159, 177
Montana iv, 2, 11, 57, 62, 63, 72, 98, 99, 119, 127, 130-132, 137-142, 146, 152, 156-159, 162-172, 183
Montana State University 63, 156, 183
Moore, Michael 20
Morley, Alex 151
Morrison, Seth 94
Morrow Snowboards 134
Mosely, Jonny 131
Moser-Pröll, Annemarie 117
Mountain biking 133
MSNBC 155
Mt. Belvedere 12
Mt. Rainier National Park 45, 65
Mt. Rose Ski Tahoe v, 11, 14

N

Naches, Washington 115
Nagano, Japan 131
Nagel, Donna 64, 119, 150
Nagel, Jack 47, 48, 53, 55, 58, 155
Nakagawa, Yoshitada "Yosh" 66, 68, 71, 186
NASCAR 20
National Association of Ski Areas (NSAA) 127
National Forests
   Adirondack Mountains 108
   Arapaho 5, 44
   Baker-Snoqualmie 57
   Beaverhead-Deerlodge 167
   Custer Gallatin 164
   El Dorado-Toiyabe 89
   Gallatin 146, 164
   Green Mountain 50
   Humboldt-Toiyabe 14
   Medicine Bow-Routt 70
   Roosevelt 44
   Sawtooth 82
   Sierra 128
   Snoqualmie 57, 123
   Tahoe 63, 186
   White Mountain 96
   White River 10, 23, 33, 40, 135
National Outdoor Leadership School 11
National Ski Association (NSA) 12
National Ski Patrol (NSP) iv, 12, 24, 36, 46, 48, 119
Navy ROTC 49

NBA 20
NCAA 32, 56, 62, 63, 67, 120, 170
Nedved, Troy 151, 172
Nelson, Carl 35
Nelson, Cindy 122
Nevada 11, 14
New Hampshire 61, 90, 96, 131, 136, 138, 160
New Mexico 127
New York 3, 11, 13, 61, 75, 103, 104, 106, 108, 109, 112, 127, 131, 132, 136, 179
New Zealand 138, 139
NFL 20
Nick, Megan 122, 179
Night skiing 123, 135, 141, 146, 157, 167, 175
Nike Corporation 11
Nobel Laureates 20, 65
Non-profit 63, 159, 180
Noonan, Rich 3, 4, 140, 152-157, 162, 165-170, 176, 177, 182, 183
Nordica Boots 74, 75, 93, 139
Nordic combined 62
Nordic skiing 67, 178
Nordic trails 102
North America 33, 40, 66, 88, 104, 138, 146, 150, 159, 172
North Dakota 132
Northern Rocky Mountain Division of PSIA 2, 119, 165
Northstar Ski Area 139
Northwest Ski Hall of Fame 150
Norway 4, 58, 66, 116, 130, 131, 137
Norwich, Vermont 137

O

Oakes, Nancy 122
Ogilvie, Bev 119, 182
Oklahoma 26
Olin Ski Company 95
Olympic Games iv, 1, 3, 23, 41, 58-63, 66, 67, 71, 80, 88, 93, 94, 99, 100, 103-118, 120-128, 130-137, 160, 174, 177, 178, 180
  1896 Olympic Games 111
  1948 Olympic Games 116, 122
  1948 Olympic Games 116, 122
  1952 Olympic Games 116, 122
  1956 Olympic Games 41, 67, 116
  1960 Olympic Games 67, 116, 122
  1964 Olympic Games 116, 122
  1968 Olympic Games 58
  1972 Olympic Games 103, 120, 122, 180
  1976 Olympic Games 103, 122
  1980 Olympic Games 3, 103, 104, 107, 112, 124
  1984 Olympic Games 121, 122, 124
  1988 Olympic Games 125
  1992 Olympic Games 122, 125, 130
  1994 Olympic Games 122, 131
  1998 Olympic Games 122, 131
  2002 Olympic Games 122, 132
  2006 Olympic Games 117, 122, 136
  2010 Olympic Games 117, 122, 136
  2014 Olympic Games 61, 117, 122, 137
  2018 Olympic Games 61, 62, 122, 117
  2022 Olympic Games iv, 58, 62, 93, 99, 103, 106, 109-117, 120-126, 131, 132, 136, 174, 177
  Brundage, Avery 103, 104, 106, 113
  Hockey game: U.S. vs. Russia 114
  International Olympic Committee (IOC) 103
  Lake Placid Olympic Organizing Committee (LPOOC) 104, 105, 109, 110, 113
  Olympic Organizing Committee 103, 104

Pin trading 111
U.S. Olympic Committee 104, 121
U.S. Olympic Team 104
Olympic medalists 1, 61, 62
   Allamand, Olliver 130
   Armstrong, Debbie 121, 122, 125, 189
   Bahrke, Shannon 122
   Bergoust, Eric 131
   Bernsten, Hedda 137
   Bowman, Maddie 122, 137
   Button, Dick 111
   Carmichael, Nelson 130
   Cheryazova, Lina 131
   Christensen, Joss 137
   Cochran, Barbara 120-122, 178, 180
   Cochran, Bob 178, 180
   Cochran, Jimmy 178, 180
   Cochran, Lindy, 178, 180
   Cochran, Marilyn, 120, 178, 180
   Cochran-Siegle, Ryan 120, 178, 180
   Cooper, Christin 121, 122, 125
   Corrock, Susan 122
   Dawson, Toby 136
   Eriksen, Stein 100
   Ferreira, Alex 178
   Fraser, Gretchen 116, 117, 122
   Goepper, Nicholas 137, 179
   Groenvold, Audun 137
   Grospiron, Edgar 130
   Hall, Alexander 179
   Hamill, Dorothy 111
   Hamilton, Scotty 111
   Hattestad, Stine Lise 130
   Heiden, Eric 114
   Heuga, Jimmie 66, 116
   Howell, Dara 137
   Johnson, Bill 121
   Josserand, Marion 137
   Kauf, Jaelin 122, 179
   Kearney, Hannah 122, 137
   Kenworthy, Gus 137
   Kidd, Billy 66, 116, 186
   Killy, Jean Claude 58, 88
   Kozhevnikova, Yelizaveta 130
   Lamarre, Kim 137
   Langlois, Lloyd 131
   LaRoche, Philippe 131
   Lawrence, Andrea Mead 116, 122
   Lid, Hilde Synnøve 131
   Ligety, Ted 61, 136, 137
   Lindgren, Marie 131
   Lindh, Hilary 122, 130
   Logan, Devin 122, 137
   Mahre, Phil 3, 104, 107, 113, 114, 124, 188
   Mahre, Steve 42, 56, 58, 59, 86, 93, 104, 107, 113, 115,
      124, 139, 149, 150
   Mancuso, Julia 1, 61, 62, 117, 122, 136, 137, 186
   Martinod, Marie 137
   Matt, Andreas 137
   Mayer, Travis 136
   McIntyre, Elizabeth "Liz" 122, 131
   McIvor, Ashleigh 137
   Miller, Bode 61, 94, 136, 137, 187
   Moe, Tommy 131
   Mosely, Jonny 131
   Moser-Pröll, Annemarie 117
   Nelson, Cindy 122
   Nick, Megan 122, 179
   Onozuka, Ayana 137
   Pack, Joe 136
   Pitou, Penelope "Penny" 116
   Riddle, Mike 137
   Roffe, Dianne 122
   Rolland, Kevin 137
   Saubert, Jean 117, 122
   Schmid, Mike 137
   Schönbächler, Andreas 131
   Shiffrin, Mikaela 62, 117, 118, 122, 137, 178, 191
   Sigourney, Brita 122
   Snite, Betsy 116, 122
   Staub, Roger 71
   Stenmark, Ingemar 113
   Stevenson, Colby 178
   Stone, Nikki 122, 131
   Street, Picabo 122, 131
   Vonn, Lindsey 1, 61, 117, 122, 137, 141
   Weibrecht, Andrew 61, 137
   Weinbrecht, Donna 122, 130
   White, Shaun 131
   Wilson, Bryon 137
   Wise, David 137, 178
Olympic Organizing Committee 103, 104
Olympic pins 2, 105, 111, 112, 177, 188
Olympics: see Olympic Games
Olympic Village 112
Onozuka, Ayana 137
Oregon 62, 64, 66, 72, 75, 121
Orvis 134
Oshman's Sporting Goods 126
Oslo, Norway 58, 116
OU Sports 66, 68, 71, 74
Outward Bound 11

P

Pack, Joe 136
Paepcke, Walter 23
Pallavicini Trail 30, 55
Pandemic iv, 139, 172, 174
Paradise trail 170
Paralympics 60, 62
Paris, France 125
Park City Ski Area 61
Park City, Utah 128, 131, 136, 178
Parker, Bob 12, 35, 40
Pasacani, Jerry 30
Patrolling iv, 29
Pats for Sports 83
Paulson, Huck 45
Pennsylvania 127, 132
Perfect North Slopes 179
Petzoldt, Paul 11
Pfeifer, Doug 160
Pfeifer, Freidl 12, 23
Pickleball 53
Pin collection 111, 112, 177
Pinocchio's Pizza in Aspen 21, 134
Pin trading 111, 112, 177
Pitou, Penelope "Penny" 116
Plavada Ski Area 132
Playboy magazine 100
Poma lift 147, 148
Portillo, Chile 119
Post, Ned 87, 105
Po Valley Campaign 12
Poulsen, Wayne 14, 63
Powder 29, 95, 132, 170, 187
Powder Bowl Ski Area 132
Powder fats skis 95

President Bill Clinton 20
President George W. Bush 20
President Gerald Ford 20
President John F. Kennedy 20
Pre Skis 88, 90, 91
Prothman, Marge 60
Professional Ski Instructors of America (PSIA) iv, 2, 3, 4, 12, 32, 42, 43, 62, 95, 119, 121, 122, 140, 142, 144, 152-154, 157-165, 169, 179, 183
   Clinics 75, 79, 142, 145, 152, 153, 161, 172, 175
   Demo Team 121, 122, 144, 163
   Northern Rocky Mountain Division 2, 157, 163
   PSIA-AASI 153, 158, 161, 162, 163, 165, 169, 183
Pueblo, Colorado 24
Puerto Rico 131
PyeongChang, South Korea 117

R
Racer chaser 106, 120
Races 59, 94, 99, 116, 117, 120, 125, 178, 180
Racing 3, 32, 42, 47, 55-58, 61-65, 72, 84, 92-94, 100, 104, 106, 113-118, 120-126, 130, 139, 149
Red Lodge Mountain 158, 162-164
Reines, Frederick 20
Reno, Nevada 14
Rhinehart, Don 160
Richardson, Robert Coleman 20
Richmond, Vermont 178, 180
Riddle, Mike 137
Rideout, Percy 12, 23
Ride Snowboards 134, 138
Riva Ridge 12, 41
River rafting 133
R.L. Winston Fly Rod Company 130
ROC 130
Rochester, New York 131
Rocky Mountain National Park 27, 28
Rocky Mountains 29, 47
Roffe and Demetre 126
Roffe, Dianne 122
Rolland, Kevin 137
Roosevelt National Forest 44
Rope tows 16, 147
Rossignol Skis 75, 78, 80, 81, 83, 85, 94, 126
Rueck, Suzanne 122
Russia 4, 111
Rust, Julie 119
Rutland, Vermont 120
Ryan Cochran-Siegle 178

S
Sabich, Spider 78, 84, 187
Sacramento, California 78
Sage Fly Rod Company 100
Sailer, Erich 141, 190
Sakry, Cookie 7, 8
Sakry, Paul 9, 148
Salem, Oregon 75, 121
Salesforce 68-72, 75, 80, 84, 98
Salesperson 3, 65, 83, 97, 98
Salida, Colorado 6, 7, 15-20, 55, 91, 109
Salisbury, Harrison 20
Salmon, Idaho 170
Salomon Bindings 66, 85, 92, 126, 134, 139
Salomon, Georges 92
Salt Lake City, Utah 136
Sam's Grill in San Francisco, CA 78, 79, 135
Sandpoint, Idaho 99, 102
San Francisco, California 49, 78, 79, 83, 135, 149

Santa Barbara, California ii, 135, 176, 179
Sapporo, Japan 103, 120, 121, 178
Sarajevo, Yugoslavia 121
Saubert, Jean 117, 122
Sawtooth National Forest 82
Schaeffler, Willie 32, 56
Schaffgotsch, Felix 82
Schauffler, Sandy 32
Scheiblener, Leo 48
Schmid, Mike 137
Schönbächler, Andreas 131
Schweitzer Ski Resort v, 99, 102
Schwinn Bicycles 88
Sears, Bill 27, 30, 45, 48, 50, 55
Sears, Bill and Betty 30, 55
Seattle, Washington 9, 35, 51, 52-57, 64-69, 76, 80, 86, 99, 101, 121, 139, 152, 174
Sedona, Arizona 121
Seibert, Pete 13, 34, 35, 40
Selkirk Mountains 102
Semmelink, John 93
SeniorSkiing.com website 168
Serac Ski Clothing 101
Shanks, Bob 3, 4, 66, 166, 168, 177
Shaw, Marie Russell 122
Shepard, Morrie 34, 36, 55, 71-75, 88, 92, 93
Shiffrin, Mikaela 62, 117, 118, 122, 137, 178
Showdown Ski Area 166, 190
Sidecut 94, 95, 134
Siebert, Pete 12, 34, 40, 43
Sierra Club 11
Sierra National Forest 128
Sigourney, Brita 122
Silver medal 6, 52, 66, 116, 117, 121-125, 130, 131, 136, 137, 178, 179
Simmons Mattress 104
Simms Fly-fishing 130, 134
Simonson, Henry (Hank) 65
Simonson, Jimmy 55, 74, 75
Simpson, Jennifer 122
Skiable acres 5, 10, 14, 28, 40, 44, 50, 57, 63, 70, 82, 89, 96, 102, 108, 115, 123, 128, 135, 141, 146, 151, 157, 164, 171, 175, 180
Ski areas iv, 3, 127, 132, 133, 138, 165
   Afton Alps Resort 138, 139, 162
   Alpental Ski Area 121, 125
   Arapahoe Basin Ski Area iv, v, 11, 12, 17, 27, 30-34, 42, 50, 55, 56, 133, 148, 160
   Aspen Snowmass Ski Resort v, 11-13, 17, 21-23, 34-37, 39, 61, 78, 100, 134, 139, 159, 160, 178
   Bald Mountain 82
   Bear Paw Ski Bowl 166
   Beaver Creek Resort v, 40, 127, 139
   Big Sky Resort 3
   Blacktail Mountain Ski Area 168
   Bousquet Mountain Resort 152, 157
   Brantling Ski Center 131
   Breckenridge 34, 133, 138, 139
   Breckenridge Ski Area 34
   Bridger Bowl 63, 119, 141, 151, 165
   Brighton Ski Resort 175
   Buck Hill 61
   Buck Hill Resort v, 45, 141
   Bugaboos v, 71, 72, 73, 76, 138
   Cannon Mountain 61, 136
   Cochran's Ski Area v, 120, 178, 180
   Crested Butte 139
   Crystal Mountain Ski Resort iv, v, 11, 45-48, 51-69, 81, 119, 155

Dartmouth Skiway 131
Deer Valley Ski Resort v, 128
Discovery Basin Ski Area 165
Eaglebrook School 4
Echo Summit 132
Edelweiss 132
Epic Pass members 139
Great Divide Ski Area 167
Heavenly Ski Resort v, 89, 138
Heavenly Valley Ski Area 84, 85, 119
Hidden Valley Mountain 130
Hidden Valley Ski Area v, 27-30, 130
Holiday Valley 136
Howelsen Hill 4
Ikon Pass members 2022-23 139
Iron Mountain 132
Jackson Hole Mountain Resort v, 150, 151
Kauf, Jaelin 122, 179
Keystone Ski Resort v, 32, 119, 133-138, 160
Kirkwood 139
Lake Tahoe 84, 89, 101, 132, 136, 138
Lookout Pass Ski Area 167
Loon Mountain Resort v, 90, 96
Lost Trail Ski Area v, 170, 171
Loveland Ski Area 2, 5, 11
Maverick Mountain Ski Resort 167
Missoula Snow Bowl 131
Monarch Mountain iv, v, 3, 15-18, 24, 119, 159, 177
Mt. Rose Ski Tahoe v, 11, 14
Northstar 139
Park City 61
Perfect North Slopes 179
Plavada 132
Powder Bowl 132
Schweitzer Ski Resort v, 99, 102
Showdown 166, 190
Ski Cooper v, 3, 4, 7, 10, 11, 177
Sky Tavern Ski Area 178
Snow Bowl Ski Area 170
Squaw Valley/Palisades Tahoe v, 58, 61, 63, 93, 116, 131, 136, 149, 159
Steamboat Springs Resort v, 66, 67, 70, 119, 130
Stevens Pass 139
Stratton Mountain Resort v, 45, 50
Sugarbush Ski Resort 11
Summit at Snoqualmie v, 121, 123
Sun Valley Resort v, 60, 68, 81-84, 88, 119, 125, 131, 148, 160
Tannenbaum 132
Telluride 139
Teton Pass Ski Resort 169
Turner Mountain Ski Area 168
Vail Resort ii-v, 3, 4, 11-13, 22, 34-46, 51-55, 62-66, 71, 92, 107, 119, 133, 136, 138, 149, 173, 174, 179
Whiteface Mountain Ski Resort 11
Whitefish Mountain Resort 11, 99, 131, 159, 166
White Pass Ski Area v, 115
Winter Park Resort v, 11, 32, 37, 41-44, 66, 93
Yellowstone Club 169, 170
Ski ballet 125
Ski boots 8, 25, 26, 47, 55, 90, 93, 100, 159
Ski Cooper v, 3, 4, 7, 10, 11, 177
Ski Cross 62, 136
Ski Hall of Fame 121, 150, 190
Skiing
  adaptive 108, 158, 166
  alpine 4, 58, 61, 62, 88, 91, 105, 116-118, 121, 126, 137, 158, 160, 162, 174, 178
  cross-country 58, 62, 67, 88, 90, 100, 109, 120, 158

freestyle 14, 40, 62, 84, 121, 125, 130, 131, 136, 137, 139, 158, 164, 178
telemark 90, 158, 170
Skiing Cochrans 120, 178, 180
Ski instructors 3, 12, 18, 26, 39, 65, 119, 158, 159, 160
Ski jumping 32, 62, 104, 106, 109, 178
Ski lifts iv, 5, 10, 14, 18, 23, 25, 28, 33, 34, 40, 44, 49, 50, 57, 63, 70, 76, 82, 89, 96, 102, 108, 115, 123, 128, 135, 141, 146, 147, 150, 151, 157, 164, 171, 175, 180
Ski Magazine 80, 152, 183
Ski News magazine 52
Ski Patrol iv, 12, 22, 24, 27, 30-36, 41, 46-53, 71, 119, 134, 149
Ski racing 58, 61-63, 93, 104, 116, 118, 120
Ski Safety Research Project 45, 48
Ski School 26, 34, 36, 42, 46, 48, 53, 55, 60, 61, 64, 67, 71, 92, 119, 142, 143, 155, 159, 160, 161, 162, 163, 169, 172, 175
Ski School Director 36, 48, 92, 119, 163, 169
Ski shops
  Anderson's Sporting Goods 75
  Bill's Ski Shop 9
  Dick's Sporting Good 133
  Gart Brothers 88
  Gorsuch Ski and Sports Shop 119
  Leipheimer's Ski Shop 99
  Oshman's Sporting Goods 126
  OU Sports 66, 68, 71, 74
  Pats for Sports 83
  Sportsman's Ski Haus 99
  Stan's for Sports 79, 126
  Swiss Ski Sports 149
  Wilson Sporting Goods 105
Ski Team 32, 58, 59, 60, 61, 71-78, 84, 93, 119, 120, 121, 141, 178
Skofic, Pavel 94
Sky Tavern Ski Area 178
Slalom 58, 59, 62, 66, 67, 94, 106-109, 113-117, 120-125, 130, 136, 137, 178
Slifer, Rod 34
Smith Goggle Company 105
Smith, Shawn 122
Sneathen, Chris 14, 141, 155, 156, 170, 172, 179, 182, 183
Snite, Betsy 116, 122
Snoqualmie National Forest 57, 123
Snoqualmie Pass, Washington 123
Snow biking 175
Snowboards 62, 94, 95, 127, 134, 143, 166, 168, 176, 178
Snowboarder 141, 143
Snowboarding 62, 121, 131, 143, 158, 161
Snow Bowl Ski Area 170
Snowcat 10, 18, 44, 95, 148
Snowplow 26, 159
Snyder, Frank 50
Sochi, Russia 117, 137
Sodergren, Mariam 122
Soil Conservation Office 19
South Korea 117, 136
Spar Gulch 21
Spielberg, Steven 20
Spokane, Washington 99
Sportsman's Ski Haus 99
Squaw Valley, California v, 58, 61, 63, 93, 116, 131, 136, 149, 159
Squaw Valley/Palisades Tahoe v, 58, 61, 63, 93, 116, 131, 136, 149, 159
Stan's for Sports 79, 126

Staub, Roger 71
Steadman Clinic 107
Steadman, Dr. J. Richard 107
Steamboat Resort v, 66, 67, 70, 119, 130
Stenmark, Ingemar 113
Stern, Edgar 128
Stevenson, Colby 178
Stevens Pass Ski Area 139
Stingel, Carl 13
St. Moritz-Corviglia, Switzerland 116
Stone, Nikki 122, 131
Stratton, Charles, Jr. 141
Stratton Mountain Resort v, 45, 50
Street, Picabo 122, 131
Subaru 166, 171
Sugarbush Ski Resort 11
Sula, Montana 170, 171
Summit at Snoqualmie v, 121, 123, 139
Sun Valley, Idaho 60, 68, 81-84, 88, 119, 125, 131, 148, 160
Sun Valley Resort v, 82, 148
Super-G 62, 117, 125, 130, 131, 137, 178
Surface lifts 147, 148
Suzy Chapstick 121
Swan, Dick 72-75, 78
Sweden 66, 131
Swiss Ski Sports 149
Swiss technique 149, 159
Switzerland 67, 71, 91, 116, 119, 125, 131, 137, 139, 160, 179
Sync skiing 154, 177

T
Tahoe National Forest 63
Tancik, Joe 6-8, 15, 17, 19, 26, 56, 109
Tancik, Thelma iii, 3, 6-8, 15, 16, 27, 56, 109
Tannenbaum Ski Area 132
TaylorMade Golf 134
T-Bar 9, 16, 17, 147, 148
Teaching iv, 12, 20, 26, 29, 39, 41, 58, 59, 62, 64, 71, 91, 119, 138-145, 152-156, 158-165, 170-181
Team U.S.A. 131, 137
Technica Ski Boots 139
Telemark skiing 90, 158, 170
Telluride Ski Area 139
Temple, James 70
Terrain parks 14, 18, 40, 50, 62, 70, 89, 96, 102, 146, 151, 164, 167, 175
Teton Pass Ski Resort 169
Texas 26
Texas Instruments (TI) 106
Thanksgiving 17, 37, 64, 82, 132, 172, 176
TheSkiDiva.Com website 153
The Washington Post 104
Thurlow, Whitney 122
Tilden, Brad 20
Title Nine 121
Toboggan 25, 31, 36-38, 74
    Akia tobaggan 37, 38, 74
Tokyo, Japan 174
Torino, Italy 136
Tourist Trap 41
Trail difficulty 162
Trams 150
Tubing 18, 40, 44, 50, 96, 102, 115, 141, 157
Turin, Italy 117
Turner Mountain Ski Area 168
Tweedy, Jack 34
Twilight skiing 102
Twin Bridges, Montana 130

U
Unger, Geoff 169
Uniforms 55, 104-106, 126
United States 4, 11
University of California 135
University of Colorado 21, 24, 59
University of Denver 32
University of Utah 59
University of Virginia 97, 100
University of Washington 52, 133
University of Wyoming 59
U.S. Air Force 26, 34, 42, 43, 166
U.S. Air Force Academy 26
U.S. Alpine Team 178
U.S. Army 7, 11, 13
    10th Mountain Division iv, 8, 10-14, 24, 34, 91, 93, 127, 139, 167
    Camp Hale 7, 8, 11-13
    Mt. Belvedere 12
    Po Valley Campaign 12
    Veterans 11-13, 32, 33, 50, 133, 168
U.S. Congress 174
U.S. Department of Justice 133
U.S. Forest Service 11, 41, 45, 158, 159, 170
U.S. National Championships 116, 170
U.S. Olympic Committee 104, 121
U.S. Olympic Team 104
U.S. Park Service 11
U.S. Ski Team 58-61, 75, 78, 84, 93, 118-121, 141, 178
USSR 111
U.S. Team 104, 107, 137, 178, 180
Utah 6, 15, 46, 59, 61, 72, 124, 127, 128, 131-136, 159, 175, 178
Uzbekistan 131

V
Vaccines 174
Vail Associates 4
Vail, Colorado ii, 34, 40, 41, 62, 119, 136, 179
Vail Resort ii, iv, v, 3, 4, 11-13, 22, 34-46, 51-55, 62, 65, 66, 71, 92, 107, 119, 133, 136, 138, 149, 173, 174, 179
Vail Resorts 119, 133, 138, 174
Valar, Paul 160
Vancouver, Canada 117, 136
Vandergriff, Jim 94
Vashon Island, Washington 83
Vermont 11, 45, 50, 62, 120, 138, 178, 180
Vertical drop 5, 10, 14, 18, 23, 28, 33, 44, 50, 57, 63, 70, 82, 89, 96, 102, 108, 115, 123, 128, 135, 141, 146, 151, 157, 162, 164, 171, 175, 180
Vertical feet 74, 169
Veterans 11-12, 13, 32, 33, 50, 133, 168
Vienna, Austria 125
Volant Skis 94
Volkl Skis 75, 139
Volunteer ski patrolmen 48
Vonn, Lindsey 1, 61, 117, 122, 137, 141

W
Walmart 20
Walton, Sam 20
Warren Miller iv, 14, 35, 77, 123-126, 131, 138
Washington 11, 45, 51, 52, 57, 59, 62, 64, 66, 72, 80, 83, 88, 98, 99, 100, 104, 115, 123, 125, 127, 133, 141, 155, 174
Washington Post 104, 155
Washington State University 59
Wayne, John 20

Wedge 140, 143, 159, 169
Weibrecht, Andrew 61, 137
Weinbrecht, Donna 122, 130
Werner, Wallace "Buddy" 41, 67
Werner, Gladys "Skeeter" 67, 119
Werner, Loris "Bugs" 67
West Virginia 127
Whiteface Mountain Ski Resort v, 11, 61, 104, 106, 108, 109, 113, 137
Whitefish Mountain Resort 11, 99, 131, 159, 166
White Mountain National Forest 96
White Pass Ski Area v, 115
White River National Forest 10, 23, 33, 40, 135
White, Shaun 131
Wiley, Milt "Uncle Milty" 36
Willet, George 166
Willits, Deb (Ackerman) 122
Wilmington, New York 108
Wilson, Barbara 51
Wilson, Bryon 137
Wilson Sporting Goods 105
Winfrey, Oprah 7
Winter Park Resort v, 11, 32, 37, 41, 42, 44, 66, 93
Wisconsin 127, 134
Wise, David 137, 178
Witte, Bill 104, 106, 110

Women in skiing iv, 116-123
Wong, Wayne 84, 121
Woodruff, Gary 105, 106, 110
Woodward, John 65
World Championships 117, 121
World Cup 58-61, 100, 104-106, 117, 120, 125, 140, 149, 174, 178
World War II 7, 13, 14, 24, 32, 33, 68, 91, 159, 178
Wright, Dick 13
Wright, Robert 50

X
X Games 23

Y
Yanqing National Alpine Ski Centre 178
Yellowstone Club 169, 170, 191

Z
Zahm, Amy 122
Zip lining 133
Zue, Dick 68, 75, 78, 79, 81
Zurich, Switzerland 179

ABOUT THE AUTHOR

Mike Ewing first learned to ski in Colorado at the age of nine. That began a lifelong love for the sport. He dropped out of college to pursue a career in skiing. At the time it seemed a bit risky but, 60 years later, it seems like a winner!

Through skiing, Mike has had the good fortune to work for world-class resorts like Vail, Arapahoe Basin, Crystal Mountain, Bridger Bowl, and Big Sky. He also worked for ski industry giants like A&T Ski Company, Lange Ski Boots, and K2 Skis.

Along the way, Mike was one of three founders of Simms Fly-fishing company and an executive at R. L. Winston Fly Rod company. Working at something you love can barely be called work!

Mike lives in Bozeman, Montana with his wife of 55 years, Barbara, and their cat. They both regularly ski in the winter and fly-fish in the summer with friends and family.

Mike currently teaches skiing near Bozeman, Montana. If you would like to book a lesson, email him at Stlheadmike@gmail.com.

Books shown:
- Boy Scouts of America (1958). *Merit Badge Series: Skiing.* Compiled by Harold M. Gore.
- National Ski Patrol (1952). *Ski Patrol Manual of the National Ski Patrol System of America.* Edited by Edward F. Taylor.

www.ingramcontent.com/pod-product-compliance
Lightning Source LLC
Chambersburg PA
CBHW050157130526
44590CB00044B/3378